A Miraculous Escape and Selected Writings on Jewish Themes

by

Rabbi Dr. Chaim Simons

Grosvenor House
Publishing Limited

This book is published by
Grosvenor House Publishing Ltd
Link House
140 The Broadway, Tolworth, Surrey, KT6 7HT.
www.grosvenorhousepublishing.co.uk

A CIP record for this book
is available from the British Library

ISBN 978-1-80381-030-0

CONTENTS

PREFACE

- Over 40 years, I have written a variety of papers in English and in Hebrew on Jewish themes, which of course include Israel.
- Many of these papers have been published either as books, papers in scholarly journals, or articles or letters to the Editor in various newspapers.
- Recently I published two selections of these papers in book form, and I am now publishing a further selection. Some of these papers are scholarly articles. Another is an in-depth study of a man escaping from an Indian jail, in which he was being held for an extended period prior to any trial, under the most inhumane conditions, and as a result was suffering from a life-threatening disease Another is a history of my family who perished in the Holocaust. Finally, I have included a selection of autobiographical events in my life.
- Since the papers contained in this book were written at different periods, there is no consistency in the format of the references at the end of each paper. Likewise, transliterations of Hebrew words to English are not necessarily consistent for the same word throughout the book.
- I have made some small stylistic changes in the papers.

Section One

A Miraculous Escape

AN IN-DEPTH STUDY OF AN
ESCAPE FROM INDIA

Rabbi Dr. Chaim Simons

(written in 2012)

NOTE TO THE READER

Needless to say, this book should not be taken as an endorsement for drug smuggling. It is a very serious crime. However, there have been a number of cases where highly respected people with good hearts, were asked to take a suit case, which they were told contained, for example, clothes, to another country. Unfortunately, completely unknown to the carriers, drugs had been secreted in the suit case. This has often resulted in these innocent carriers finding themselves in jail and then being put on trial, often after several years of incarceration. Should, however, after a fair trial, a person be found guilty of knowingly smuggling drugs, that person should, unquestionably be punished accordingly.

[The name of the escapee in this book has been replaced by PA, the initials of "Ploni Almoni." It is used for anonymous and is to be found in the Biblical Book of Ruth chapter 4 verse 1]

INTRODUCTION

PA then a young Israeli in his early 30s, married and one young daughter, was arrested at Mumbai airport in June 2004, on suspicion of trying to smuggle drugs into India. Whether in fact this was the case, or he was just an innocent person carrying for someone as a favour a suitcase whose contents he was unaware of, is outside the scope of this book.

What is relevant is that a person suspected of committing any crime is entitled as a basic human right to a speedy trial. Periodically, during the course of his incarceration, he was taken to the courthouse, but instead of the judge arranging for a trial, he was repeatedly remanded. It is reported that instead of the judge listening to the details of his case, the judge kept dozing off!

Meanwhile he was kept in the Mumbai Arthur Road Jail under the most inhumane and life-threatening conditions, which were in complete violation of even a convicted prisoner's most basic rights. In this jail there was a gross overcrowding; the food contained ants and stones; both the sanitary conditions and medical treatment could well be described as non-existent, so much so, that prisoners regularly contracted life-threatening diseases from which some died. All these above-mentioned facts will be substantiated in the course of this book.

It was in this jail, that PA contracted malaria and his life was in serious danger. His only salvation was to escape. This fact was also realised by highly respected Rabbis and Organisations who would try and assist him to achieve this objective. According to PA's book "Escape from India" and his subsequent lectures, these included Rabbi Yitzchak Grossman of Migdal Haemek, the Rishon Lezion and former Chief Rabbi Ovadiah Yosef, and the Chabad and Habayit Hayehudi Organisations.

A positive result of PA's incarceration was that he went into jail as a "secular" Jew and came out as a Jew who despite the horrendous prison conditions observed as many mitzvot (Jewish religious precepts) as he could.

The purposes of this book are:

1. To use the text of the book "Escape from India" in order to reconstruct details of PA's escape journey from the JJ hospital in Mumbai (Bombay) in India until Ben Gurion Airport in Israel. To accomplish this aim, maps and various timetables and other information were utilised. The book often gave very sketchy details of PA's escape route and it was therefore not always possible to reconstruct the precise route, and sometimes some guesses had to be made, or several alternative routes put forward. It was also found that the times given for getting between various places were sometimes incorrect, but this is understandable, since PA could not be expected to remember such details precisely.

2. To give detailed background information on the various places PA passed through, the various organisations he came in contact with, the different modes of transport he utilised, the Jewish religious practices he observed on his journey, and many more things.

The method which will be used in this book will be to bring in *italics* brief quotes together with the page number from the book "Escape of India" (by Avigail Myzlik, English translation by Shoshie Nissenbaum, second edition, 2009), when necessary, with my interpolations in brackets, and this will be followed by my commentary in normal print.

This book is meticulously documented and where internet references are given, the prefix http:// is omitted. It should be pointed out that since this book is "an in-depth study" and not an "advertising brochure," as far as possible, the names of businesses, restaurants, hotels etc. have been intentionally omitted. Since the names of such places are often to be found on the various websites quoted, such names have been replaced by ***.

PA's escape was clearly hashgacha pratit (Divine providence) – a journey with miracle after miracle. There were so many opportunities on this long escape journey for PA to have been intercepted by the authorities and returned to the jail in Mumbai. But despite this, he succeeded in returning to Israel.

PA's escape from India began on Tuesday, 27 September 2005, at the JJ Hospital in Mumbai ...

[Because of his malaria, PA was taken to the JJ Hospital.] *When we arrived at the hospital we went to the reception desk at the entrance. (p.319)*

There are a large number of hospitals, both governmental and private[1] in Mumbai. Amongst them is the JJ Hospital, which is situated in a large campus near the Ramchandra Bhatt Marg (Babula Tank Road) and the Sir Jamshedjee Jejeebhoy Road in the Byculla area of South Mumbai.[2]

It was in 1834, that Sir Robert Grant, the Governor of Bombay (Mumbai), seeing the lack of medical care in his city, proposed the establishment of a medical school and a teaching hospital. A few years later, the First Indian Knight & Baronet, Sir Jamshedjee Jejeebhoy, offered an enormous donation for this purpose. Simultaneously, with the foundation of the Grant Medical College (named after Robert Grant), a hospital (known as the Sir JJ Hospital after the donor), was then built and it was opened in May 1845. In 1958, the whole JJ Hospital building was torn down and replaced by a seven-story building. Today there are numerous buildings on this campus which extend over 44 acres of ground. Since the various buildings were added over a long period of time, they are of various styles of architecture. In addition to the Main Building of the JJ Hospital, these buildings include the Grant Medical College, the Central Medical Library, a Pharmacology Department, a Pathology Department, an Anatomy Hall, and a number of residential facilities for doctors, nurses, hospital workers and medical students. [3]

The hospital has 30,000 admissions each year and treats over half a million outpatients, and being a government hospital, all this is free of charge to the patients. There are 45 wards with a total of 1,352 beds. An average of 57 operations are performed there each day.[4]

7

They gave me a small cup to bring them a urine sample. (p.319)

One of the non-invasive medical tests performed on a patient is to analyse a sample of his urine. This is known as urinalysis. These tests include: colour and appearance, measuring of specific gravity to determine whether a person is dehydrated, and an analysis of whether certain other substances such as ketone bodies, bilirubin, glucose and hemoglobin are present and/or at what concentrations.[5]

Urine tests (in addition to other tests, such as saliva and blood tests) are also performed if a person has, or is suspected of having malaria.[6] Malaria is a mosquito-borne infectious disease transmitted from the bite of a mosquito infected with the parasite. It can then take a week or even months for the symptoms of malaria, such as fever, shivering, vomiting, anaemia, retinal damage and convulsions to appear. Malaria is widespread in tropical and subtropical regions, including parts of the Americas, Asia, and Africa. Each year, there are approximately 250 million cases of malaria in the world, of which about one million are fatal.[7]

Tests and experiments which have been performed within the last 20 years show a correlation between the contents of a person's urine and the presence of malaria. For example, experiments performed in the year 1991, on urine samples of patients with a certain species of malaria showed that 85 per cent of them had elevated levels of proteins in their urine.[8] Experiments performed in Sudan in the year 2000 on 600 patients whose clinical picture was suggestive of malaria, suggested that malaria might have a significant effect on the urine, especially the presence of albuminuria.[9]

In a paper which was received by the editorial board of the "American Journal of Tropical Medicine and Hygiene" in August 2006, it stated that in India "about 2 million confirmed malaria cases and 1,000 deaths are reported annually." However, it goes on to strongly dispute these figures and quotes the WHO [World Health Organization] South East Asia Regional Office, who estimate that there are "15 million cases and 20,000 deaths" annually.[10] More specifically, "The Times of India" gives numbers for Mumbai for the period 1 January 2005 to 15 September 2005

– the period when PA contracted malaria in Mumbai. The figures given in this paper are 1,117 cases.[11]

It was suggested that the record monsoon rain towards the end of July that year – more than 65 centimetres in one day, the heaviest recorded in India's history! – had caused an increase in the number of cases of malaria. This caused water-logging and hence an increased breeding ground for the mosquitoes. The city workers therefore sprayed insecticide to try and prevent the spread of the malaria.[12]

However, high numbers of cases of malaria were also reported in Mumbai in 2002[13] and in 2006.[14] The high numbers of malaria cases in Mumbai led to "Travel Medicine" of 2008 stating: "Malaria risk occurs year-round in the tropical cities of Mumbai ..." [15]

PA was suffering from malaria and thus one can see why he required a urine test. However, there is no mention in the book of any other tests such as blood or saliva, but it is possible that they would have performed other tests had PA then not escaped.

⚜ ⚜ ⚜ ⚜ ⚜ ⚜ ⚜ ⚜ ⚜ ⚜ ⚜

The guards took me to the end of the hall where there were three bathroom stalls. Despite the fact that India toilets are nothing more than holes in the ground, two out of three were broken. (p.319)

Almost all toilets found in Western countries are the sitting toilet. However, the majority of the world uses "squat toilets," which essentially consists of a hole in the ground. As the name suggests, these toilets are used by squatting rather than by sitting. Except for the most primitive of places, there is a system to flush water into these squat toilets.

These toilets are mainly to be found in the Middle East and countries such as India, China and Japan. Depending on the country, they are of slightly different design, but the common denominator is that they are all essentially consisting of a hole in the ground.[16] According to a BBC News report of July 2010, a few of these squat toilets were installed in England in a Greater Manchester shopping centre after its bosses went on a cultural awareness course.[17]

Numerous arguments have been put in favour of using this type of toilet rather than the sitting type. These include: they are less expensive; they are easier to clean; they eliminate physical contact between the body and the toilet; the body posture when using them protects the nerves that control the prostate, bladder and uterus from becoming stretched and damaged and relaxes the puborectalis muscle.[18]

There are also arguments against this type of toilet. These include: their use requires certain balancing skills; they can be difficult to use by the elderly, those with joint problems or limited mobility and those recovering from leg injuries.[19]

[Whilst in the toilet, PA] *noticed a small window around twelve inches* [30 centimeters] *wide. It had glass shutters and a wire screen. ... I took the inner shutters and tried lifting them out of the track. They broke in two in my hands ... I decided to check out the strength of the screen. I pushed it lightly with my hand and the bottom support flew out wildly ... The next section of the shutters ... also* [easily] *broke into two. ... There was only one layer of glass left. I took the screen and gave it a little knock. The right support flew outside. (pp.320-21)*

In a properly looked after building, especially a public building, the shutters and screen should not break with just the slightest of pressure! But these were not the only deficiencies with this immediate area of the building. Two out of three of the toilets were broken. The building was not maintained as it should have been. This was not the only part of the JJ Hospital that was in a state of disrepair. Adjacent to the main building of the JJ Hospital is the "Grant Medical College."

In his book "Bombay Gothic," which was published in 2002, Christopher W. London wrote: "the Grant Medical College is in a

10

state of serious disrepair."[20] The trustees of the JJ Hospital realized the state of the Grant Medical College building, that they brought in a team of "Conservation Architects and Historic Building Consultants" to survey it and submit their preliminary recommendations for repairs and renovations. Their report is undated, but since it quotes from Christopher London's book, it is obviously dated later than 2002. There they give a long list of repairs and renovations that were in need. These include structural repairs, elimination of water seepage and repairs to windows. Some of these defects they attributed to atmospheric conditions.[21]

It is true that this building was constructed in 1845, whereas the main building of the JJ Hospital only in 1958 and thus one would thus expect a greater deterioration if the older building had not been looked after. One of these deteriorations in both of these building would be rusting.

"Rust" is a general term used for a series of iron oxides. However, the term is generally used for the red oxides which are formed by the reaction of iron and oxygen in the presence of water or air moisture. Given sufficient time, the oxygen and water will convert any iron entirely into rust causing the iron to disintegrate.[22]

Thus after nearly 50 years, (until 2005, the year of PA's escape), monsoon rain and other weather conditions would have certainly caused the metal bars on the outside windows of the JJ Hospital to become thoroughly rusted over and shutters to become very brittle. Thus the little pressure exerted by PA, was sufficient to cause them to break. The rusting of these window bars was also referred to in a newspaper article quoted later.

[Although PA had not prepared himself to escape that day, since he had already broken the windows and the shutters, a fact which he could not disguise, he decided to then escape.] *There was one thing preventing me, the window was at the height of my head and there was no toilet to climb onto to hoist myself through the*

11

window. Suddenly I noticed that protruding from the wall two metal pipes coated with cement. (pp.321-22)

As already stated, the toilets there were the squat type and not the seat type and hence PA had no seat to stand on.

What were these two metal pipes doing in this toilet? Maybe these pipes were for the water for a sink in this toilet cubicle, (or maybe one was for a sink and the other to flush the toilet) and over the years these pipes had broken and instead of repairing them, they had been cemented over and the sink removed. We have already seen the neglect of at least this part of the building. Two of the three squat toilets were broken, the bars and shutters on the window were in a very derelict state and this very likely explains why there were the remnants of two pipes in the wall of this cubicle.

I climbed up the pipes [in the toilet cubicle] ... *I pulled myself up slowly until my legs were already out of the window. (p.322)*

The next day, Wednesday, 28 September, PA's escape was reported in several Indian newspapers. "The Times of India" wrote "around 12.30 pm, PA *(his name was spelled incorrectly in this newspaper article)* told the policeman he needed to use the toilet. The duo escorted him and waited outside the toilet and asked him not to bolt the door. Investigating inspector Laxman Vakhare said PA, however, managed to bolt the door from inside. The policeman waited outside for a few minutes and then began knocking on the door. When they realised that PA was trying to break out through a window, they raised an alarm. However, the well-built Israeli had by then broken the rusted iron rods on the window and fled. The policeman reported the matter to the JJ police station." (One of the buildings on this campus is the JJ Police Station which is situated about 150 metres to the west of the JJ Hospital.[(23)]) This paper also commented that "this is the third such incident in one month" and also that the police commissioner had given "instructions to his men to take extra care while escorting foreign nationals under trial."[24]

Another Indian newspaper reporting, also on 28 September, this incident was "DNA" (Daily News and Analysis). They described this incident in a similar manner: "[PA] was brought to the hospital along with other detainees under police escort for regular medical check-up. After the check-up he requested two Local Armoury police personnel to allow him to use the washroom. In the intervening period, one of the constables went to the Pathology department, while another escorted him to the toilet. When he did not come out of the toilet after a few minutes, the constable suspected foul play. Even after banging the door, the accused did not relent. The constable climbed the door to peep inside and was shocked to find the accused bending the iron grills of the toilet window and sneaking out."[25]

There are two significant differences between PA's account and both newspapers' account of his escape from the toilet. Firstly, he had to give a sample of urine, and this is always done in a modest manner in a toilet and this was obviously the reason he was in the toilet, and not that he had asked to use it. Secondly, it would seem according to PA's account, that he had already escaped from the toilet before the police discovered he was no longer there – he does not mention any banging on the door of the toilet; in contrast, according to the newspaper reports he was still breaking the window bars when the police caught on to what he was doing.

I [ran]*... to the* [boundary] *wall* [of the hospital], *but I realised it was too high to climb. ... I looked to my right ... and saw two armed guards ... guarding to the entry of the hospital.... I turned to my left and I saw ... a mound of sand piled next to the wall. I ran up the hill and jumped with all my strength and landed on top of the wall. (p.322)*

In the long list of repairs given in the above mentioned Report, which needed to be done on the Grant Medical College building is an item which concerns the entire JJ Hospital campus: "Boundary Wall, fencing, gate restoration" at a cost of one million Indian rupees.[26] For security reasons, in order that terrorists should not enter the campus, and that prisoners who had be brought to the JJ Hospital for medical reasons should not use the opportunity to escape, one needs to have a boundary wall and also armed guards at the gates.

It is thus most important that the boundary wall be in top condition and repairs to it should be given top priority. One of the components required to repair a wall is sand, and it is likely that this was the reason that there was a "mound of sand piled next to the wall." This conveniently placed mound of sand enabled PA to climb over the high wall.

There are 14 gates in the boundary wall around the JJ Hospital campus,[27] each gate having a number. For example, Gate 3 is on Ramchandra Bhatt Marg opposite a motor cycle dealer;[28] Gate 12 is on JJ Road opposite a hotel.[29] Due to the deteriorating security situation, it was reported in 2010, that 8 of the 14 gates had been closed.[30]

I jumped down to the other side [of the boundary wall]. ... *I saw that I had landed in a busy street. (p.322)*

The front entrance to the JJ Hospital is on a road called Ramchandra Bhatt Marg. Originally this road was called Babula Tank Road.[31] In fact many roads in Mumbai have had their names changed. This was as a result of nationalist sentiment which prompted the removal of old European names in favour of ones that honour Indian heritage.[32] The origin of the original street name "Babula Tank Road" is that it is called after the babul or acacia Arabica – a thorny mimosa tree found in most parts of India.[33] Another reason for this name, possibly more plausible, is given below.

On both sides of Ramchandra Bhatt Marg are buildings. These house many diverse activities. There are shops which include those selling clothing for men and women, and there is also one which sells ladies, gents and children's footwear. Also, amongst these shops is one of the biggest bookstores in Mumbai providing medical books, and whilst on the medical subject, there is also a medical store. One who desires dried fruit will find a shop selling it there. In addition to the shops, there are several manufacturers whose factories are located on this street. One of them manufactures all sorts of nozzles for making and decorating cakes, and also icing sets, dessert moulds and many other similar accessories. There are other manufacturers who produce printing materials such as brochures, catalogues, diaries and calendars, and there is also a manufacturer for carbon seals. If one wants to organise a party or a wedding, there is a wedding hall on this road for this purpose. Finally, Municipal Office buildings are to be found there.[34]

From all the above, we can see that there would therefore be numerous workers, customers and public officials going along this road during the daytime. Thus we can easily understand PA describing it as "a busy street."

We might also mention in passing, that Ramchandra Bhatt Marg has been the scene of some skirmishes between the Shias and the Wahhabis (Sunnis), but such skirmishes have been limited to just the throwing of soda water bottles.[35] Shia and Sunni are the two major denominations of Islam, and over the years Shia-Sunni relations have been marked by both cooperation and conflict, with conflict predominating.[36]

I glanced quickly across the street and noticed a small alleyway. I ran towards it and went down its narrow confines. (p.323)

On the opposite side of Ramchandra Bhatt Marg opposite the JJ Hospital about 60 meters east of Laxman Narayan Jadhav Marg and parallel to it, there is a very narrow road.[37] This very narrow road is of length about 250 meters.[38] About half way along this very narrow road is situated a municipal secondary school. At the end of this road is Imamwada Road and situated at the junction, is a municipal primary school.[39] It is also opposite the Mughal Masjig[40] which is an Iranian Mosque. It is at this Mosque that the Shiite Moslems have a ceremony during the first ten days of the first month, called Muharram, of the Islamic calendar. This ceremony includes self-mutilation.[41] This is likely the "small alleyway" which PA saw.

About half way along this very narrow road is a small garden called Babula Tank Garden.[42] In past generations, water tanks were the only source of water in Mumbai. Of the ten tanks in the city, one was named Babula Tank, and was named after a philanthropic citizen who donated the money for this tank.[43] It could be that this garden is the location of the Babula Tank (or at the least, close to it). The tank was filled up in 1907.[44] This is thus another possibility for the original name for the road now called Rachmandra Bhatt Marg.

🕉 🕉 🕉 🕉 🕉 🕉 🕉 🕉 🕉 🕉 🕉

I continued running for another fifty meters... I noticed that ten meters away was a taxi. The alleyway was so narrow that the taxi was blocking the entire street. (pp.323-24)

About 50 metres from the Ramchandra Bhatt Marg end of this very narrow road is an extremely narrow path going from west to east.[45] Quite possibly the taxi was parked on this path thus blocking it.

🕉 🕉 🕉 🕉 🕉 🕉 🕉 🕉 🕉 🕉 🕉

I ran to the taxi, got in quickly and ordered the driver ... 'drive'. (p.324)

The taxis in Mumbai are easily recognisable, since they have distinctive black and yellow liveries with the bottom half painted black and upper half painted yellow. There, the taxis can either be hailed on the street or hired from taxi-stands, and thus PA was

16

easily able to hail the taxi in the street. In the main city districts of Mumbai, auto-rickshaws are banned, thus giving taxi drivers a monopoly.[46]

By the Indian Government's regulations, all taxis are required to have a fare-meter. However, enforcement of this regulation is lax and many taxis operate either without a fare-meter or with a defunct one. In such a case, the fare is decided by bargaining between the customer and the taxi-driver.[47] However, on this method, a knowledgeable user of taxis advises the public "Chuck him [the driver]. There's no dearth of taxi drivers in Mumbai!"[48] In fact it has been said: "There are more taxis per square inch than buses [in Mumbai]."[49]

Many scams and rip offs by taxi drivers in Mumbai have been reported by users of such taxis.

In April 2005, "greenchutney" wrote: "The guy [taxi driver] forgot to put the meter ... when I reminded him he should put it ... he said it's not working and it gives a low reading ... and said he will settle for 400 rupees for the trip to a suburb ... he actually started yelling at me when I said for him to drop me back to the airport since this is illegal and I said I will take him to the cops ... anyway he settled down when I said I will pay what the meter comes up and it came to 234 rupees for the trip ... which seemed about right..."[50]

This comment was answered by "PeakXV" who wrote: "Has anyone ever got an honest rate with a metered ride? If it's not the broken meter, it's the meter with doctored gear that spins around like a watch's second hand on steroids, or the curry-stained extrapolation chart that you need a PhD in math to get your head around. No thanks, I'll haggle it out **before** I step in and not leave the final bill to a meter and a prayer."[51]

The final word came from "goangoangone" who wrote: "Best one I've seen is in Dubai. There's a notice on the dashboard stating: **If the meter is not working, your journey is free.** I think it'll take a while for that to hit India."[52]

A case of a rip off by a taxi driver in Mumbai was reported in January 2010 by "Ali-Monbeam," a parent of a child from Bradford in the north of England. The child had been charged

300 rupees for a journey which would take just five minutes by foot. "Aadil" who lives in Mumbai answered: "Even if he took the cab he should have paid by the meter and he would have paid just 14 rupees instead of 300 rupees!!!" "RPD" was not so sympathetic and wrote: "It's a fair price, because the definition of fair price is whatever both parties freely agree on. US$7 [300 rupees] for a lesson is not bad; western Universities charge much more than that and teach less." The final word came from "jspyder136" who was just about to go on a "massive backpacking adventure all over India" and he indicated that he had learned a lesson from this incident and wrote that "now that I read this, I am not letting ANY taxi driver in India charge me 300 rupees for a taxi ride unless he plans on driving me back home to America."[53]

He [the taxi driver] *turned around and looked at me and asked "To where?"* ... *Suddenly I remembered hearing there was an Israeli restaurant that was not far from where I was.* .... *Then I remembered hearing that the restaurant was in Kolaba* [Colaba]... *'to Kolaba'. (pp.324-25)*

There is a restaurant near the Colaba area of Mumbai, which could loosely be called an "Israeli Restaurant." It advertises its cuisine as "Mediterranean"[54] but the "Hotelier Caterer," India's Only Hospitality Business Weekly, describes its fare as "hovers on Mediterranean fare with a bent on Turkish, Moroccan, *Israeli* and Italian paired exclusively with wines" *(emphasis added)*.[55] A video prepared for this restaurant mentions Israeli dishes several times.[56] Furthermore, one of the patrons in a review written in December 2005, writes that the "Oaf Memulay was interesting."[57] "Oaf Memulay" is the Hebrew for stuffed chicken, and it would seem that these Hebrew words appeared on the menu card.

This restaurant is run by a Jew born in Mumbai who moved to Israel where he worked in a kibbutz restaurant for 6 months. During the course of his career, he worked in the kitchens of non-Jewish hotels in Mumbai and London, and also in a Tel-Aviv hotel.[58] In 2003 he opened his own restaurant in the Colaba area of Mumbai and since then has also opened several cafes in Mumbai.[59]

From the reviews alone of people who have eaten at this restaurant, it can be seen that the food does not conform to Jewish dietary laws - it is not a kosher restaurant. The writer of one review written in December 2005 wrote: "The Harissa Prawns were excellent all round... The bread was grilled to the right level. Not too hard, but just firm to hold the prawns."[60] Prawns are seafood which is not kosher.[61]

Another reviewer gave the menu he and his friend had: "We started with a Cheese Fondue and were busy with it for the next 5 minutes... Main course: 1 Expresso Chicken ... the meat was extremely soft and well cooked ... 1 Beaten Fillet Steak (Yummy yummy beef) .... And a Baked Philadelphia Cheese Cake with a candle."[62] Such a menu does not conform to Jewish dietary laws, since one need not look any further than the fact that they served a cheese dish immediately after a meat dish.[63] Furthermore, the publicised opening times of this restaurant include Shabbat.[64]

This restaurant is situated in a refurbished old bungalow.[65] From this alone, it can be clearly seen that this was not the destination PA was seeking. What he was seeking was on the fourth floor of a hotel. (There is today another restaurant in in Colaba which could be called an "Israeli restaurant," but it was only opened in 2008.[66])

The [taxi] driver drove in a strange and dizzying way using a meandering route. ... We travelled for a long time on side streets and alleyways and when we reached a main highway we were a long distance from the hospital ... then we crossed a big bridge, which passed right by the courthouse. ... The taxi ... crossed over into a different neighborhood, open, with big modern buildings and filled with tourists. The taxi driver stopped the car and announced, 'This is Kolaba [Colaba]'. ... I got out of the cab and

started to look around. I was in a large shopping area, with many
stands and stores and a lot of tourists all around. (pp.325-26)

In the area where the taxi ride began there are a whole maze
of side streets and alleyways.[67] There are two big bridges in the
area which cross a number of parallel railway lines. The more
northerly bridge is the Elphinstone Bridge.[68] The second one is
about one kilometre south of it, and thus a greater distance from
the JJ Hospital, and is called the Carnac Bridge.[69] About one
kilometre south of the Carnac Bridge is the Chhatrapati Shivaji
[Rail] Terminus (Victoria Terminus).[70] It is at this terminus
that all the rail lines finish and so there is no bridge south of the
Carnac Bridge.

There are a number of bridges in Mumbai. They are made of
stone and were built from 1866 onwards. However, after nearly
140 years, their state of preservation has deteriorated and in an
article in "The Times of India" in December 2004 appeared an
article under a rhymed heading "'Bridges to wealth' are in poor
health." Towards the beginning of this article is written: "But the
city [of Mumbai] also has a formidable engineering heritage
in its historical stone bridges many of which, sadly, are in bad
shape today." The writer goes on to quote heritage enthusiast
Ragavendra Kannan who asks why they are "not listed along with
some of Mumbai's historic buildings?"

These bridges were built "to enable the easy passage of large
quantities of goods and people between the walled Fort area and
the docks" and also "to avoid the [railway] level crossings which
apparently took hours to traverse because of suburban trains"[71]

At the time of this article (December 2004) the Elephinstone
Bridge, built in 1868, was in the course of being rebuilt. This
bridge is named after Elephinstone, a former Governor of Bombay
(Mumbai).[72]

Four years earlier in 2001, "The Times of India" had reported
that the Carnac Bridge, which also spanned a number of railway
lines was in a state of urgent repair. Trucks would park bumper to
bumper on either side of the bridge, even though this was illegal,
but the traffic police did nothing about this and as a result of the

excess weight of these trucks, this bridge could one day buckle. When the assistant commissioner of the police was confronted with this illegal parking, he answered that "he was not aware of the problem" adding "However I will look into it and do the needful." The article adds that there were no plans for restoration work.[73] This bridge is also named after a former Governor of Bombay – James Rivett Carnac who held this position between 1839- 1842.[74]

Much further south in Mumbai is the area of Colaba, and it indeed forms the southern tip of Mumbai. The name "Colaba" comes from kolabhat which is a word in the Kolis language. The Kolis were the indigenous inhabitants of the islands before the arrival of the Portuguese. At a later date, the Portuguese Princess, Catherine of Braganza (sister of Alphonso VI, the then Portuguese monarch) gave as her dowry the area of Colaba (and the neighbouring cluster of islands) to her newly wedded husband the British monarch King Charles the second.[75]

Colaba is today a major shopping district for both tourists and locals and it is regarded as a "one-stop shop" where one can buy anything one wants and it is also the place for the cheapest clothes after bargaining a bit. There, there are numerous international world-renowned chain stores selling all manner of clothing, such as jeans, shoes or athletic apparel. For food, one can find numerous grocery stores and supermarkets. The visitor will have no difficulty in finding fast food shops, pizza stores, cake shops and restaurants in the area. Some are vegetarian whilst others are not. There are also markets in Colaba where one can buy such things as vegetables, fish and clothing. The most famous market in Colaba is the "Colaba Causeway Market." There one has a choice of three languages – Hindi, English and Marathi. This market is famed for its silver jewellery, shoes and books. If one wants one's name to be written on a grain of rice, they say that this is possible in this market![76]

Colaba has been described as having an old English charm and at the same time having a very modern feel.[77]

There are a large number of hotels in Colaba, which as in any other place, are of differing standards – ranging from 5 star to budget. It is now common for visitors at hotels to write their comments on the internet. Some of these comments will be favourable, whilst others will be otherwise. As an example, for hotels in Colaba, in October 2005, "thestens" wrote on a hotel he had stayed at: "Scruffy, dirty hole. The first thing we saw on arrival was a rat - and it didn't get any better! We arrived at 3 am after booking on line, so had no option but to stay. We have travelled extensively on a budget in India, so aren't unrealistic, but this was scruffy rip off! We didn't discover any! The room we had booked with en suite bathroom didn't have one." In answer to this uncomplimentary comment, "Watson" wrote: "Weird? I stayed at both their guest house directly on Colaba road and at the main complex and I thought that both the rooms I had were clean, spacious and sunny. Friendly staff and well an all-around good place to spend the night. They gave rooms at the guesthouse for around 995 rupees. It's a bit loud, but pretty ok."[78] In an attempt to resolve these two contradictory comments, it would seem that the writers had mixed up two different hotels that happened to have the same name!

The main road through Colaba is Shahid Bhagat Singh Marg (Colaba Causeway Road). This is a vibrant road which is full of offices, shops and restaurants, and in addition things are sold on its sidewalks.[79]

From the above it can be seen that in Colaba there is, as stated in PA's book, a "large shopping area, with many stands and stores" and the presence of many hotels indicates that there will be "a lot of tourists all around."

Let us now try and reconstruct the route taken by PA's taxi from the alleyway near the JJ Hospital to Colaba, allowing for the fact that the details given in the book are very sketchy. Here is a possible route which conforms to almost all these points: The taxi went southwards through a whole maze of side streets and alleyways, crossing the main road Sardar Vallabhai Patel Road,[80] and continued until it reached Lokmanya Tilak Marg (Carnac Road), turned left and after a very short distance crossed the big Carnac Bridge and reached the main highway P.D. Mello Road (Frere Road), which was several kilometres from the JJ Hospital.

The taxi turned right at the P.D. Mello Road and continued on it for about one and a half kilometers until it reached Walchand Hirachand Road. There it turned right and at the T-junction with Dr Dadabhai Naoroji Road (Hornby Road) turned left. It continued until the T-junction with Mahatma Ghandi Road (Esplanade Road) and veered left and continued, passing the Sessions Court, until the roundabout. It exited from the roundabout at Shahid Bhagat Sing Mart (Colaba Causeway Road) and continued until it reached Colaba.[81]

A problem is that PA wrote: "Then we crossed a big bridge, which passes right by the courthouse." In fact, there is no "big bridge" close to a courthouse. Furthermore, PA is almost certainly talking about the "Sessions Court" to which he was regularly taken for a further remand. This court is several kilometres away from even the nearest bridge – the Carnac Bridge. It is very likely that the taxi went passed this courthouse but it was at least ten minutes after crossing the Carnac Bridge and thus his account of the taxi ride is inaccurate in this detail.

The "Session Court" of Mumbai is the court which hears criminal cases. Its decisions can be appealed to the Bombay High Court, which was inaugurated in 1862. It is of interest to note that even when the name of the city was changed in 1995 from Bombay to Mumbai, the High Court retained the name "Bombay High Court."[82] There are also many other courts in Mumbai. One of them is the "Small Cases Court" which hears civil cases. Other courts are the Coroner Court, the Industrial Court and the Juvenile Court.[83]

I ... asked him [a religious Jewish man standing close by] *if he knew if he knew if there was an Israeli restaurant nearby. 'Yes it's at the end of the street on the left. There is a hotel there and the restaurant is on the roof.'... I ran fast following the man's directions and easily found the building. ... I ran inside and pressed the button* [of the elevator] *for the last floor. ... I reached*

the fourth floor and saw a door with "Or HaYisrael" on it. I knocked on the door. ... I went in. (pp.326-27)

The "Israeli restaurant" was in fact the "Bet Chabad" (Chabad House) of Mumbai and the sign on the door read "Bet Chabad."[84] It would seem that the author of the book made these changes so that there would be no repercussions on Chabad for their having assisted his escape from jail. However, since PA, in the lectures he gave, states that he went to the "Bet Chabad" and more especially that Chabad in at least two of their publications[85] state this fact, there is no reason not to mention it here.

How did PA get to Shelley's Hotel, which then housed Chabad House, after alighting from the taxi? It would seem that PA got off the taxi at Apollo Bandar Road, or maybe in Sahid Bhagat Singh Marg opposite Apollo Bandar Road. Following the instructions he received, he went about 300 meters along Apollo Bandar Road till he reached the end of this road and just around the corner after turning left into in P.J. Ramchandani Marg (Strand Road) was Shelley's Hotel.[86]

Shelley's Hotel (which closed towards the end of 2007[87]) was situated at the southern end of Ramchandani Marg, right on the coast, and in the proximity of three other hotels.[88] The building is four storied and has an elevator. It was built in 1935, at the period of the British Raj, and the building has been declared a "Protected Heritage Structure."[89] It had 42 air conditioned bedrooms, which had wall to wall carpets with private bathrooms. Some of the rooms were de-luxe and had added facilities such as a refrigerator. The hotel was regarded as one of the best budget hotels in Mumba.[90]

As with many hotels, there are both positive and negative reviews on Shelley's Hotel. On the positive side, there is: "Good location, very nice small colonial hotel, delux *(sic)* sea facing room spacious and well furnished, large comfy bed, good amenities." On the negative side: "Rude, surly staff at front desk, price I was quoted by email was increased for an additional childs matress *(sic)* on the floor, despite my request stipulating the room was for 3."[91]

Chabad House of Mumbai was set up at the beginning of 2003 in a rented room on the top floor of Shelley's Hotel, by a newly married couple, Rabbi Gavriel and Rivkah Holtzberg. It catered to the city's local Jewish community and travelling Jewish businessmen as well as to Israelis, especially those who had just finished their army service, who were on the way to "party hotspots" such as Goa and Rajasthan. The conditions in Shelley's Hotel were far from ideal for the needs of Chabad. They had no kitchen, little space and a highly disagreeable owner. However, at a later date, they managed to expand their space at this hotel. Despite all these difficulties, they would serve meals. Since there were no kosher chickens available, Gavriel, who was also a shochet would slaughter hundreds of chickens each week.[92] Chabad House in Mumbai offers numerous services which include an Israel Center, a Women's Group, Kitchen Koshering, Food Package Distribution, a Library, and Medical Services.[93] In addition, this Chabad House offers Prison Visitation, and on a number of occasions Gabriel was able to visit PA when he was incarcerated in the Arthur Road jail.[94] [At a later date, in 2006, the Holtzbergs purchased a nearby building, Nariman House, which became the permanent Chabad House of Mumbai, but tragically, in 2008, the Holtzbergs were murdered in a terrorist attack.[95]]

The Chabad House in Mumbai is just one of several thousand Chabad Houses worldwide which can be found in over one thousand cities throughout the world. It was the seventh Lubavitch (Chabad) Rebbe, Rabbi Menachem Mendel Schneerson who founded these Chabad Houses. Each Chabad House is run by a rabbi and his wife and provides educational and outreach activities.[96] Some of these are to be found in well-known cities with large Jewish population, examples being, Jerusalem, Tel-Aviv, New York, London, Manchester, Moscow and Melbourne. However, others are to be found in more obscure places, examples being, Tallinn in Estonia, Seoul in South Korea, Yerevan in Armenia, Lagos in Nigeria, Kinshasa in the Congo, La Paz in Bolivia, and Queenstown in New Zealand.[97]

Chabad – Lubavitch is a Chasidic movement which was founded in the late 18th century by Rabbi Shneur Zalman of

Liadi. The name "Lubavitch" comes from the Russian town Lyubavichi, where the group was based until the early 20th century. In 1940, it transferred to New York, where they purchased 770 Eastern Parkway, which has been their world headquarters since that date. Lubavitch Chasidim all over the world have built replicas of this building in locations which include Kfar Chabad in Israel, Los Angeles, Melbourne, Milan, Brazil and Argentina.[98]

[When PA arrived, Rivkah Holtzberg was in Bet Chabad but not Rabbi Gavriel] *She* [Rivkah] *prepared for me five thousand rupees, a clean white shirt, a baseball cap ...* [PA quickly changed his clothes since he] *was sure that the police would show up at any moment and after thanking her for everything ran outside. (pp.327-28)*

In an article in "Beis Moshiach" published by the Lubavitch in New York, PA describes how Rabbi Gavriel Holtzberg did the maximum to help him whilst he was incarcerated. Every two weeks, he would visit him in jail, or send someone from Chabad House. On Succot he brought him the arba'at haminim, on Purim he read him the megillah, and when he became ill because of the terrible sanitary conditions in the jail, he bought him expensive medicines. Rabbi Holtzberg would also give bribes to those in charge of the jail, so that PA and the other Israelis in the jail would enjoy certain advantages – baksheesh was the way things worked in India! With regards to his escape from jail, PA stated: "When I managed to escape after a year and a half in prison, the first place I went to was the Chabad House, although R' Gabi [Rabbi Gavriel Holtzberg] had asked me not to do so since it could jeopardize their work. Only his wife was there, and when she saw what condition I was in she let me in and gave me some of her husband's warm clothes, money, food and a water bottle."[99]

The courageous assistance given to PA by Rivkah, after he had managed to escape from jail, is also mentioned in an article which appeared in the magazine "Mishpacha" following the brutal murder of her and her husband: "[PA] made his way to Chabad House. Rivka was home alone at the time. Despite her fears, she calmly gave [PA] food and drink, provided him with money and even gave him some of Gavriel's clothes and a hat."[100]

According to the Israeli newspapers, the police learned during their search for PA that following his escape, he had been at the Chabad House, where he had been given clean clothes.[101]

I decided to try and hide in a private hospital called George Kennedy Britz, which is on a small street near the ocean and I hoped they [the police] *wouldn't look for me there. (p.328)*

Although there are numerous hospitals in Mumbai, some governmental, some municipal, and others private, there is no hospital with the name "George Kennedy Britz." It is a mishearing of the "Breach Candy Hospital", which is one of the major private hospitals in Mumbai.[102] It is likely that the miswriting of the name of this hospital arose as follows. The word "Breach" transliterated into Hebrew letters would be bet-reish-yud-tsadi *with an apostrophe symbol after it* to give it the sound "ch." Were this apostrophe to be omitted, it could be read as "britz." "Candy" when transliterated into Hebrew letters without vowel points can easily be read as "Kennedy." Where then does "George" come into the name? George Kennedy is a famous person in show business and by the process association of words, the word "George" became, in PA's mind, part of the name of this hospital!

The Breach Candy Hospital is situated on the coast at 60 Bhulabhai Desai Road, (better known as Breach Candy or Warden Road), in a niche up-market residential and semi-commercial locality of South Mumbai, an area which has high rise buildings.[103] This hospital was established in 1958 and has 173 beds. It has many departments and is regarded as a prestigious hospital, so much so, that even a former Prime Minister Atal Bihari Vajpayee utilised its services. The hospital's many facilities include pediatric services, artificial kidney services and a medical research centre. It is renowned for its medical expertise, excellent nursing care and quality diagnostics.[104]

☗ ☗ ☗ ☗ ☗ ☗ ☗ ☗ ☗ ☗ ☗

I exited the [Shelley] *hotel* [where the Chabad House was situated] *and caught a taxi and headed towards the* [Breach Candy] *hospital. The taxi traveled along the coast far from the main streets. When we arrived at the hospital I immediately realized that I couldn't hide there. It was a small quiet place and I would stand out too much. (p.328)*

Probably the shortest route from Shelley's Hotel to Breach Candy Hospital goes via the main streets of Mumbai, including passing the Sessions Court, and only a relatively small part of this route is on the coastal road.[105] This does not seem to conform with the route taken by this taxi carrying PA. Due to the lack of detail in the book as to the route taken, there are a number of possibilities that the taxi could have taken, to reach the coastal road. One of such possibilities was to go along Apollo Bander Road, turn left at Shahid Bhagat Singh Marg, turn right at the secondary road Fourth Pasta Lane and then veer right to a road near to the coast, Prakash Pethe Marg (Cuffe Parade Road). This road continues into Jagannath Bhosle Road; then one turns left at the junction with Madame Cama Road, which terminates at the coastal road, Netaji Subhash Chandra Bose Road (Marine Drive). One then turns right at this coastal road and continues along it until the Breach Candy Hospital; the name of the road changes several times along this coastal road.[106]

☗ ☗ ☗ ☗ ☗ ☗ ☗ ☗ ☗ ☗ ☗

I ... looked for a store with an international public phone [where he telephoned his wife who was naturally very excited to learn that he had escaped and told her his immediate plans and asked for the family's practical help]. *(pp.328-29)*

The earliest "telephone" can be traced back to 1667 when Robert Hooke invented a string telephone that conveyed sounds over an extended wire by mechanical vibrations. The electric telephone was invented about two hundred years later, but the credit for its invention is disputed and has been attributed to at least six people![107]

In the early days of the telephone, there was no direct dialing – the service was manual. The customer lifted the receiver off its hook and asked an operator to connect him to a requested number. Automatic dialing only came into existence at the beginning of the 20th century.[108] But this was only for relatively short distances. Long distance calls known as "trunk" calls still had to be made through an operator. Initially, they had to be booked in advance and the operator would tell the customer when it could be put through. In about 1920, this procedure was shortened allowing an immediate connection, but still via an operator.[109]

A historic milestone occurred in 1958 when the Queen of England made the first long distance telephone call without an operator when she telephoned from Bristol to Edinburgh,[110] a distance of about 600 kilometres.[111] But that was about the limit in those days.[112] The term "STD" (Subscriber Trunk Dialing) then came into the English language and this means that subscribers can dial trunk calls without using an operator.[113]

Since the late 20th century, most international calls can be dialed directly.[114] Each country has been given a country calling code, for example for Israel it is 972 and for India it is 91.[115] This is then followed by the area code, for example, Jerusalem area is 02, Haifa and Northern area is 04, but the 0 is not used when dialing from outside Israel,[116] and this is followed by the recipient's own telephone number.

From this it can be seem that PA in 2005 was able to dial directly from India to Israel. Incidentally the term "STD" is still used in India to describe any national call made other than one's local unit.[117]

29

I decided to walk along the beach because I was afraid of checkpoints. ... I walked slowly for two hours on the beach. ... I returned to the street, stopped a taxi and ordered him to take me to the Dadar train station, which is very far from the hospital and the prison. After fourty (sic) minutes of smooth driving with no checkpoints, we arrived at the train station. (pp.329-30)

The Breach Candy Hospital is right on the coast and for a reconstruction of the route of PA's two-hour slow walk on the beach, there are a number of possibilities. He could have walked in a northerly direction, in a southerly one, or just backwards and forwards. Following this walk, he returned to the street, namely the coastal road, and took a taxi to Dadar Railway Station. The time for a taxi ride between the hospital and the railway station is about 14 minutes.[118] Since his taxi ride took 40 minutes, it would seem that this two hour walk was in a southerly direction, thus making the taxi ride to Dadar Railway Station much longer than 14 minutes.

Dadar Railway Station is about 8.5 kilometres by road from the JJ Hospital, and about 5.5 kilometres, also by road, from the Arthur Road jail.[119] These distances would accord with PA's expression of "very far from the hospital and the prison."

Dadar Railway Station is just one of the numerous stations on Mumbai's extensive suburban railway system. This railway system began its operations in 1857 and today has a system length of over 300 kilometres. The railway has two lines, namely, the Western Railway and the Central Railway. The Central Railway also has a branch line known as the Harbour Line, since it has stations such as Dockyard Road. Each of the lines has both a fast track and a slow track. Having two such tracks enables some of the trains not to stop at every station and they can therefore overtake trains using the slow track. The fast tracks are also used by long distance (namely, out of Mumbai) trains and by freight trains. Both of the lines begin their operations almost at the southern tip of Mumbai, the Western Railway at a station called Churchgate and the Central Railway at a station called Mumbai C.S.T.[120]

I went to the cashier [at Dadar Station] *and inquired about purchasing a ticket to either Amdabar* [Ahmadabad], *the capital of* [the state of] *Gujarat ... or* [to the state of] *Rajasthan ... The teller informed me that the train to Rajasthan leaves only at night and the train to Gujarat leaves at seven o'clock in the evening* [which was in four hours' time]. *(p.330)*

In addition to the suburban trains which go through Dadar Station, there are also interstate trains which go from Mumbai via Dadar Station to states such as Gujarat and Rajasthan. For example, there is a train called the "Gujarat Mail" which starts at Mumbai Central and goes via Dadar Station, Surat and Vadodara, and whose final destination is Ahmadabad which is in the state of Gujarat; this is a journey of about 500 kilometres and takes about eight and a half hours.[121] The Gujarat Mail is one of the oldest and most prestigious overnight superfast mail trains running on this route. Although it is still titled "mail" it does not (at least since March 2006) carry postal mail anymore.[122] An example of a train which starts at Mumbai Central, whose destination is Rajasthan, and which goes via Dadar Station is the "Jaipur Superfast Special." This train goes via Surat, Vadodara, Ahmadabad, Abu Road, Ajmer Junction and whose final destination is Jaipur which is in the state of Rajasthan; a journey of over 20 hours and of length of over 1,100 kilometres.[123]

Gujarat and Rajasthan are two of twenty-eight states which together with seven union territories are collectively called the Republic of India. These states and territories are further subdivided into districts. Each state has its own legislature, executive and judiciary, the later right up to the level of the state's High Court. Situated in New Delhi, the Federal capital of India, is the Central Government, which comprises three independent branches. These are a bicameral Parliament, whose membership are the representatives of the various states and union territories, the Executive branch of government, and the India Supreme Court whose functions includes appeals from the various state high courts. India is the seventh largest country in the world by geographical area, the second most populous country with a population of 1.2 billion people and the most populous democracy in the world. The name "India" is derived from Indus, which is derived from the Old Persian word Hindu. Its official languages are Hindi and English and there are also numerous recognised regional languages.[124]

I decided that the train was the safest option. The station was full and busy, with thousands of passengers on the train. (p.330)

Dadar is the only railway station which is common to both the Western and the Central lines on the Mumbai Suburban Railway and this makes it a transit point from one line to the other, and as a result, this railway station is the most crowded one on the Mumbai Suburban Railway. Thus PA felt that this station would be the safest way from which to leave Mumbai. In total, this suburban railway carries over six million passengers every day and it has the highest passenger density of any urban railway system in the world. Another record which this railway holds, but far less pleasant, is that more than 3,500 people get killed annually due to their trespassing on the railway tracks, or are electrocuted by the overhead electric wires when they sit on the train roofs to avoid the crowds.[125]

I decided to wait until seven o'clock, and in the meantime I left the station and went to a market nearby. The market was crowded with many Indians shopping. (p.330)

Senapat Bapat Marg (Tulsi Pipe Road) is the road outside Dadar (Western) Railway Station. On exiting from this station and turning left and after going about 300 meters along this road, one reaches the Dadar Manish Market.[126] It is thus likely that this is the market that PA refers to in the book.

Dadar Manish Market is open every day of the week with the exception of Sunday.[127] There are numerous clothing shops of all sorts in this market, with clothes for men, woman and children[128] and one also can buy computer accessories thee.[129] It is also a wholesale market for fruit, vegetables and flowers.[130] A visitor who was at this market early one morning wrote: "People of all ages, in colourful dresses were milling about, negotiating price and picking the best fruit and veg that they could find. During the night lorries arrive from all over India with the fresh produce. Men in shabby and worn shirts, with scarfs in bright colours covering their heads were busy unloading the produce from the backs of lorries. Eager hands receiving the nylon bags and carrying them over to the selling ground. Others were loading small vans, even taxi cabs with the day's purchases to sell at other markets around Mumbai."[131] Dadar Manish Market is just one of more than seventy markets in Mumbai. There is even another market in Mumbai with the name "Manish Market." Of the Mumbai markets "Frommer's India" writes: "It's worthwhile to spend a couple of hours exploring at least one, not so much for the shopping as for the human spectacle of it all."[132] From a list of "important tips" given to the shopper in Dadar, one can see how crowded this area is: "While the area is generally crowded at any given time of day, it is best to avoid going there after 5p.m. If children are in tow, keep a tight grip on their hands as they can easily get lost in the crowds. Keep an equally tight grip of your handbags; ensure that the outer pockets are properly zipped up."[133] Again, because of the crowds at this market, PA felt that it was a safe place to pass the time until the train left.

I went into a coffee shop and ordered a drink ... I sat there for three minutes and suddenly I got a nervous sensation. I was frightened that maybe someone in the coffee shop would realize who I was or maybe the police would come looking for me. ... I had to move constantly and not stop for a minute. (pp.330-31)

The book does not state any identification details of this "coffee shop." However, it is possible that PA looked for a place which was vegetarian since any kashrut concerns would have been minimised. Although there are a number of eateries in the area of Manish Market, it would seem from the wording in the book that the "coffee shop" he went to was situated inside the market. There, there is a snack bar situated on the ground floor of a building, and it is open from nine in the morning until nine in the evening on every day except Sunday. This snack bar states that it is pure vegetarian and its menus are advertised as "fast food, Indian, Punjabi, snacks." It is possible that PA went to this snack bar, but it is of course by no means certain.[134]

I had three hours to pass [until going to Dadar station at six o'clock to buy a ticket for the train]. ... *It was finally six o'clock and I headed towards the train station. At the exact moment I crossed the street I saw a large truck with the words 'Mumbai Security' stop fifty meters away from me. The doors swung open and dozens of police officers started pouring from the truck. ... Some explored the station and some searched the market and the surrounding streets ... They were looking for me! (pp.332-33)*

At about six o'clock PA went back along Senapati Bapat Marg until he reached opposite Dadar Western Railway Station and he then crossed this road in order to get to this station,[135] and it was then that he saw numerous members of the local police force.

The Mumbai Police, which is also known as the Brihanmumbai Police (and these words appear on their logo) is the police force of the city of Mumbai. It has the primary responsibilities of law enforcement and investigation in Mumbai and its motto "Sadrakṣaṇāya Khalanigrahaṇāya," which appears in Sanskrit on its logo, when translated is: "To protect the good and to punish the evil." It is said that although it is considered to be one of the best police forces in the world for solving high profile, high stakes crimes, it is also thought to be influenced by local politicians.

It has a large manpower of over 40,000 policemen of various ranks and has 89 police stations under its jurisdiction. Its many vehicles have the sign, in Marathi which is the main language spoken in Mumbai, "Mumbai Police." It has more than 20 units, which include Crime Branch, Traffic Police, Narcotics Cell, Missing Persons Bureau and Riot Control Police. Each unit has its own Commander.[136]

I saw that to my left was a small crowded alleyway which seemed to be a continuation of the market. I quickly turned around and headed in that direction. ... I continued walking and suddenly I saw at the end of the alley was a checkpoint and police officers were checking every passerby. I quickly turned around. ... But twenty meters ahead I saw two groups of officers spreading out across the alleyway coming slowly towards me. ... I walked straight towards them. ... I continued to walk and I then passed them. They didn't see me. (p.333)

Standing outside Dadar Western Railway Station and looking across the road towards the left, one can see a whole maze of alleyways between Dr. D'Silva Road and MC Jawle Marg (Dadar Road), and they are situated about 150 metres to the right of the Dadar Manish Market.[137]

One of these alleyways is called Smruti Kunj[138] and in it there is a restaurant which recently celebrated its centenary and it describes itself as "the tiny hole-in-the-wall restaurant; it is one of Mumbai's oldest surviving restaurants.[139]

Also in these alleys is the Kirtikar Market,[140] which was built by the Pathare Prabhu. They are one of the Hindu communities of Mumbai and were amongst the earliest settlers in the city. They were amongst the first of the Hindus to adopt to British educational practice. They advocate widow re-marriage which was an act considered a taboo in the orthodox Hindu society at that time.[141]

There are also a large variety of shops in D'Silva Road and Jawle Marg. These include, amongst many others, those selling clothes, electronics, medical supplies, jewellery, stationery, office furniture and household appliances.[(142)] Furthermore, these same two roads, have for many years been a place where illegal hawkers would sell their products, but the police and local council lacked the will to stop them.[(143)]

It can thus be seen that any time of the day there are crowds in this area and this is especially so in the evening hours, the time when PA was there.

It would seem from the description given in the book, that the police checkpoint at "the end of the alley" was at the junction with the main road Saraswatibai Joshi Marg or a little before it. On seeing the police, PA made an about turn and continued back towards the main road Senapati Bapat Marg,[(144)] without the police noticing him.

I left the alleyway and returned to the main street next to the station. ... [On the main street] I saw a taxi waiting at the side of the road. I jumped inside and told the driver ... the name of a different train station located near the city's [Mumbai's] exit and I told the driver to go there. (p.334)

At Dadar Railway station, the two lines of the Mumbai suburban railways, namely the Western Line and the Central Line, converge. The Western Line which is of length 120 kilometres goes through the northern suburbs of Mumbai and then exits the city; stations on this line include Bandra, Borivali, Vasal Road, Virar, Palghar and the final station is Dahanu Road. The Central Line goes in an easterly direction and then branches off into two lines, one in a north-east direction to Kasara station and the other in a south-east direction to Khopoli station, both of which stations are outside the city of Mumbai; stations before the branching off include Sion, Thane and Kalyan.[(145)]

The book does not give the name of the railway station that PA requested the taxi driver to go to. It just states "located near the city's exit." Geographically, there is Mumbai City and adjoining it in the north is Mumbai Suburban District and outside that area is Thane District and Navi Mumbai. Taken literally, a station near the exit of Mumbai City could be, for example, Mahim or Bandra.

🧍 🧍 🧍 🧍 🧍 🧍 🧍 🧍 🧍 🧍 🧍

[Following some thought] *I was afraid that there would be more officers searching for me at the other train stations ... I ...*[instructed] *the driver ... 'Find me a bus station with busses* [sic] *to the North* [of India]'*, He continued driving and we found a tour company which operated bus lines. There was a bus filled with tourists which was about to leave for Goa* [which is south of Mumbai.]. *... The driver went to ask the travel agent where we could find a bus heading north and he directed us to an area called Sim* [Sion] *where there were many buses leaving for the north. I asked the driver to point to the direction of Sim to make sure we would not return to the search area. It was towards the city exit so we headed off for Sim and arrived there twenty minutes later. It was already seven o'clock in the evening. (pp.334-335)*

The details given here in the book are vague and thus they beg a number of questions. At what stage was the taxi driver instructed by PA to change route and go to a bus station with buses to the north? Where was this travel agency situated? Which route was taken to reach Sion?

There was one hour, namely from 6 to 7 o'clock from the time he returned to Dadar Railway Station until he arrived in Sion. Let us try and reconstruct what PA did during this hour. At six o'clock, he saw the Mumbai police arriving at Dadar Station, and he accordingly hurried back to the area of the Manish Market. After managing to avoid the police checkups there, he succeeded in returning to the main road and he boarded a taxi. One could estimate this to have taken about 15-20 minutes.

He then instructed the taxi to go to a station located near the city's exit. It is possible that the taxi went along Senapati Bapat Marg, since this road runs parallel to the Western Line railway

37

track.[146] At some period during this journey, he decided that it was safer to take a bus, rather than a train, northwards, since there were sure to be police checks for him at all the Mumbai stations. He therefore instructed the taxi to find such a suitable bus. As we shall see, that in order to fit in with the time schedule given in the book, it is possible that he came to this conclusion somewhere in or approaching the area of Bandra.[147]

The taxi driver looked for a tour company and found one where a bus with tourists was about to leave for Goa. In the Kalar Nagar area of Bandra East, there is a tour company which has an office there.[148]

There are numerous bus companies who run bus lines between Mumbai and Goa. Many of them have a boarding point in Bandra. Most of these buses begin their journeys from Borivali, which is in the north of Mumbai, or from Dhobi Talao, which is in the south of this city, or from Mumbai Central. These buses are also of different degrees of comfort. Some are Volvo, some are air-conditioned, some have sleeping berths, whilst others have slumber seats.[149]

Goa is the smallest by area of India's 28 states and the fourth smallest by population. Per capita it is the richest of India's states. It is located south of the state of Maharashtra (where Mumbai is situated). For about 450 years it was a Portuguese territory. In 1961, the Indian army conquered it and annexed it to India. Goa is renowned for its beaches and is visited by numerous tourists each year.[150] This includes many young Israelis after their army service and some of them visit the Chabad House in Mumbai on their way to Goa.[151]

Let us now try and reconstruct a possible route that this taxi took. The distance by road from Dadar Railway Station to Kala Nagar is about 6 kilometres and the journey time is about 13 minutes.[152] The route of this journey begins along Senapti Bapat Marg; one then continues along Mahim Sion Link Road and turns left to Sion Bandra Link Road where one continues until one reaches Kala Nagar.[153]

There are three ways to travel from Kala Nagar to Sion. In one of them, one starts by travelling northwards, namely in the direction of the exit from Mumbai. The fact that the driver pointed in that direction indicates that this was the route the taxi took. For this route, one travels in a north-easterly direction along Bandra Kurla Complex Road (MMRDA Road) and then turns a very sharp right and continues in a southerly direction along Lal Bahadur Shastri Road (Agra Road) until one reaches Sion.[154] (The other two routes begin by travelling southwards, namely in the direction of deep into Mumbai.[155]) The travel time from Kalar Nagar to Sion on this (first stated) route is about 14 minutes and the distance by road about 7 kilometres[156] and we can assume that this was the approximate time taken for the taxi to go between these two points.

When allowing for the time for the change in route (namely, instead of going to an outlying train station, going instead to a bus station) and the time taken to make inquiries of a bus to the north, the total time of one hour (from 6 to 7 o'clock) seems reasonable.

In conclusion, one cannot however exclude other solutions for the route of this taxi journey and the travel agency visited.

There were many travel agents there [in Sion] *and ... I found a company that operated bus lines to Gujarat with a bus scheduled to depart for Amdabar* [Ahmadabad] *at eight thirty* [that evening], *arriving at seven thirty the next morning. It cost five hundred Rupees. (p.335)*

Numerous tours and travels agents are to be found in Sion. Although most are open for about nine hours each day and are closed on Sundays, there are a few who are open for 24 hours a day, seven days a week. The ratings by users for these Sion travels agents vary from "excellent" to "average."[157] One reviewer wrote: "Very good travel agency for any kind of travel. Personal approach and hassle free job."[158] For a different travel agency, a reviewer wrote: "They are govt. authorized travel agency. My passport was submitted on time and I got it in 28 days, door delivery, timely update was given to me and I found them to be the best travel agency so far for their good work and good service to their customer."[159]

There are a large number of buses which run each day between Mumbai and Ahmadabad. Some of these buses begin at Mumbai Central but have no further boarding points in Mumbai, whilst others have additional boarding points, which on some of the buses is at Sion, and a few even begin their journey in Sion.[160] There is also an interstate bus depot adjacent to Sion Circle.[161]

I wandered around amongst the stores and restaurants [in Sion] *and bought some bananas, apples and cigarettes. (p.335)*

In the immediate area of Sion Circle are to be found a large number of stores which sell a variety of products, such as men's, women's and kid's footwear, furnishings and carpets, novelty stores, and computers and laptops. There are also shops selling cakes, sweets and dried fruits.[162]

Numerous restaurants are also to be found in this immediate area and they serve all manner of foods, both vegetarian and non-vegetarian.[163] One of these restaurant's specialty is South Indian, Chinese and Punjabi foods "and special mention must be made about the CHAATS and MINI MEALS." On this restaurant a reviewer wrote: "The Southy stuff served with Sambhar in small copper kadhais and red and white coconut chutney. I tried the Rava Masala Dosa which was really yummy, no excess oil and tasted perfect. I just hope they wouldn't make the Sambhar sweet." He added that at peak times this restaurant is very crowded, so much so, that one must expect to wait 15-20 minutes.[164] Some of the restaurants even offer a home delivery service.[165]

The book gives no indication where PA bought the fruit and cigarettes. It could possibly be in one of the restaurants, or from one of the many stores in Sion Circle. In addition, there is a shopping centre at the junction of Road No. 8 and Road No. 29 which is just a few minutes' walk from Sion Circle[166] and, just a little further out at the junction of Road No. 8 and Jaishankar Yagnik Road (Flank Road West), there is a Bazaar, which has a co-operative departmental store.[167] PA was wandering in this area for an hour and a half and therefore had plenty of time to go to these areas or even further afield for these purchases.

At exactly eight thirty a new luxury bus pulled up. I got on the bus ... and was amazed at the luxury! ... I leaned back and felt like a millionaire. (p.335)

There are numerous firms who run buses between Mumbai and Ahmadabad. Some of these firms are private firms. In addition to the private firms, there are also public road transport corporations running interstate services. As with the buses running between Mumbai and Goa, there are different degrees of comfort on the private buses running between Mumbai and Ahmadabad; some are air-conditioned whilst others are not; some have sleepers, others semi-sleepers (chairs which tilt backwards), whilst others have just seats. As to be expected, the fares on the public buses (and almost certainly the degree of comfort) are lower than those on the private firms.[168]

After a year and a half in jail with its horrendous overcrowded conditions, PA could really appreciate a luxury bus, that he could honestly say that he "felt like a millionaire."

The bus was ... mostly filled with Indian businessmen. After a few minutes the bus pulled out of the station [in Sion]. (pp.335-36)

The location of the boarding points in Sion might depend on which firm's bus is selected and the locations include cafes, hotels, travel agents and possibly also the bus station.[169] It is not clear whether the word "station" which is used in PA's book means the Sion Bus Station or one of these various firms' boarding points.

Occasionally police officers came on the bus and ask passengers to present their passports. ... [This caused PA to be afraid.] ... I said the prayer for wayfarers more intently than I ever had before. (pp.336-37)

Since most of the passengers on this journey were Indians why should they be asked to produce a *passport*? Maybe it was some sort of identification that they had to show.

When beginning a journey, one has to recite the "Prayer the Wayfarers." In this prayer, one asks the Almighty that the desired destination will be reached safely and that one should be rescued from any enemy, ambush, robbers and wild beasts which one might encounter on the journey. One only has to say this prayer once in a particular day and it should preferably be recited during about the first four kilometres after leaving the city limits.[170] PA was in far more of a danger than most travelers and one can therefore understand why he recited it more intently than he had ever said it before.

[After about four hours travel] *the bus finally stopped next to the guardhouse* [at the border between the states of Maharashtra and Gujarat] *on the side of the road. The driver got off the bus with all the receipts with the names of all the passengers and brought them to the border guards. ... After a few minutes the driver returned to the bus alone ... and we continued our journey ... into the Gujarat State. (p.337)*

The details given in the book on the crossing of the interstate border raise many questions. It states that the driver gave the border guards a list of the names of the passengers. The book would surely have stated if PA had been asked his name when buying his bus ticket and if so, did he give a fictitious name, since it would be very unadvisable to give his own name. In any case, one does not have to produce an identity card or passport to cross a state border within India.[171] Sometimes one has to pay a tax to bring a vehicle into a state.[172] Furthermore, customs duties have to be paid for certain goods if they are transferred across states.[173] Any border checks would thus be for customs charges. In addition, in Gujarat alcohol is forbidden except for non-Indians. This is the only state in India with such a law.[174] As a result, it is smuggled in from the neighbouring states which include Maharashtra.[175] Even truckloads of alcohol are smuggled in![176] It was probably connected with these taxes, customs duties and alcohol smuggling that the bus driver was speaking to the border officials. Due to mental strain, PA obviously thought the worst and that they were checking who the passengers in the bus were.

The location of the border between the states of Maharashtra and Gujarat is just before Bhilad, which is on the Gujarat side. Bhilad is a village whose population is about 7,000 inhabitants and it is situated within the district of Valsad. It is named after a small nearby hill called Bhilkhai hill. This village even has its own railway station and this is also utilised by those living in nearby villages. Since it is surrounded on all sides by industrial areas, it is very popular for residential purposes.[177]

The journey by road from Mumbai to Ahmadabad goes almost entirely along National Highway 8. The total extent of this Highway is from Mumbai, the financial capital of India, to New Delhi, the federal capital. Its total length is nearly 1,400 kilometres. The first 550 kilometres of this highway is from Mumbai to Ahmadabad. In the stretch of Highway 8 within Mumbai, it is popularly known as the "Western Express Highway."[178] On the portion between Mumbai and Ahmadabad, the National Highway 8 goes through a large number of small cities and towns. These include Kasa Khurd, Vapi, Chikhli, Bharuch and Vasad.[179] The various settlements on this route are on the whole spread out and each one is tens of kilometres from the neighboring settlement.[180]

This National Highway 8, is just one of the numerous highways in India. They are maintained by the National Highways Authority of India and each Highway has been designated by a number – the Mumbai-New Delhi Highway as number 8. The majority of these Highways are just two lanes wide, namely, one in each direction. However, in more developed areas, they may broaden into four lanes and closer to big cities, even to as many as eight lanes. Although the Highways in India are only about two per cent of the total road network, they in fact carry nearly 40 per cent of the total road traffic.[181]

One might mention that in addition to the National Highways, India has also begun to construct National Expressways, which are usually four lanes wide. The first one, which was opened in 2004, and goes from Vadodara to Ahmadabad, is about 100 kilometres long, and is, on part of its route parallel with National Highway 8. When travelling from Mumbai to Ahmadabad, one can transfer from National Highway 8 to this Expressway 1, and shorten the time of one's journey by about an hour and a half.[182]

The bus travelled through dark forests, far away from urban life. (p.338)

There are many areas in the state of Gujarat in which there are forests, some of which are classed as dense forests; these areas include Bharuch, Surat and Valsad.[183] It was presumably through these forest areas that the bus that PA travelled on from Mumbai to Ahmadabad travelled.

We reached Amdabar [Ahmadabad] *early in the morning. (p.338)*

The duration of the bus journey between Mumbai and Ahmadabad is about 9 –14 hours.[184] The book states that they departed from Sion in Mumbai at eight thirty in the evening. Thus they arrived in Ahmadabad "early in the morning." On that Wednesday, 28 September, sunrise in Ahmadabad was just before 6.30 in the morning[185] and thus it would be reasonably light soon after six o' clock.

The book did not state where exactly in Ahmadabad PA alighted from the bus. There are in fact a number of bus stops (for example: Ankur, Gulab Tower, Laxminarayan Nagar, Wadaj) and bus stations (for example: AMTS Nava Vadaj, Lal Darwaja, Naroda, Vasna) in different parts of the city (although it is unlikely that an interstate bus whose route is Mumbai to Ahmadabad will go to the parts of Ahmadabad where some of these bus stops are situated).[186] Since PA intended continuing his journey as quickly as possible, it is likely that he alighted close to Ahmadabad Railway Station or the Central Bus Station. (Incidentally, adjacent to the Central Bus Station there is a leprosy hospital.[187])

Most of the residents of Amdabar [Ahmadabad] *the capital city of Gujarat are Muslim. (p.339)*

The city of Ahmadabad was founded in the year 1411 and is named after its founder Sultan Ahmad Shah. The city is renowned as a great textile and commercial centre and is referred to as the "Manchester of the East." It is a prosperous, thriving city and is the largest in the state of Gujarat and the seventh largest in India. It has a population of over four million inhabitants and is the fastest growing city in India. The official languages in this city are Hindi, English and Gujariti. During the course of the year, a number of fairs are held in Ahmadabad, most of them bearing some relevance to some religious belief or event.

Ahmadabad was the capital city of the state of Gujarat between the years 1960 and 1970. During that period, the city of Gandhinagar, named after Mahatma Gandhi, and situated 23 kilometres from Ahmadabad, was built. In 1970, Gandhinagar became the capital city of Gujarat in place of Ahmadabad.[188]

As with almost every city in the world, Ahmadabad's inhabitants practiced a variety of religions, with not all the religions having the same number of adherents. It is incorrect to state that most of the population of Ahmadabad are Muslims. According to the 2001 census of that city 84.62% of the population in Ahmadabad are Hindu, whilst only 11.4% are Muslim. However, despite its relatively small size, the community

45

of Muslims is culturally significant in Ahmadabad, and dates from the times of the sultanate.[189] The rioting between Muslims and Hindus in Ahmadabad has resulted in there being separate Muslim and Hindu areas in the city.[190] The Hindu areas are beautifully kept and are clean, whereas there is a stench of overflowing garbage in the Muslim areas, as a result of the municipality garbage workers refuse to enter these areas fearing for their lives.[191] However, despite this racial tension in the city, in April 2003 a Muslim woman was elected as mayor of Ahmadabad, and what is more, this occurred just a year after the city was ravaged by its worst communal riots in recent time.[192]

I wanted to buy clothing from one of the stores so I could disguise myself as a Muslim. (p.339)

Muslim dress is different from the dress of other religions, since under Islamic law, there are strict regulations regarding modest dressing for both women and men. A woman must cover her entire body with the exception of her face and hands. For a man, the minimum amount to be covered is between the naval and the knees. Although this may seem sparse compared with a woman's clothing, there are pertinent reasons for this ruling. Many Muslim men are employed as construction workers, farmers, and some spend most of the day working under a hot sun, and thus the wearing of as much clothing as a woman would be impractical. The term "hijab" refers to the way a Muslim man or woman dresses. For both women and men, the clothing must be thick enough not to be see-through. It must also be loose so as not to outline or distinguish the shape of the body. For this reason, men often wear a loose, long-sleeved robe extending from the neck to the ankles, which comes in various colours. Such a garment is known as a "thobe" or a "thawb."[193] It is normally made of cotton, but heavier materials, such as sheep's wool is used during colder seasons.[194] This thobe was quite possibly the garment that PA wanted to buy and it would have

46

been quite different from the garments he was then wearing and thus it would act as a disguise.

I hired a rickshaw and asked the boy to take me to an area where I could find a clothing store. We circled the empty streets for about forty minutes, going from one closed store to another. (p.339)

There is no shortage of ways to travel around the city of Ahmadabad. Although the black and yellow coloured taxis that are found in Mumbai are rare in Ahmadabad, there are private taxis which can be hired. With regards to public transport, there are numerous municipal buses run by the Ahmadabad Municipal Transport Services and they cover all the areas of the city. Also, they charge a very nominal price for their services. Although they do not have a fixed time schedule, they operate on a regular basis.[195]

For short distance, people prefer rickshaws. Originally, these were two or three wheeled vehicles which seats one or two persons and they would be physically pulled along by a human. In fact the word "rickshaw" originates from the Japanese word "jinrikisha" which literally means "human-powered vehicle.[196] Such rickshaws were later replaced by a three wheeled tricycle rickshaw which was pedal driven by a driver.[197] At a still later date, this was replaced by a motorized version – often called an "auto." Today this latest version is common all over India and provides clean and efficient transportation.[198]

Every rickshaw driver has a fare chart which states how much the fare should be for different distances. There is also a meter to measure the distances travelled. The passenger is advised when entering such a vehicle to ensure that the driver sets the meter to zero and he should also look at the fare chart and pay accordingly.[199]

It was early in the morning that PA went around Ahmadabad with the rickshaw driver but they found that the clothing shops were not yet open. Although a few shops might open at about ten o'clock, most do not open until about eleven o'clock or even eleven thirty[200] and thus it was not surprising that PA did find one which was open so early in the morning.

The book does not specify in which area of Ahmadabad they looked for a shop selling Muslim clothes but it was quite possibly in the area of the Central Bus Station. One of the shopping malls in this area which sells, amongst many other commodities, clothing, is Manek Chowk. These include several men's clothing shops, although it is not known whether they stock Muslim garments.[201] However, in this area is situated the mosque Jama Masjid. This mosque is described as the most beautiful mosque in India and it was built in the year 1423. It has 260 pillars which support 15 domes of varying heights. It also contains the mausoleum of Sultan Ahmed Shah, the founder of the city of Ahmadabad, and also the graves of the three great rulers of the Shah dynasty in Gujarat. Until this day, this mosque serves as a prayer place for hundreds of Muslims.[202]

Since large numbers of Muslims come to pray in this mosque and there are five daily services in the Muslim ritual, this could indicate that Muslim clothing could be bought in this area.

❀ ❀ ❀ ❀ ❀ ❀ ❀ ❀ ❀ ❀ ❀

I went inside the station ... I went to the cashier and inquired about the next train to Jaipur in [the state of] *Rajasthan. (p.339)*

Jaipur is the capital and also the largest city of the state of Rajasthan. It was founded in 1727 and today has a population of nearly four million inhabitants. It is situated on the eastern side of Rajasthan and is in a semi-desert area. The streets are very well planned and are laid out into six sectors separated by broad streets. Hindi and Rajasthani are the most common languages spoken there, with English, Punjabi and Sindhi also being widely spoken. When the Prince of Wales visited Jaipur in 1853, the whole city was painted pink in his honour and until this day the avenues remain painted in pink, thus giving the city the nickname the "Pink City."[203]

To travel to Jaipur from Ahmadabad, one has a choice of a number of trains each day. The route taken by the trains is via Mehesana, Abu Road and Ajmer.[204] The length of the journey is about 625 kilometres and the time taken for the journey is about 12 hours. At the vast majority of the intermediate stations, the trains' stop time is 2 minutes, but both Abu Road and Ajmer, it is 10 minutes.[205]

However, for some reason, the train which the cashier informed PA was one which went on a longer route, namely via Udaipur, and it took much longer. Furthermore, as we shall now see, it was not a through train, but one that one would have to change at Udaipur.

In fact, it was not possible to have a through train from Ahmadabad to Jaipur, due to different rail gauges. The rail gauge on the line between Ahmadabad and Udaipur is not the same as that between Udaipur and Jaipur.[206] One must therefore change trains at Udaipur.

Rail gauge is the distance between the inner sides of the heads of the two load bearing rails that make up a single railway line. Sixty per cent of the world's railways use a standard gauge of 1.435 metres.[207] However, in India it was determined that, due to the local climatic conditions, a wider gauge of 1.676 metres, known as broad gauge, was advisable,[208] and this is the gauge between Udaipur and Jaipur.[209] However this is not the only gauge on the Indian railways. In fact, three other gauges are to be found,[210] one of them being the metre gauge on the line between Ahmadabad and Udaipur.[211]

I bought a ticket [to Jaipur] *and ran ... in the direction of the train. ... I went into a carriage panting... I went from car to car looking for a place to sit. All the cars were full, but after a long*

49

search I found an empty seat. ... I sat on a bench opposite an Indian family. (p.340)

As at 2005, the Indian railway system spanned over 63,000 route kilometres. It comprised more than 8,000 stations and more than 13 million passengers travelled each day on 14,000 trains.[212]

The trains run on diesel fuel or electricity depending on the route. At the front of each train are the driver and his assistant, and at the tail end is the guard who is in charge of the train. As with other countries in the world, in India there are various classes of travel and the more ones pays for one's ticket, the better travelling conditions one receives, but compared with western prices, the fares are very cheap indeed! These classes of travel include second class general compartment, second-class sleeper compartment, air-conditioned second-class sleeper, and first-class compartments. The second-class sleeper class is the main chunk of a typical express train with each coach holding about 72 passengers and the bunks which are three tiers with each three tiers facing a another three. Each train has a luggage van attached at the ends of each train and most long-distance trains also have a pantry car which serves meals, snacks and drinks.

In almost all the classes of travel, tickets can be booked up to 60 days in advance of travelling and a reservation made. In fact, the only tickets that one can buy at the railway station, and one can even do so when the train is standing at the platform ready for departure, is for a second-class general compartment. There are no seat reservations in this class of travel. In this class, there are often two such carriages at the front of a train and two at the back. The seats are wooden and are in rows of two facing each other. There are no sleeping berths and thus if one was on a long journey, one would have to sleep in a sitting position. The physical conditions on this class are a bare minimum. There are four squat toilets for each carriage, two wash basins and fans.[213]

Since PA purchased his ticket immediately before travel, he obviously travelled in a second-class general compartment. This is confirmed by his comments that he "sat on a bench opposite an Indian family" which is the layout of seats in this class of travel.

These carriages are often overcrowded and one will have to search for a seat. Even after finding a seat, there is no guarantee that you will be able to hold on to it for the entire journey. Should one leave it unattended even for a few minutes, someone else may meanwhile occupy it![214] It indeed took PA a long time to find a seat due to the overcrowding.

⚜ ⚜ ⚜ ⚜ ⚜ ⚜ ⚜ ⚜ ⚜ ⚜ ⚜

It was a nerve wracking trip which lasted the whole day. The train stopped every twenty minutes in a different village. ... At many stations the locals would come on to the train and sold [light refreshments]. *(p.340)*

On which train did PA travel? A train which in September 2005, "stopped every twenty minutes in a different village" was the Mewar Fast Passenger.[215] This train started from Ahmadabad and its final destination was Udaipur. As stated above, there could physically not be any through trains from Ahmadabad to Jaipur, due to the change in railway gauges, and as a result one would have to change trains at Unaipur.

This train departed from Ahmadabad at 7.05 in the morning and arrived at Udaipur at 17.15 in the late afternoon. Between Ahmadabad and Udaipur there were thirty stops, the average distance between each stop was about twenty minutes and the train waited at each stop for two minutes. The stops included Naroda, Talod, Sunak, Lusadiya, Jagabor, Shalashah Thana, Semari, Zawar and Umra. An exception was Himmatnagar which was a junction, where the stop was for ten minutes.[216] Himmatnagar, which literally means the "Town of Courage" has two palaces in the town and is also famous for Asia's best Horse Training Centre.[217] For the first part of the journey from Ahmadabad, this train only stopped at every other station. For stations such as Sahijpur, Jaliya Math and Khari Amrapur,[218] it did not stop. Only local trains that travelled relatively short distances stopped at these stations.[219]

51

Between Lusadiya and Jugabor is the border between Gujarat and Rajasthan,[220] but PA made no special mention of crossing this border. He does however comment that at each station on this entire route, police looked at the passengers in each carriage, but almost certainly not specifically for him.

One may well ask why PA did not take a direct express train all the way from Ahmadabad to Jaipur.

In 2005 (the period of PA's escape) there were several trains each day which went between Ahmadabad and Jaipur. There was the Ahmadabad-Delhi Mail which departed on this route every day at about 10 o'clock every morning. There was also the Ashram Express which made this daily run, departing from Ahmadabad at 17.45. The first of these two trains took about thirteen and a half hours for the journey, whilst the second was a little faster and took just under eleven hours.[221]

In addition there were the Bandra-Jaipur Express and the Bhuj-Bareilly Express which began their journeys before Ahmadabad where they arrived at 5.45 and 19.15 respectively and they then went on to Jaipur.[222]

There were also the Uttaranchal Express, and the Portbandar–Delhi Sarai Rohilla Express, which took this route but they did not make this journey on Wednesday, which was the day that PA travelled by train from Ahmadabad.[223]

All these trains would have been much quicker that going via Udaipur. On the other hand, PA would have had to wait about an additional three hours in Ahmadabad for the earliest of these trains, namely the Ahmadabad-Delhi Mail. Not having secured the Muslim garments to act as a disguise, PA obviously wanted to travel as far away from Mumbai as quickly as possible. It is also possible that the only information that the cashier gave him was for the next train, namely, the slow train via Udaipur.

[A passenger informed PA that] *the train wouldn't reach Jaipur until one o'clock in the morning. ... Everyone* [in Jaipur] *would be*

sleeping [at that hour] *and I wouldn't find a place to sleep. It would be very dangerous to sleep in the street without a passport. I decided to get off the train at Udaipur, a big city that the train would reach at eight thirty at night. [p.341]*

From a study of railway timetables, it seems that the times of day given in the book are not accurate. PA left Mumbai on a bus to Ahmadabad at eight thirty in the evening. He arrived in Ahmadabad "early in the morning." The earliest time that this could have been, when taking into account both the minimum time a bus would take to go from Mumbai to Ahmadabad and the time of sunrise that day, would be soon after six o'clock. PA states that he then drove around in a rickshaw in Ahmadabad looking for a shop selling Muslim clothes for a period of forty minutes. He then went to the railway station, made enquiries regarding a train to Jaipur, and later returned to the station and just managed to catch this train. It would seem that the train was the Mewar Fast Passenger which departed at 7.05. According to the book, there was a lot of activity between soon after six o'clock and 7.05. It is thus quite possible than his time on the rickshaw was rather less than forty minutes.

A further time inaccuracy was regarding the time he arrived in Udaipur. According to the timetable, the scheduled time was quarter past five, whereas he stated in the book that it was half past eight. It is also possible that this train arrived much later than the timetable time, namely at eight thirty - something which is not unusual for trains in India! [224] However, as we shall soon see, the next stage in PA's journey seems to confirm that he arrived in Udaipur well before eight thirty.

PA states that a passenger told him that they would arrive in Jaipur at one o'clock in the morning. Either the passenger was incorrect or the time he told PA is incorrectly reported in the book. Since PA adds that he was worried that he would not find a place to sleep at that time of night in Jaipur, it would seem, as we shall now see, that the passenger erred regarding the arrival time.

In 2005, around the period of PA's escape, the Chetak Express departed daily from Udaipur at 18.15 hours and arrived in Jaipur at 5.20 in the morning[225] – a journey of 436 kilometres and of duration about eleven hours. This would have been a reasonably good connection with a train arriving at Udaipur at 17.15 hours. A less good connection was the Lake City Express which departed daily from Udaipur at 20.50 hours and arrived in Jaipur at 7.15 in the morning.[226] Thus, even on the earlier of these two trains, PA could not have arrived at Jaipur at one o' clock in the morning

Udaipur, which is situated at the southern end of the state of Rajasthan, is known as the "City of Lakes." It was founded by Maharana Udai Singh II in 1559. It is also known as the "Venice of the East" and is also nicknamed the "Lake City." The lakes in this city include Fateh Sagar Lake and Lake Pichola and they are considered as some of the most beautiful lakes in this state. Furthermore, the city is also rated as one of the most beautiful cities in the world. There are also a number of palaces in the city, the largest palace complex being known as the "City Palace." This palace was built on a hill top which gives it a panoramic view of the city and its surroundings. Other beautiful palaces include the Monsoon Palace which is also known as Sajjan Garh Palace. Udaipur has a population of just over half a million.[227]

[From Udaipur, PA telephoned his wife – Wednesday, 28 September - and she told him] *This morning all the newspapers* [in India] *were filled with articles about you and your escape along with pictures. Even here in Israel the Yediot Achronot had an article about you this morning* [which included details of PA's escape and of details of his family.] *(pp.342-43)*

On Wednesday, 28 September, there were indeed articles on PA's escape in at least two English language Indian newspapers,[228] but no articles appeared that day in the Israeli newspaper Yediot Acharonot, nor did they appear that day in Ma'ariv. However, on the following day, there were articles in both of these newspapers, but not in Ha'aretz nor in the Jerusalem Post.

The larger by far of the two articles was in Yediot Acharonot and occupied about a third of a page with a massive headline: "Israeli flees from Indian Jail." It began by stating that "the Mumbai police were making a massive manhunt after PA aged 33, who had been arrested with a suitcase full of hashish and had succeeded two days earlier to escape from under the noses of the police." The article continued that PA "had denied any connection with the drugs which had been found in his possession and argued that he had arrived in India in order to purchase clothes for his brother's shop." The article then went on to state how he had been sitting in jail for over a year awaiting trial and how in India one can wait many years until the end of one's trial. On his family status, it said that PA was married and had two children. It then reported how he was not feeling well, was taken for tests to a hospital, asked to use the toilet, closed the door and fled through the window, without the police guarding him realising what had happened.[229]

The article in Ma'ariv was just a small part of a single column and was headed "Israeli Citizen Escaped from Jail in India." This paper also stated PA's family status, and that several months earlier he had contracted malaria and had been brought for treatment to a local hospital. The article then commented that the guarding of him was not as efficient as it should have been and thus he managed to escape.[230]

⚜ ⚜ ⚜ ⚜ ⚜ ⚜ ⚜ ⚜ ⚜ ⚜ ⚜

[In this telephone conversation, PA's wife also told him about a man called] *Avraham who lives in Varanasi. He has a place there called 'Ohel Avraham' ... He is waiting for you. (p.343)*

As in the case mentioned above in Mumbai, where the book changes the "Chabad House" to "Israeli restaurant', the author also here changes the name of the place to "Ohel Avraham" and the person running it as "Avraham." However, in his lectures he identifies the name of the place as "Habayit Hayehudi" (the Jewish House) and also gives the name of the person then running it as Eliezer Botzer. We shall therefore also use these names.

[Since all trains to Varanasi went via New Delhi, PA was afraid that the police would be looking for him there. He therefore opted for a taxi.] *I went to an area with a lot of taxis ... and I found a driver who agreed to take me* [to Varanasi]. *....We left at ten o'clock. The driver told me it would take around thirty hours to get to Varanasi. ... At four in the morning we reached the border between* [the Indian states] *Rajasthan and Uttar Pradesh. ...* [The border guards told the taxi driver] *that he would have to pay three thousand five hundred rupees to get a permit to enter Uttar Pradesh. ... even if we combined all our money it would not be enough* [to cover this amount]. *(pp.344-45)*

It would seem that the shortest and quickest route from Udaipur which is in the state of Rajasthan to Varanasi, which is in the state of Uttar Pradesh is to travel almost due east and go via Chittaurgarh, Kota, Shivpuri, Jhansi, Orai and Fatehpur. This is a distance of about 1,120 kilometres and the journey takes over 16 hours.[(231)]

The disadvantage of this route, as far as PA was concerned, was that it involves crossing two state borders - Rajasthan to Madhya Pradesh and Madhya Pradesh to Uttar Pradesh - with the consequent additional possible border inspections.

The book clearly states that the border PA intended crossing was between Rajasthan and Uttar Pradesh. No further details of the route taken are given, but there are several possibilities based on a reasonable assumption that the border crossing chosen by PA was the one just beyond Bharatpur.

One of these routes in Rajasthan is via Beawar, Ajmer, Jaipur, Mahwa and Bharatpur; another is via Bhilwara, Shahpura, Kekri, Chaksu, Dausa and Bharatpur; a third is via Bhilwara, Shahpura, Tonk, Gangapur, Bayana and Bharatpur. After crossing the border into Uttar Pradesh, to reach Varanasi one goes via Agra, Kanpur and Fatehpur. The journey is about 1,250 kilometres, which is only slightly longer than the above due east route and takes about 18 hours.[232] PA had obviously preferred to minimise the number of state border crossings and chose a longer route in which there was to be only one state border crossing, namely direct from Rajasthan to Uttar Pradesh.

The journey by car (or taxi) from Udaipur to the border with Uttar Pradesh, just beyond Bharatpur, is about 600 kilometres and takes nearly nine hours.[233] As stated above, the train from Ahmadabad to Udaipur arrived at 17.15 hours rather than 20.30 as stated in the book, and thus the arrival at the state border at about four o'clock in the morning could be a reasonable approximation.

The demand by the border guards to the taxi driver that he would have to pay three thousand five hundred rupees to get a permit to enter Uttar Pradesh is not at all clear. As stated earlier, there is no fee to cross a state border in India. A fee can be demanded to take certain vehicles across or to transport certain produces. It could well be that the border guards were demanding this money for their own pockets!

The only thing [solution for a source of money to pay the border guards] *was to find a branch of Western Union and ask my family to send money. The* [taxi] *driver made a u-turn and we started looking for a Western Union. [p.345]*

The Western Union Company is a financial services and communications company which is based in the United States. It was founded in 1851 in Rochester, New York as the "The New York and Mississippi Valley Printing Telegraph Company," but five years later changed its name to "Western Union Telegraph Company." Its function was to transmit telegrams all over the world and this service continued until 2006, and it was the best-known United States company in the business of exchanging telegrams. In 1871, the company introduced its person to person money transfer service, based on its extensive telegraph network. As the telephone replaced the telegraph, money transfers became its primary business. As of December 2005, the company had 250,000 Western Union agent locations in over 195 countries and territories.[234] This of course included many agents in the area of Rajastha[235] where PA then was.

After an hour and a half we reached a little village in the middle of the desert. ... It was a wealthy village with huge, well-kept homes. The houses had private swimming pools and fancy cars next to them.... I couldn't believe how a village of millionaires blossomed in the middle of the Rajasthan desert. (p.345)

About sixty percent of the total geographical area of the state of Rajasthan consists of desert. This desert is the Thar Desert, (it is also known as the Great Indian Desert) and it also extends into the southern portions of the states of Haryana and Punjab and into the northern portion of the state of Gujarat. The desert also forms a natural boundary which runs along the border between India and Pakistan. The area of this desert is more than 200,000 square kilometres and is the seventh largest desert in the world. There are three principal landforms is this desert region. They are the predominantly sand covered Thar, the plains with hills including the central dune free country and the semi-arid area surrounding the Aravalli range.[236]

The book gives no further details as to the identity of the village that PA reached, or even more precise details as to its location. Furthermore, to state that that village is situated *only* an hour and a half's drive from the border with Uttar Pradesh, *and* that it is in the middle of the Rajasthan desert cannot be correct. The Thar Desert does not extend so far east as to even approach the border with Uttar Pradesh. One would need to travel far more than one and a half hours to reach this desert at all, and even considerably more to reach the *middle* of this desert.

I submitted the following question in April 2010 to IndiaMike in the hope that this village might be identified: "Wealthy village in Rajasthan: I read about a certain little village situated in the desert in the state of Rajasthan about one and a half hours drive from the border with the state of Uttar Pradesh. This village is very wealthy and has large houses with luxurious furniture, carpets, televisions and private swimming pools, and the owners have expensive cars. Can anyone please help me identify this village? Thank you." However, even after about 450 people had viewed this question over a long period of time, there was not even one suggested answers to this question.[237]

Some days after I had submitted my question to IndiaMike, "chooper786" sent my question to "Phasor." There, there were a couple of replies to this question. "NucleusFermi" wrote: "There can be many such [in the east of Rajasthan], and "nikjerry" wrote: "I have heard about this wealthy village in Rajasthan."[238] However, as can been seen, these two answers did not advance my identification of this village,

A possibility that could be put forward is that this village is situated in the Shekhawati area of Rajasthan. This area, whose size is nearly 13,800 square kilometres, is situated in the north-eastern part of the state and it is a semi-desert area.[239]

The name Shekhawati is named after a great warrior named Rao-Shekha, who established this area. He ruled over this territory for many years and died in the year 1488, near Ralawta.[240]

The Shekhawati area includes the districts of Sikar and Jhunjhunu. There the Shekhawats built many imposing buildings. Some specific examples are Roop Niwas Kothi, which was established as a large country house by Rawal Madan Singh who was the former ruler of Nawalgarh. This house sits on an area of over 0.4 square kilometres and its facade is painted in charming colour ochre. Another example is Mukundgarh Fort, which today has been converted into a hotel. It was built in 1859 in a traditional style and spreads over over 8,000 square metres. It has several courtyards, balconies which look as if they are hanging in the air, arched windows and corridors which display the richness, diversity and tradition of the Shekhawati wall paintings.[241]

However, there are numerous villages within these two districts and it is impossible from the book to know which one PA is referring to. It can be said, however, that within these two districts in the Shekhawati are to be found the types of homes described in the book. There, wealthy business magnates live in palatial buildings adorned with fresco paintings in different colours and shades.[242] Artists were commissioned to paint frescos in these houses and these frescos are noted for depicting mythological themes. The buildings are known as "havelis," which is the term used for a building of personal residence in the Shekhawati area. This word is of Persian origin, meaning "an enclosed place," since they used to be closed from all sides with one big strong main gate. The largest havelis could have up to three to four courtyards and were two to three stories high.[243]

The distance from the border to these areas is just over 300 kilometres and it would take about five hours to reach them, (by avoiding crossing state borders)[244] and not just an hour and a half as stated in the book, although in the middle of the night, when there is very little traffic on the roads, as it was in the case of PA, it could well be less.

We asked someone if there was a branch of Western Union there and he told us that a few houses down the road lived the manager of the local Western Union branch. ... We went to the house that we were directed to. [The manager fed PA with fruit salad, allowed him to take a shower and made the necessary arrangements for money to be transferred to PA via Western Union.] *(pp.345-349)*

Since we do not know the location of this village, it is not possible to identify which Western Union branch, he was manager of. There are numerous Western Union agents in the Jhunjhunu area, some of which are located in the city of Jhunjhunu, and others located in Chirawa, Bagar and Dhundlod. There are also a large number in the Sikar area, some of which are located in the city of Sikar, and others located at Jakhal and Nawalgarh. These branches are to be found in a whole variety of places - banks, post offices, travel agents, various stores, cafes, gas service stations. They are usually open each day from about 9 or 10 in the morning until the evening hours, with many being closed on Sundays.[245] It is possible that it was at one of these branches that he was the manager.

'I [the Western Union manager speaking to PA] *have a driver who I work with who would be happy to take you to Varanasi. ... I am going to join you on the trip. ... We have twenty-four hours travel ahead of us.'* ... *We travelled on for many long hours through the desert.* [Several stops were made during the course of the journey so that they could take short naps.] *(pp.347-352)*

A route from Jhunjhunu to Varanasi goes via Alwar, Agra, Kanpur and Fatehpur.[246] The world famous Taj Mahal is in Agra. This building is regarded as one of the most beautiful buildings in the world, and it is reported that in 2003, more than three million people visited it. In 2007, this building was voted as one of the "New Seven Wonders of the World." It was built as a mausoleum by the Mughal emperor Shah Jahan in memory of his third wife in the first half of the seventeenth century. It took over twenty years to build and utilised thousands of artisans and craftsman.[247]

The distance from Jhunjhunu to Varanasi is just under 950 kilometres and the journey normally takes a little over 13 hours.[248] Even if the time taken when they stopped and slept amounts to 4 hours, it still leaves about 7 hours unaccounted for. However, the book states that they travelled for many long hours through the desert. But Jhunjhunu is right at the edge of the desert. However, it is possible that the manager did not go directly to Varanasi but attended to various items of his own business in places situated within this desert for these 7 hours.

'Ohel Avraham' [Habayit Hayehudi in Varanasi] ... [is] *surrounded by a maze of narrow alleyways that are restricted to pedestrian traffic. The driver brought me as close as possible. ... I found an old man who agreed to escort me there ... It was a relief when I saw a building with Hebrew letters saying 'Welcome to Ohel Avraham of Varanasi'. (pp.352-53)*

Varanasi is one of the oldest inhabited cities in the world and it is reputed to be at least three thousand years old, and it is situated in the south eastern side of the state of Uttar Pradesh. This state is the most populous state in India and accounts for over sixteen percent of the total population of the country. Other names for Varanasi are Benares and Kashi. It has a population of over 1,300,000 people and it is situated on the banks of the Ganges River, 320 kilometres from the state capital Lucknow. It is a holy city for Hindus and is one of seven most holy places for them in India, with more than a million pilgrims visiting the city every year.[249]

Varanasi is famed for its "ghats." A ghat is a very special type of embankment, which is actually a long flight of wide stone steps leading down to the river. Hindis will use some of these ghats to go into the River Ganges for a ritual bathing. Some of the ghats are used for cremation purposes. In the course of nearly seven kilometres on the Ganges waterfront are to be found nearly one hundred ghats. Some of them are big, whilst others of them are small. They were built during the eighteenth and nineteenth centuries.[250]

This city is also a pilgrimage site for Buddhists and Jains. In addition, the city is famous for its fine arts and crafts and especially so in the field of silk weaving. It is also a seat of learning, having several universities and colleges teaching a whole variety of subjects.[251]

Varanasi's "Old City," which is situated near the banks of Ganges, consists of a maze of crowded narrow winding lanes that are flanked by road-side shops and scores of Hindu temples.[252] Some of the alleys are so narrow that cars cannot fit through.[253] In fact, taxis are only allowed to go up to a certain point, and thus

PA's taxi could not go as far as Habayit Hayehudi. These alleys are full of many pedestrians, motorcyclists, bicyclists and cows. In fact cows are quite common in Varanasi and other forms of traffic have to work around them.[254] There are numerous advertisement boards in these lanes. Naturally, some are in Hindi, but there are also many in English to attract the tourists and there are even some in Hebrew.[255] One restaurant even advertises in its menu "Israeli pitza."[256]

This maze of streets in the Old City is confusing to the tourist, one of whom wrote in a review: "We would not venture to the Old City ourselves because it is a maze of extremely narrow streets and we knew we would never be able to find our way out. The guide was well worth it or I would still be lost in there instead of writing this review."[257] It was thus fortunate that PA found an old man who was prepared to escort him to Habayit Hayehudi!

In summary, Varanasi is often referred to "the city of temples," "the holy city of India," "the religious capital of India," "the city of lights," and "the city of learning."[258]

As stated above, we see from PA's lectures that the book changed the name of the place PA went to in Varanasi from "Habayit Hayehudi" to "Ohel Avraham." Although in most places in the world, Chabad were the pioneers to set up houses to draw people back to Judaism, in India the first organisation to do so was "Habayit Hayehudi" who began its work there in 1997.

The first Habayit Hayehudi established in India was set up by Rabbi Michi Yosefi in Dharamsala in northern India, and at a later date they were directed by Rabbi Eliezer Botzer, who originally came from Safed in Israel.[259] Their activities included lectures, workshops and singing and were run by suitable young people who were involved in education. Those attending the activities were in the main non-religious Israelis.[260]

A number of branches of Habayit Hayehudi were established in India, including one in Varanasi. The Varanasi one was in operation over each Pesach and also over the period of the Tishri Festivals.[261] It was just a few days before Rosh Hashanah that PA arrived in Varanasi and Habayit Hayehudi was already open for the Tishri Festivals.

Habayit Hayehudi in Varanasi would rent a small hotel from the Indians. At first they rented a certain hotel which is situated about half a kilometre from Varanasi Railway Station and about 3 kilometres from the River Ganges.[262] At a later date they rented the Ganga Guest House[263] and this was place they were at in 2005 when PA was there.

On the second floor [of the Ganga Guest House] *I saw a large balcony. (p.353)*

The Ganga Guest House is situated amongst a maze of streets at B30/250A Nagwa. This is near Assi Ghat, which is one of the ghats next to the Ganges River.[264] The Tourist Guide booklet for Varanasi writes of this ghat: "It traditionally constitutes the southern end of the conventional city. The ghat is located on the confluence of Ganga and Asi. A dip in the river at this place is considered very holy, especially in the month of Chatiya (March/April) and Magh (Jan/Feb)."[265] This guest house is one of the Government of India's approved paying guest houses in Varanasi. It is privately owned by Kailash Nishad, who is also a famous musician.[266] The guest house building consists of five double bedrooms and has three floors and employs two people.[267] It is smaller than the previous hotel that Habayit Hayehudi rented.

Habayit Hayehudi would rent the top two floors of the Ganga Guest House which comprised four rooms. They served food and occasionally allowed people to sleep there. It was mainly non-religious Israelis who visited the place, some on a daily basis and some for Shabbat and Festivals. They would also utilise the roof and for Sukkot they would build a Sukkah there.[268]

A Jewish girl reported on her stay at this guest house: "Happy 24th birthday in Varanasi, India ... I went off to Varanasi for the first time. Here I spent Yom Kipur and Sucot which also was my birthday. It was really nice to spent [sic] it in the 'Jewish House' [Habayit Hayehudi] with a nice family and many good people .... I went on to my Daily Yoga class. In the evening I went to the

Jewish House where I met nice people, to Celebrate my (and Tal's – another Israeli birthday girl) birthday ... Under the 'Suca'."[269]

A Pesach seder was celebrated yearly at this guest house and it has been hosted by the families of Rabbi Eliezer Botzer from Yitzar in the Shomron and Rabbi Oded David from Pardes Chana.[270]

There were all sorts of instruments on the tables, guitars and drums and many books of Rebbe Nachman [of Breslov]. *(p.353)*

Music holds a central part amongst Breslov Chasidim. The numerous recordings of their songs are either a band playing, or an instrumental accompaniment to singing.[271] Thus we can understand why there were "all sorts of instruments on the tables, guitars and drums" in this guest house.

There are also many books which were written by Rebbe Nachman, which were published and disseminated mainly after his death by his closest student Reb Noson. These include "Likutey Moharan" which are Rebbe Nachman's major Torah discourses and which were transcribed by Reb Noson, who in many cases was able to check the transcript with the Rebbe; "Sippurei Ma'asiyot" are 13 stories with deep spiritual lessons; "Tikkun Haklali", are ten Psalms to be recited as a repentance for certain sins; "Sefer Hamidot" is a collection of practical advice which has been gleaned from Torah sources and is presented as epigrams or maxims and arranged alphabetically by topics.[272] It was probably these books, or at least some of them, which PA saw in this guest house.

I immediately felt at home. ... Avraham prepared a small room for me next to the roof, with a bed and a fan. The window looked out onto the Ganges River. (pp.353-54)

The Ganga Guest House is situated close to the Ganges River which is on the eastern side of the guest house and thus PA could easily see it from the window of his third floor room.(273)

[PA telephoned his wife who informed him that she had] *called Rabbi Ovadiah Yosef to ask him how I should proceed on Shabbat. 'The Rabbi said that since you are in a state of pikuach nefesh* [danger to life] *you should continue traveling on Shabbat.'* [However, when the Rabbi heard that PA was in a safe place, he said should stay there over Shabbat.] *(p.354)*

Rabbi Ovadiah Yosef was born in Baghdad in 1920 and four years later immigrated to Jerusalem. Between 1958 and 1965, he served as a dayan (Rabbinical judge) on the Jerusalem District Rabbinical Court. He was then elevated to the Supreme Rabbinical Court and in 1965 became the Sefaradi Chief Rabbi of Tel-Aviv, a position which he held until he was elected in 1973 as the Sefaradi Chief Rabbi of Israel. For the next ten years he held this position. In 1984, the Shas political party was founded in Israel under the leadership of Rabbi Yosef and he remains its spiritual leader today. This party represents the interests of the religiously observant Sefaradi Jews. Rabbi Yosef has written numerous responsa and these are noted for citing almost every source regarding a specific topic, and he is regarded as one of the greatest Rabbis of the generation.(274)

Numerous people submit religious questions to Rabbi Yosef for him to answer and amongst these questions was one by PA's wife asking what PA should do that Shabbat in view of the life-threatening conditions which he faced. There is a principle that pikuach nefesh [danger to life] overrides Shabbat and this is even so when there is a doubt whether it is a case of pikuach nefesh. Not only may one desecrate Shabbat to save lives, one is obligated to do so and the quicker one acts, the more one is to be praised.(275) Even if afterwards it were to be found unnecessary for some reason to have desecrated Shabbat, one will have still done a great thing.[276] Usually pikuach nefesh is associated with a person having some illness which could even remotely be life threatening. However, this is not always the case, A person can be completely healthy but the situation could be such that could lead to a danger to life, Examples could be if there were a fire in a building or serious flooding in the area or an electric power line had fallen in the street. In all such cases, one can desecrate Shabbat to eliminate such a danger.[277]

PA was in such a situation, since if he were to be caught by the police, he would have immediately been returned to the jail, with the life-threatening conditions there. Were it not for the temporary safety of Habayit Hayehudi, the safest solution for him would have been to travel as quickly as possible, including on Shabbat, towards getting out of India.

🏮 🏮 🏮 🏮 🏮 🏮 🏮 🏮 🏮 🏮 🏮

Avraham called me to immerse in the mikvah, which he had improvised on the roof from a water tank. ... It was an awesome experience. (p.355)

Before each Shabbat there are various preparations which are done in honour of Shabbat. One should wash one's whole body in hot water, or at a minimum, one's hands and face (and in places where one goes barefooted one's feet).[278] Some people, especially Chasidim, also immerse in a mikvah.[279] A mikvah is a ritual bath made to certain rigid specifications. In the case of a mikvah for just men, one may use ordinary tap water, as distinct from non-drawn water which has to be used in a women's mikvah.[280] For both a men's and women's mikvah, the water must be "stationery", namely there must be no leakage of water from the mikvah, and also the mikvah must not be classed as a "vessel."[281] The definition of the term "vessel" in the mikvah context will be explained below.

The placing of a mikvah on a roof, as was the case in the Varanasi mikvah, is rather unusual. However, in a book written in 1930, Rabbi David Miller writes about mikvahs and how one can easily build one in one's home!(282).. Incidentally, the book came under a lot of criticism, since he argued that the New York tap water did not come under the category of "drawn water" and therefore could be used in a women's mikvah.(283) However, here we are talking about a men's mikvah, where one can use tap water, and so even if one does not accept Rabbi Miller's views on this point, it does not affect the validity of his other points.

For the materials for the construction of the vessel for the mikvah, Rabbi Miller suggested amongst other things wood which was suitably lined to prevent water leakage, or galvanized sheet-metal. ("Galvanizing" is done by electroplating a layer of zinc on to the iron in order to prevent rusting.)(284)

Even though mikvahs are usually built at ground level or below the ground level, to avoid the problem of it being a "vessel," Rabbi Miller explains how it can be built even at a higher level. He gives a list of rules and conditions to make a vessel into a permitted receptacle to be used as a mikvah. It must first be made incapable of holding water by making a certain size hole at the bottom of the vessel. It is then set permanently on the ground or building, and only then is the hole mended, but in such a way that when the vessel is lifted from the ground or building, the repairing material will come off leaving the original hole.(285)

This is very likely the method that Eliezer used to construct this mikvah. Since he constructed it from a water tank, it was obviously made of metal.

A similar opinion can also be found in Rabbi Simchah Rabinowitz series of books "Piskei Teshuvot," where he writes that a bath tub which has a hole of 3.8 centimetres in diameter and is attached to the ground can be used according to all opinions as a men's mikvah provided it holds the correct minimum quantity of water, and the hole is plugged up to prevent any leakage.(286)

To be able to go to a mikvah after a year and a half in jail, was clearly to PA "an awesome experience."

I dressed in the new Shabbat clothes I was given, organized my room in honour of Shabbat. (p.355)

The Talmud states that one's Shabbat garments should not be like one's weekday garments.[287] The outer garments, such as a jacket and hat should be reserved especially for Shabbat and they should be nicer than one's weekday ones. They should be clean and laundered, but if they are not dirty, they don't have to be washed each week. The inner garments, provided they are clean, need not be reserved for Shabbat. However, it is nice that one's other garments, other than underwear, also be reserved for Shabbat.[288]

It is stated in the Shulchan Aruch that the house must also be arranged in honour of Shabbat. All the tables should be covered with tablecloths, which are left on throughout Shabbat. The beds should also have covers over them.[289]

PA followed all these instructions with regards to his clothes and to his room.

When the sun began to set, Avraham went up to the roof dressed splendidly in complete Chasidic garb, including a shtreimel. (p.355)

Shabbat begins just before sunset on a Friday. The duration of Shabbat is about 25 hours. On the face of it, it might seem strange that it is longer than 24 hours – the normal length of a day. The reason is that it has not been resolved as to when the Jewish day begins. It could be at sunset, or it could be when it is dark, namely, when one can see 3 medium stars. In addition, one must add some minutes to both before the commencement and after the termination of Shabbat. One therefore begins Shabbat, some minutes before sunset and finishes it some minutes after dark.[290] All this makes its length about 25 hours. On 30 September 2005, the time of sunset in Varanasi was 17.45, and according to custom, the commencement of Shabbat was at about 17.25.[291]

Before the commencement of every Shabbat, Chasidim put on their traditional Shabbat garb. Chasidism is a movement which was founded in Eastern Europe in the 18th century by Rabbi Yisrael Baal Shem Tov.[292] Today there are numerous different groups of Chasidim, who are named after the town in Eastern Europe where they originated from. These include Gerrer, Belz, Satmar, Lubavitch, Breslov, Amshinov and many many others. Almost all of these groups have their own Rebbe, which is a hereditary office.[293] A notable exception is Breslov. Their only Rebbe was Rabbi Nachman of Breslov (a great grandson of the Baal Shem Tov) who lived between 1772 and 1810, and he had no successor. Until this day, instead of appointing a new Rebbe, the Breslov Chasidim continue to turn to Rebbi Nachman's teachings for inspiration and guidance and still look on him as "the Rebbe."[294]

Many of the various Chasidic groups have a dress code for both weekdays and Shabbat, and there are some subtle and also not so subtle differences between the way different groups dress. Contrary to popular belief, the Chasidic garb has little or even nothing to do with the way the Polish nobles once dressed. A common general feature of dress is that Chasidim wear black jackets and trousers and white shirts. (Gerrer Chasidim tuck their trousers into their socks and this is called hoyzn-zokn.[295]) On weekdays, the jackets of Chasidim are often made of cloth and are called a rekel and on Shabbat and Yom-Tov, they are made of silk and is called a bekishe or kaftan. When praying, all Chasidim wear a gartel, which is like a belt, and this is worn to separate the upper part of the body from the lower part.[296]

With regards to the headgears of the different Chasidic groups, there are many differences. Although on weekdays they all wear black hats, they are of different designs depending on the Chasidic group. Some, such as Gerrer and Slonimer wear a round hat, Stolin and Emunas Yisrael a pinched hat, while Satmer have a hat which resembles a bowler hat with rounded edges on the brim.[297]

On Shabbat and Yom Tov, most Chasidim, including Breslov, Belz, Satmar, Bobov wear a shtreimel. A "shtreimel" is a fur hat made out of sable tails. It is very expensive and each one can cost many thousand dollars. Gerrer, Amshinov and a few others wear a spodik, which is also made of fur but is narrower and taller than the shtreimel. The Lubavitch, however, wear the same type of hat as is worn on a weekday.[298]

Eliezer was a Breslov Chasid. Although the book only directly mentions his shtreimel, from the expression "dressed splendidly in complete Chasidic garb," we can conclude that he almost certainly wore a bekishe with a gartel in the middle.

Many Israeli trekkers came, with long hair, covered in tattoos, and tanned from their long hours on the beaches. (p.355)

In Israel there is mandatory army service for three years for all youth reaching the age of 18. After this mandatory service, many of the youth, particular those who are far from Jewish religious observance, trek to India. They are known as "backpackers." The number, 50,000 Israelis, has been quoted as those travelling annually to India, and they are aged mainly between 22 and 35. They travel to the Far East searching for "spirituality." However, this "spirituality" is not that of Judaism. It is yoga, meditation, karma, ayurvetic healing, Buddhism and Hinduism. All these things can be found in abundance in the thousands of ashrams (religious retreats) which are scattered across India. Many of these ashrams have a guru, who is a spiritual leader whose commands must be followed. There was even a case of a Lubiner chasid who became a guru! There are numerous Jews in these Indian ashrams, some say even a greater number than Indians.[299] When interviewed, an Israeli army veteran aged 24 said: "Our souls need a permanent break from Israel... There's nothing for us back in Israel."[300]

In some places, there are so many young Israelis that there are signs in Hebrew in the stores. Frequently, some proprietors can speak some Hebrew.[301] Food and board are cheap in India. A room with a plank bed and a pink mosquito net costs just five dollars a night and sleeping under a tree is free. Kitchens with names like the "Outback Indian Israeli Restaurant" come with Hebrew-speaking Hindus who ladle vegetarian fare for a few cents a plate. (The reason for vegetarian food is that Hindus are strict vegetarians and probably not because many of the Israelis trekking in India are concerned with kashrut.)[302]

The Israelis have almost taken over Pahar Ganj which is a neighbourhood located just in front of the New Delhi Railway Station. Some of the signs in front of the cafes there are in Hebrew and the fare is Israeli salad (cucumbers, tomatoes, coriander) and falafel, made by desis (a term which refers to people, cultures, and products of the Indian subcontinent) taught by Israelis.[303]

Some of these Israeli youth have been tattooed in India. It has been written of these Israelis in India, "... a gaily decorated group of Israelis ... brightly coloured hair, multiple tattoos, more piercings than a pin cushion and toting requisite drums and other bangles, they grew greater attention than the bangled Rajasthanis. It might have been because they were so loud that everyone turned to stare, or was it their attire?"[304] In the Indian state of Goa there is even an Israeli tattoo parlour.[305] Not only are the Israelis tattooed but almost every other Israeli ones meets in Pahar Ganj has dreads (long matted hair) and multiple body piercings.[306]

The various beaches in Goa, such as Anjuna beach, which is famous for its trance parties, are full of Israelis who are sunbathing there.[307] They are often on these beaches, sometimes for 24 hours a day, with beach parties accompanied by music going on throughout the night. The noise was such that the local population lodged complaints to the authorities about it, since it disturbed their sleep.[308]

Vagator Beach is the northernmost beach of Bardez Taluka, Goa. This beach is divided into three parts, one of them being often called the "Tel Aviv beach" since it is almost entirely occupied by Israelis. It is reported that the Israelis tried to prevent the local population from using this beach, but they were warned that they would be expelled en masse if they continued to act this way. [309]

Places like Habayit Hayehudi in Varanasi gave a traditional Jewish retreat for these Israelis.

Avraham conducted the prayers with an amazing unity and succeeded in reaching everyone's heart. (p.355)

The ma'ariv (evening) service for Shabbat is preceded by a "Kabbalat Shabbat" (Welcoming the Sabbath) service. This Kabbalat Shabbat prelude is of relatively late origin and dates back only to the 16th century. It begins with six Psalms, which symbolises the six week days. This is followed by the singing of the hymn "Lecha Dodi" which was composed by Rabbi Shlomo Halevi Alkabetz, a Safed Kabbalist living in the 16th century. The verses of Lecha Dodi are in an acrostic format with the first letter of the first eight stanzas spelling out the author's name. Originally, in Safed they would go out into the fields and face the western horizon where the sun was setting in order to greet the Shabbat bride as she arrives. Today, during the singing of the last verse, the congregation turns round to face the setting sun on the western horizon, or according to other customs, the door.[310]

There are numerous tunes which are sung for Lecha Dodi, depending on the community. The Breslov have a distinctive melody for Lecha Dodi which was composed by Rebbe Nachman, and there is a recording of it with Rabbi Lazar Brody singing with a musical accompaniment by the Kisufim Trio.[311] There are some feedbacks on this recording: "It brings tears in my eyes when I watch this always," "much love and respect ... breslov is a great inspiration to me ... moshiach soon!" "MARAVILLOSO nigun!" "one of my favourite videos everrrrr *(sic)*."[312] It is very likely that this was the tune that Eliezer sung in Varanasi.

A fundamental of Breslov teachings is to always be happy and Reb Noson (who was Rebbe Nachman's closest student) told a man who had a lot of trouble, to dance every day. Indeed, Breslov Chasidim dance after almost every service, and this of course includes the Shabbat eve service. Based on kabbalistic principles, the dancing is done in a counter-clockwise direction.[(313)] It is likely that it was the melodies and the dancing which "succeeded in reaching everyone's heart" that Friday night in Varanasi.

The popularity of the Breslov Shabbat eve service may be illustrated from that held in the Breslov Synagogue in Safed, Israel, which is the largest Synagogue in that city. It is reported that in the summer, for this service the synagogue is filled to capacity with some worshippers having to stand throughout the service.[(314)]

Afterwards Avraham and his wife served a delicious meal. (p.355)

Following the Shabbat evening service, there is the Shabbat evening meal. This meal begins with the recitation of kiddush (sanctification over the wine).[(315)] The meals eaten on Shabbat should be more elaborate than those eaten on weekdays. It is recommended to have meat, fish and other nice dishes at the Shabbat meals. If one is financially strapped, it is suggested that one cuts down on one's weekday budget for food, in order to honour Shabbat with nice food. It is written in the Talmud that if one detracts from the money spent for food for Shabbat, one will have a lower income that year, and conversely, if one spends more, one will have a greater income during that year.[(316)] With regards to eating on Shabbat, Rebbe Nachman of Breslov said: "One should be extremely joyous on the holy Shabbos [Shabbat] and not show even the slightest trace of sadness or worry. Simply 'take delight in G-d' and enjoy all the pleasures of Shabbos, in food and drink, as well as in fine clothing according to one's means. For the eating of Shabbos is entirely spiritual, entirely holy, and it ascends to a completely different place than the eating of the ordinary days of the week."[(317)]

Hence the delicious meal served on Shabbat at Habayit Hayehudi in Varanasi.

Avraham shared sweet, beautiful, Torah insights and then we all joined in singing the Shabbat zemirot. (p.356)

It is customary during the Shabbat meals to sing zemirot and to discuss words of Torah. Shabbat zemirot are hymns sung at the table on Shabbat. Some are especially for the Shabbat eve meal, others for the Shabbat morning meal, others for the third Shabbat meal, whilst others can be sung at any of the Shabbat meals. The melodies vary greatly from community to community. Many of these zemirot were composed during the Middle Ages; in some cases the authorship is known and in others it is not.[318] Some of the zemirot are universally known and appear in almost every zemirot book and siddur. Others such as "Shalom lecha Yom Hasheviyi" by Rabbi Yehudah Halevi are much more difficult to find.[319]

The Breslov Chasidim are famous for their treasury of rich and varied melodies. They have brought out a large number which appear on CDs, and also on the internet and they can sometimes be downloaded. Music has in fact held a central part amongst the Breslov Chasidim and their families place a tremendous emphasis on singing the zemirot on Shabbat. Many of these melodies were composed by Rebbe Nachman.[320] On the subject of zemirot, it is written in "Likutei Moharan" that Rebbe Nachman would repeatedly tell Jews to sing zemirot on Shabbat and would get angry at anyone who did not make the effort to sing zemirot on Shabbat and motzaei Shabbat. Until his final illness, he himself would throughout his lifetime sing many zemirot on Shabbat and motzaei Shabbat.[321] No details are given in the book of the "Torah insights" which Eliezer gave that night, but it is quite possible that he gave material from the Rebbe Nachman's "Sippurei Ma'asiyot," stories with deep spiritual lessons,[322] and/or from "Likutei Moharan"[323] on that particular week's parashah (Reading of the Torah) which was Nitzavim.

I saw how the Israelis enjoyed themselves, chatting together. *(p.356)*

Since the policy of Habayit Hayehudi is to provide meals for all those Israelis attending, it is most likely that most, if not almost all, of the Israelis who came to the service stayed for the meal. In addition, places like Habayit Hayehudi and Chabad Houses act as meeting places for the various Israeli backpackers in the area to meet each other and exchange news.

Even outside the framework of Habayit Hayehudi and Chabad Houses, Israeli backpackers who were completely secular in Israel, would get together in the Far East and have a Shabbat service and dinner together, the service often being conducted by a person who was formerly religious. One of those who attended such a service wrote: "I never went to synagogue in my life [in Israel] and I'm sure I'll never go when I come back. I'm not religious and I think the haredim [ultra-Orthodox Jews] *(bracketed words in original)* are one of the biggest problems in Israel ... But here, it's a whole other thing..."[324] Another secular Israeli wrote: "In Israel I can't get into this without putting myself in a bad situation. It's either all or nothing over there ... Tonight was different. I'm really interested in my Jewish side, and I love all those old Hasidic songs too ... I can think about religion in a completely different way here. In the East it's OK for me to be with other hilonim [secular Jews] at a Shabbath *(sic)* service. And it's a kind of a relief, to tell you the truth, to see that I don't have to go to an ashram to be spiritual."[325]

There is also a comradeship between Israeli backpackers, who meet for the first time in the Far East. One of them wrote that when he had severe food poisoning, a "group of Israeli strangers" nursed him back to health, even though this caused them a two-day delay in their trip. He described this as "Israelis stick together."[326]

After the meal I went to sleep on a real bed! (p.356)

In addition to eating at Habayit Hayehudi, they would occasionally let people sleep there over night.[327] Needless to say, this was a world of difference from sleeping in Arthur Road Jail!

This jail was built in 1926 and is Mumbai's largest and oldest jail.[328] It is located in the southern part of Mumbai on Sane Gurugi Marg (Arthur Road), and very near to a Jewish Cemetery.[329] In 1994 it was upgraded to become a central prison and its official name became Bombay Central Prison. However, it is still popularly known as "Arthur Road Jail."[330]

The conditions for those in Arthur Road Jail were (and still are) horrendous and do not even meet the minimum conditions for human dignity, which even a person convicted of the most heinous crimes is entitled to. Furthermore, a person could wait for a number of years just for his trial, whilst incarcerated in that very same jail.

To begin with, this jail which houses most of Mumbai's prisoners, is infamous for its overcrowding. Its official capacity is 820 yet there more than 3,400 inmates. In a cell designed to house 50 prisoners are crammed 180 prisoners! There is certainly no room for beds for all these prisoners. They therefore have to sleep in awkward positions or have to sleep in shifts of about three hours.[331]

During the previous year and a half, PA had been incarcerated in Arthur Road Jail in Mumbai, awaiting a trial. There he never had "a real bed" and one can thus fully understand when PA said that that night in Varanasi he slept on a "real bed."

Apart from the lack of sleeping accommodation, the cells are grossly unsanitary. A prisoner there in 2006 described it "the dirtiest place in the world."[332] Most of the toilets do not have doors and the inmates have to take showers in groups as the water supply is limited.[333] Because of these unsanitary conditions, there are life threatening illnesses such as HIV, tuberculosis, and malaria, which are rife in the jail, and these sometimes result in the death of the prisoners.[334] It was in this jail that PA contracted malaria.

The medical facilities, if one can call them that, are ludicrous. As one prisoner summed it up: "Even if we have 10 different ailments, we are given the same medicine. This has become a joke amongst all prisoners."[335]

This type of "medical treatment" was not limited to Arthur Road Jail. A similar comment was made at about the same period by a prisoner in another Mumbai jail: "The medical conditions were horrendous. Doctors gave you paracetamol for any illness, no matter how serious."[336]

A young woman from the South of England, who spent five years in Mumbai jails before being found innocent, described the food given in Arthur Road Jail: "All we ever ate was lentils and rice which were full of stones which cracked my teeth. And it wasn't unusual to find maggots and other insects in the food."[337]

A report issued by "Amnesty International" in August 2000, stated that inmates at this prison had repeatedly been beaten and tortured by the guards and had been threatened by reprisals if they complained to the authorities.[338] Although this report is from the year 2000, this had not changed by the time PA was there. We can see this from an article written by someone who was in this jail in July 2006 who wrote: "If you complain you are beaten mercilessly.... The warden can beat you, push you around... Nobody is there to question him actually."[339] Furthermore, towards the end of 2008, a judicial report strongly condemned the brutal beating of prisoners for two hours by the prison authorities using batons, lathis, belts and stones, in June 2008 at Arthur Road Jail.[340]

However, in complete contrast, for members of crime syndicates who are incarcerated in this prison, their life is one of luxury! They generously bribe the officers and guards in this jail and in return can live in style! As a prisoner summed this up: "If you have money and are highly influential then you can enjoy jail life."[341] PA was not in this category!

I appreciated the fan as the heat in Varanasi was unbearable.
(p.356)

Varanasi experiences a humid subtropical climate with large variations between summer and winter temperatures. The summers are long and extremely hot, with temperatures ranging between 32 – 46 degrees Celsius and last from April to October. The summers are also humid, since Varanasi lies at the Tropic of Cancer. Torrential rain and high humidity accompany the monsoons which usually come in late June or early July and last for about two months. There are also hot dry winds. During the winter there are warm days and cold nights and fog is common.[342] According to historical weather records, on 30 September 2005, the day PA arrived in Varanasi, the temperature there ranged from 25 – 35.7 degrees Celsius, which can be classed as very hot. The mean humidity was 71 per cent, which is relatively high and makes sweating less effective and makes one feel hotter. The mean wind speed just 2.8 kilometres per hour, namely almost no wind.[343]

There is a journal written by someone who was in Sunauli which is on the border with Nepal and is situated in the north of the state of Uttar Pradesh. On the weather conditions of 1 October 2005, he writes:

"... it is broiling hot and muggy here. There's so much humidity that you can't see very far, and the sun is reddish near the horizon. Sitting in the shade, I can feel the sweat pouring off of my body."[344]

The question to be asked is whether one could make the same comments on the weather that day in Varanasi? Unfortunately, there are no extant records for 30 September 2005 or the days around it, for the area of Sunauli, so that one cannot make a direct comparison with the records for Varanasi. However, there are extant records for that day for Gorakhpur,[345] which is about 70 kilometres south from Sunauli, and from them one can see that the temperatures were similar to those of Varanasi. The extant records for the area of Sunauli are extremely patchy, but a direct comparison can be made for the temperatures during September 1999 between Varanasi[346] and the area of Sunauli[347] and they can be seen to be reasonably similar. One can therefore understand PA's comments that "the heat in Varanasi was unbearable."

After two hours I suddenly awoke. There was no air ... Everything around me was dark ... [Eliezer then informed PA] *It seems there is a power outage. It happens all the time. (p.356)*

In their review on their stay at a hotel, which is situated in the same area as the Ganga Guest House, one of the visitors who had stayed in this hotel in the year 2006, commented regarding power outages: "There is a large and noisy generator outside that gets going whenever the mains electricity goes (quite often)" *(brackets in original)*.[348] Another reviewer from the same year on the same hotel wrote: "The air conditioning kept going off the entire 1st night because of the water filtration the city installed that drains the power ... so that wasn't good because it's India hot over there ... but the fan stayed on!"[349]

A power outage on Shabbat can cause an unpleasant situation, since it is not permitted to turn on an electric light or appliance on Shabbat. For this reason, it is thus extremely likely that in a place like Habayit Hayehudi, some corridor and/or bathroom light would be left on throughout Shabbat. In addition, by looking out the window at the surrounding area, one would see some lights. However, with a power outage, everything would be in the dark. Due the heat and the high humidity, without a fan, one would, as PA stated, feel a lack of air.

[Eliezer then said to PA] *I want to ask the* [non-Jewish] *landlord to turn on the generator, because I have a small baby and it's dangerous for him to sleep without a fan in this heat ...* [but] *on*

Shabbat you can't ask him directly, but only with a hint [Following this hint the landlord replied] *I am already turning on the generator for you. (pp.356-57)*

It can be seen from this, that just as the above hotel (and most likely other hotels in the area) had their own generator, so did the Ganga Guest House, due to the regular power outages in the area.

Not only is it forbidden for a Jew himself to switch on the generator on Shabbat, it is also, in general, forbidden for a non-Jew to do this (or indeed any other forbidden labour) on behalf of a Jew. There are several reasons for this which include that by allowing a non-Jew to work for a Jew on Shabbat, it would cause a laxity of attitude towards the sanctity of Shabbat.[350] Furthermore, should a non-Jew do such a labour for a Jew it would be forbidden for the Jew to benefit from that labour throughout that Shabbat and even for a certain period after Shabbat.[351]

However, it is permitted to hint to a non-Jew in a passive manner to do a forbidden labour, and in a case where the Jew does not get direct benefit from this labour, he could utilise the indirect benefit. For example, if a Jew would hint to a non-Jew, "the light is on and I cannot sleep" and the non-Jew would turn off the light, the Jew could remain in the room and go to sleep, since the non-Jew did not introduce a new benefit, but just eliminated a nuisance. If however, a Jew would hint to a non-Jew, "it is dark in this room and I cannot see to read" and the non-Jew would turn on the light, since the Jew would now be getting direct benefit from the light, he would be forbidden to utilise this light to read.[352]

However, there are some cases where a Jew can directly instruct a non-Jew to do a labour for him on Shabbat. One of them is for a non-life-threatening illness. (For a life-threatening illness, a Jew himself may, or in fact must, do the labour himself.[353]) Included in this category of non-life threatening illnesses is putting on the heat on a cold day,[354] or during a heat wave, putting on a fan or the air-conditioning,[355] and this is especially so for a young child.[356] For this reason, Eliezer did not have to hint to the

81

non-Jewish landlord but could have asked him directly to turn on the generator. However, had the weather been such that putting on an air conditioner would have given no benefit even for a small baby, then hinting to a non-Jew regarding an outage of electricity would not be permitted.

Around twenty Israelis came for the afternoon meal. We all enjoyed the delicious cholent and the meal lasted until havdala. (p.357)

On Shabbat morning there is a longish service[357] which includes Reading of the Torah.[358] This is followed by the Shabbat morning meal.[359]

The book does not refer to a morning service held there or to the meal eaten afterwards. It would thus seem that Eliezer and PA prayed individually and ate their morning meal without outside company.

One of the important requirements of Shabbat is hot food and since one of the 39 forbidden labours on Shabbat is cooking, many communities make a cholent before Shabbat. The basic ingredients of cholent amongst Ashkenazi (European) Jews are meat, potatoes, beans and barley and some add a kishke (a chicken neck skin stuffed with a flour based mixture). Sefaradi (Oriental) Jews often use rice instead of beans and barley, and chicken instead of meat and they also include eggs in their shell. These ingredients are cooked before Shabbat in a pot which is kept on the boil on a permitted type of covered gas or hotplate until required during the daytime of Shabbat.[360]

This meal with the twenty participants eating the cholent, obviously was accompanied by zemirot and further Torah insights.

It was once the custom for people to eat just two meals each day, one at the beginning of the night and the other about midday. Since one is commanded to make Shabbat into an enjoyable day, one adds a third meal which is consumed usually during the latter part of the afternoon of Shabbat,[361] and it often continues until after the termination of Shabbat.[362]

At the termination of Shabbat, one makes the havdalah ceremony. This ceremony makes the formal separation between Shabbat and the weekday. This ceremony is made using wine, and also includes the smelling of spices, and the blessing over a flame[363] which by tradition was first made by the first man, Adam, following the first Shabbat after the Creation of the World.[364]

After havdalah, Avraham took out drums and guitars and everyone played and sang on the porch. (p.357)

PA was in Varanasi for Shabbat 1 October 2005. The termination of Shabbat is determined by the time one can see three medium stars which are in close proximity. Many communities calculate this as the time when the solar depression is eight and a half degrees below the horizon. For that Shabbat in Varanasi it was at 6.19 p.m. India Standard Time, which is Greenwich Mean Time plus five and a half hours.[365]

After the termination of Shabbat, a fourth meal called a melave malka is eaten[366] and like the other meals on Shabbat, it is accompanied by zemirot.[367] Many of these zemirot are built around Eliyahu Hanavi (Elijah the Prophet) who by tradition will in the future arrive at the termination of Shabbat.[368] Although playing a musical instrument is not directly one of the forbidden labours of Shabbat, there is a Rabbinical enactment not to play such an instrument, since one might come to repair it should it go wrong.[369] Thus on Shabbat, one cannot have a musical accompaniment to the zemirot. Naturally, this is not the case with the zemirot at the melave malka.

As stated above, music plays an important part in the life of Breslov and there are songs for all occasions, some dating back two centuries. These include a number of songs which are sung at a melave malka, with a number of them about Eliyahu Hanavi.

One of the Breslov's many recordings is a DVD entitled "Breslov Melave Malka."[370]

It is very likely that the songs sung that evening in Varanasi were from these songs. The porch referred to was probably the roof of the Ganga Guest House.

I sent Avraham's worker to the taxi station to find out the distance from here [Varanasi] *to Sunami* [Sunauli], *and to find a driver who would take me. He returned and told me the trip would take eight hours, and that there was a driver who could take me at midnight. (p.357)*

The distance between Varanasi and Sunauli is just over 300 kilometres and the journey between them takes between four and a half and five hours.[371] One can go almost all the way on National Highway 29 by taking the route Varanasi, Saidpur, Ghazipur, Ghosi, Chillipur, Kauriram, Gorakhpur, Pharenda and finally Sunauli. There is also a slightly shorter route, which for much of the way utilizes several State Highways in Uttar Pradesh. This route goes via Lalganj, Azamgarh and Jiyanpur and then joins up with National Highway 29 just before Chillipur.[372]

We do not know which route PA took. According to the above routes, 8 hours is plausible because one cannot discount that since it was the middle of the night, the taxi stopped on route so that they could take a rest.

Furthermore, in contrast to the four and a half to five hours suggested by "Google Maps" for this journey, a traveler in November 2005 reported on a 10 hour bus ride from Varanasi to Sunauli, also commenting that it was "very uncomfortable."[373] Similarly, another traveler in March 2009, reported that a direct bus from Varanasi to Sunauli took 9 hours, but did not add any comment regarding the comfort![374]

Sunauli is a very small town in the district of Maharajganj in the north-eastern area of Uttar Pradesh, a district which came into existence in October 1989.[375] The international border between India and Nepal passes through Sunauli.

[After PA explained to Eliezer his plan to cross the border at Sunauli, Eliezer replied] *'You can't even try to cross a border without a good passport and without a serious plan. ... the only thing I could think of is giving you my passport ... and five hundred dollars in case you need to bribe the guards.' ... [PA] looked at the picture on Avraham's [Eliezer's] passport [and saw that] he has red hair and red beard and blue eyes. I didn't understand how anyone in the world could think that this passport belonged to me. (pp.358-60)*

A passport is a document, issued by a country which certifies, for the purpose of international travel, the identity and nationality of its holder. Amongst the information contained in the passport is the name, date of birth, sex, and place of birth. A passport does not itself entitle the holder to enter another country.[376]

All passports have a formal request printed at the beginning which takes the format: The Foreign Secretary requests and requires all those whom it may concern to allow the bearer to pass freely without let or hindrance and to afford the bearer such assistance and protection as may be necessary.[377] A similar request can even be found in the Bible: "Moreover I said unto the king, 'If it please the king, let letters be given to me to the governors beyond the River, that they may let me pass through till I come to Judah'."[378]

A passport also has a photograph of the bearer and such a photograph has to be made to a number of rigid specifications. These generally include that the photograph must be in colour and not black and white, a light grey or cream background, free from shadows, eyes open and clearly visible, no hair across eyes, the subject looking in a forward direction, a neutral expression, mouth closed and a sharp focus.[379]

As can be seen, although in the past, black and white photographs were used in passports, this is no longer the case in almost all countries and the photographs must be in colour. It would thus seem that the photograph in Eliezer's passport was in colour and thus any border official would immediately see that the colour of the hair, beard and eyes in the passport photograph did not match that of PA's!

In addition to Eliezer giving PA his passport, he also gave him money, in case he would have to bribe a guard. From a report issued precisely at the period of PA's escape (September 2005) by the "Indian Institute of Planning and Management" it can be seen that bribery was the norm in India. On this it states: "Our bureaucracy is equally corrupt to the core and thrives on bribery. 23% of city dwellers in India (assuming Mumbai is typical) [bracketed words in original] are victims of bribery, whereas only 0.2% of the citizens in USA have the same experience. Thus incidence of bribery in India is more than 100 times that in a country like USA."[380]

A statistical survey of the bribery in India came out in a report entitled "India Report 2009," which was brought out by "Business Registry for International Bribery and Extortion (BRIBEline)." This is a project which collects data about "bribe solicitations made by official, quasi-official and private sector individuals and entities." Of the bribe demands, 91% originated from Indian government officials. In order of decreasing frequency, they were from national level government officials, the police, state/provincial officials and employees, and city officials. Bribe demands were also reported being made from individuals affiliated with the Justice System, Visas and Immigration, Mines and Minerals, Construction, Defense, Energy, Foreign Affairs, Forestry, Health Service, Information/Communication and Land. Almost everyone who had been solicited once had been solicited on further occasions, even as many as twenty times! The forms of bribes invariably requested were cash. Just over three quarters of the bribes were related to the avoidance of harm.[381]

I ... got into the waiting taxi and was on the way to Sunami [Sunauli]. *... We arrived at ... eight o'clock in the morning ... at the entrance to the village* [of Sunauli]. *(p.362)*

Sunauli is situated about 70 kilometres north of Gorakhpur and 3 kilometres south of Bhairawa (which is in Nepal), and there is only one main road to it. The nearest railway station is Nautanwa which is about 7 kilometres away.[382] Sunauli's does not appear on "Google Maps" even with maximum magnification – namely 2.8 centimetres for 20 metres, and "Google Maps" cannot even identify the name. Its claim to "fame" is that it straddles the border between India and Nepal. The Nepal side of the village is officially called Belahiya and this does appear on the "Google Maps." Sunauli's total population (on both sides of the border) is about 70,000.[383]

It is not easy to find accommodation in Sunauli and most of what there is, is geared towards catering to the truck drives. These accommodations have been described as not the nicest of places to stay and are not recommended to women travelling alone, Sunauli also has a government hotel for pilgrims.[384] Needless to say, Sunauli is not a popular place for tourists and there is no shortage of non-complimentary comments about it. One of them says: "Most people will want to stay here for the least amount of time possible. In fact, most people would wish they never came here."[385] A tourist writes: "The border town [Sunauli] looks like a wild west mining settlement, noisy dirty, confusing, intimidating. You'll be assailed by rickshaw wallahs as soon as you get off the bus ..."[386] "Wikitravel" describes this place as "small, congested, dusty and dirty ... and the quicker" one can get out of it "the better."[387] A tour operator writes on tours to Sunauli: "Sunauli tours are not about a pleasurable and lingering tour. It is a significant border crossing point where one can avail few services and which features negligible Sunauli attractions."[388]

There were three stone gates on the main road [marking the border crossing into Nepal] ... *The main road was crammed with stores ... The merchandise partially spilled onto the road. The road was already filled with locals with colourful shopping baskets. (p.363)*

One of the major crossing points, and indeed the most popular[389] between India and Nepal runs through the middle of Sunauli. This crossing point has been described as "one of the liveliest in the world."[390] One can also clearly see this from photographs taken at this crossing point. There, there are numerous pedestrians, bicycle riders and rickshaws and large lorries crossing the border. One can also see in these photographs how the streets in the immediate area of the border crossing is cluttered up with merchandise and unattended bicycles. In addition, there are numerous pedestrians, some of whom are carrying shopping baskets and have obviously come to do their shopping and carry it across the border.[391] PA's description of the scene at Sunauli almost exactly corresponds with what can be seen in these photographs.

In the area of the border, on both sides, there are numerous signposts in English with instructions. An example is "Stop. India Immigration. Check post Sonauli. Maharajgadj U.P." and directly underneath this board, another board reading, "Foreigners are requested to stop and get their passports stamp on arrival/departure in India. Check post officer. Sonauli. Maharajganj U.P." The upper board has a line in written in Hindi after the English instruction.[392] U.P. stands for Uttar Pradesh, the name of the State. Maharajganj is a District in Uttar Pradesh in which Sunauli is situated. Sunauli is spelled Sonauli on these boards. There is also a rectangular archway on which is written in English "India Border Ends," but this time the Hindi written on this board precedes the English. Although the meaning of the words in English is not that clear, it means that at that point one is leaving India. Some metres further away, there is a board saying in English "Welcome to Nepal." A few metres further on is a V shaped archway which also has on it in English, the words "Welcome to Nepal."[393]

These are not the only boards welcoming arrivals to these countries. Examples of additional boards state "Wel come (sic) to Nepal. Nepal Police" and "Welcome to Nepal. Nepal Indo Friendship Association" and beside them there is also a small board on which is written "Belhiya" which is the official name of Sunauli on the Nepal side of the border.[394] Likewise, on the other side of the border on the rectangular arch is written "Welcome to India."[395]

I headed towards the [border with Nepal] ... *when suddenly a police officer stood in front of me and motioned for me to come forward.* ... [The policeman then said] *"passport please'...* [Following a short conversation with the policeman and his superior officer who had then showed up, the officer] *glanced at ...* [the passport including Eliezer's photograph in it] *for a minute and flipped the pages to find the visa* [for Nepal, which was not in this passport. PA then made a joke and the] *officer started laughing* ... [Whilst sharing the joke with the other police in the area PA] *gently took the passport from his hand* [crossed through the first gate] *and walked slowly towards the Nepal side* [of the border] ... *I walked forward.* ... *The Nepali guards looked straight ahead and didn't notice me.* ... *After a few minutes of walking I realized I was in Nepal! Nobody stopped me! (pp.363-65)*

To go from India to Nepal (and vice versa) there are two border posts each of them supported by two side pillars. On the Indian side there is a horizontally placed lintel and on the Nepal side it is V shaped.[396] It is therefore not clear why the book writes "three stone gates." Before the border post is a barrier which can be lifted. In all the many photographs where one can see this barrier, it is in the open position.[397]

Needless to say, the official way to cross this border is by presenting the necessary documents to both the Indian and Nepalese officials. However, in a guide published in 2001 on travel in India and Nepal, it states: "It is possible to walk across the border [at Sunauli] without being questioned."[398] A traveller, under the nickname of "neilpollick," relating his experiences in crossing this border in November 2008, writes: "There's an archway at the border line that says you are leaving India. But before you get that far make sure you check in with Indian emigration, a small eminenetly *(sic)* overlookable open fronted office on the right about 100 metres before the border itself. Walk under the arch and then you'll be in Nepal, unchallenged. You'll need a visa to be in Nepal, one you get at the border itself but don't expect anybody to stop you, nobody will insist they stamp your passport or take your money. It's actually possible to walk right across the border, right past the Neplai *(sic)* visa office and disappear into the dark interior of the country without ever stopping to collect your Nepali visa but be warned, if you do that and you get into trouble with the authorities later on you will face a fine big enough to embarass *(sic)* even a wealthy westerner."[399] When summarising the main points of his travelogue, "neilpollick" writes: "You will not be stopped as you cross the border, unless your Kalashnikov is showing."[400] In another travelogue from November 2003, the writer states: "The border crossing [from India to Nepal] was a very lax affair. We knew we needed to get our exit stamp on the Indian side. There appeared to be a large archway dividing the international boundary, and most people just walked or drove through. If there were any guards, they must have gone home."[401] In a report brought out in 2010 by a body concerned with the illicit trade in tobacco products, they state: "International borders between India and Nepal are non-existent; it is no-man's land. India and Nepal share an open border policy."[402]

From all this it can thus be seen how PA managed to cross this border unchallenged.

However, the legal way to enter a country is, in general, with a visa. A visa is a document showing that a person is authorised to enter the country which issued such a visa. Sometimes, a visa takes the form of a document, but more often it is a stamp endorsed in the applicant's passport. In some cases, the visa can be obtained at the border, and in others, prior application is required. The country which issues the visa usually attaches various conditions of stay such as for which period the visa is valid, and the dates of validity. Sometimes two countries will have a reciprocal arrangement which waives the visa requirement. In some cases, a visitor to a country has to pass a security and/or health check on arrival at the border.[403]

All non-Indian citizens (except those from Nepal and Bhutan) require a visa to enter India and they can obtain a tourist visa, which in general has to be obtained in advance, and it is valid for a period of six months from the date of issue.[404] Visas are also required to travel to Nepal and these can be obtained at any Nepal embassy or consulate and at any border crossing point.[405] This of course includes Sunauli.[406] Such tourist visas are valid for 60 days.[407] It is reported that "crossing the border [from India to Nepal] can be a slow tedious business unless 'baksheesh' is offered to officials."[408]

At the border there are Nepal immigration and customs offices, which are officially open for 24 hours a day, although during most of the night, one has to wake up the officers. There is also a Nepal Tourist Office at this border who will give information on the best and cheapest ways to where one wants to go. At this border, one can, and in fact needs to, change one's money from Indian Rupees to Nepalese Rupees, since Indian Rupees will only rarely be accepted in Nepal. There are legal money changers and also black market operators to be found at the border, the latter not giving a good rate of exchange.[409]

I kept walking forward until I reached a large area with buses and taxis. (p.365)

Buses do not cross the border between India and Nepal, even if one has booked a through ticket from a travel agent![410] One has to get a bus to the Indian border, walk across and then get another bus on the Nepal side of the border. The Sunauli Nepal bus station is just a few minutes' walk from the border.[411]

The travel guides do not talk about the Nepal side of Sunauli (Belahiya) in a complimentary manner. They write that it "is a thoroughly disagreeable place – an unflattering introduction to Nepal if you're just arriving, and a rude send-off if you're leaving. Trucks backed up waiting to cross the border and buses trying to enter and leave the bus park produce appalling traffic jams on the Nepal side ... The general mood among travellers finding themselves in this hell is despair, or in the case of those who discover upon arrival that they were cheated by the travel agent in Gorakhpur..." [412]

Buses are the main form of public transport in Nepal. They are both incredibly cheap and very often incredibly uncomfortable! The government bus company is Sajha Yatayat and has distinctive blue and white buses. They are very shabby, poorly maintained and rarely run to schedule and consequently they are not recommended. There are also dozens of private bus companies, some of which have just one bus. Here there is a great range of comfort or discomfort. [413]

The bus booking office in Sunauli Nepal is at the bus stand and it opens at four o'clock in the morning. Since most buses in Nepal travelling in a northerly direction start their journey in Sunauli, if a passenger wants a good seat he is advised to embark there. Buses can be reserved in advance, but only on the day of their departure. [414] From this bus station there are also many daytime buses to the capital city, Kathmandu. [415]

I hired a rickshaw driven by a robust young Nepali. I asked him to take me to the closest hotel. He told me it was around forty [incorrect translation – should be four] kilometres. We set out for the city [of Bhairawa]. (p.366)

A handbook on Nepal writes that "jeeps and rickshaw provide easy and regular transport between the two [Sunauli Nepal and Bhairawa]." [416] The four kilometre journey between Sunauli

(Belahiya) to Bhairawa (also known as Bhairahawa), goes along the Siddhartha Highway (National Highway 29).[417]

PA had a choice of different modes of transport to go from Sunauli to Bhairawa. Since he obviously wanted to get as far away from the border as quickly as possible, it is likely that he chose the first transport that was available, and that happened to be a rickshaw.

Bhairawa and Sunauli (Belahiya) Nepal are in general only visited by people crossing the border or those visiting or making Buddhist pilgrimages to Lumbini.[418] (Lumbini, the birth place of Buddha, is about 25 kilometres from Bhairawa and about a 50 minutes drive.[419]) Although Bhairawa was renamed Siddharthanagar, after Buddha's childhood name, it is still more commonly referred to as Bhairawa.[420] Bhairawa is a town with a population of about 60,000. Although Nepali is the national language, most of the Bhairawa residents speak the local language Bhojpuri.[421] A number of good schools are located there and this attracts pupils from other parts of Nepal.[422] It has a better selection and quality hotels and restaurants than Sunauli.[423]

As we neared the city [of Bhairawa] *Nepali guards at a checkpoint stopped us. ... Fortunately after a short conversation ... the guards gestured the driver to continue. 'What did the guards wanted?' I asked the driver. 'In Nepal there is a serious problem of rebellion against the government. Because of that there are checkpoints everywhere and you'll see the city is full of police and soldiers who are looking for the rebels. (p.366)*

Between the years 1996 to 2006, there was the Nepali Civil war in which there was a conflict between Nepali government forces and Maoist (Communist Party of Nepal) rebels. The aim of this conflict was that the Maoists wanted to overthrow the Nepalese monarchy and establish a "People's Republic of Nepal." During the course of this conflict, nearly 13,000 people were killed. Finally, most of the Maoist demands were conceded and a peace agreement signed. A Constituent Assembly election was held and the monarchy in Nepal was abolished.[424] However, PA's escape was prior to the termination of this war and hence the numerous police and soldiers on the roads. In the months prior to PA's escape, a packed passenger bus ran over a Maoist landmine resulting in the killing of 38 civilians and injuring over another 70. In addition, the Maoists had killed 40 security men.[425]

As a result of these acts of terrorism by the Maoists, the Nepalese government established in 2001, an Armed Police Force, a paramilitary force which was organised as combat brigades and whose aim was to crack down on these acts of terrorism. Each combat brigade was responsible for a different region of the country. This Armed Police Force has 12 roles which include controlling any ongoing or would be armed conflict, controlling armed rebellion or separatist activities, and controlling terrorist activities and riots within Nepal. The service is voluntary and the minimum age for enrollment is 18 years. It started with 15,000 members taken from the police and army personnel and by 2010 it had grown to about 40,000.[426] No figures have been found for September 2005, but one could estimate it to be over 20,000 members. This Armed Police Force is distributed throughout the country, and around border areas.

Shortly after, we arrived at a hotel. I went into the hotel and asked at the reception desk for a room for a few hours. They asked me for two hundred Nepali rupees. (p.366)

There are number of hotels in Bhairawa and many of them are situated on Bank Road which runs to the west off the Siddhatha Highway. One first passes Market Road and just under half a kilometre further on, one reaches Bank Road.[427]

As to be expected, the various hotels in Bhairawa are of different degrees of comfort. For example, one of them in a handbook of Nepal from the year 2006 is described as "a typical no-frills, budget place. Rooms are reasonably large and clean but showers are cold," the price for a room with a bathroom was quoted as 200 rupees. In contrast, for a different hotel, this handbook wrote that it is "the best place in town.... [It] has attentive staff, an excellent restaurant, huge rooms and properly hot showers. Rooms are pretty much perfect and you have the option of air-con [air-conditioning]," here, as to be expected, the price was much higher and was quoted as 500-1,200 rupees.[428] For this latter hotel, a feedback by a tourist "karuna" who was there in 2007 stated "the staff ... were really, really helpful and friendly. They can arrange taxis across the border to Gorakhpur if you've had it up to the ears with buses, which I had."[429] For another hotel stayed at in 2002, "barbara" wrote that it "is basic but v[ery] friendly & the restaurant's pretty good."[430] However, there are also less complimentary comments on the hotels. A tourist who in 2009 wanted a particular hotel which the rickshaw driver could not find and thus ended up in a hotel about half a kilometre away, wrote: "He [the rickshaw driver] ended up taking me everywhere but my destination – the idiot! We ended the pseudo-journey in front of a washed-out white Hotel ... Unfortunately, I was too tired to look for any other hotel. So I succumbed to the charade and got a 1,000 rupee room that didn't even have an AC [air-conditioning]."[431]

PA does not give the name of the hotel he went to. However, the 200 rupees he paid for the room might indicate one of the less luxurious hotels.

[From the moment of his escape, PA had been in regular telephonic contact with his family in Israel. His brother Ari travelled to Nepal to meet him there and that morning they met in the hotel lobby.] *We went up to the room and let our emotions out ... we prayed an emotional Shacharit. (p.367)*

There are three services which a Jew needs to pray on a regular weekday. They are shacharit – the morning service; minchah – the afternoon service; and ma'ariv – the evening service.[432] There are definite time periods laid down in Jewish law for praying these services. Shacharit must be recited in the morning and can be done so up to until one third of the light part of the day has passed.[(433)] There are differing opinions as to how to calculate this "one third," the opinion which gives the latest time uses sunrise as the beginning of the day and sunset as the end.[(434)] In emergency, some allow one to pray shacharit until midday.[(435)]

The coordinates of Bhairawa are: latitude 27.3 N and longitude 83.3 E.[(436)] The time in Nepal is +5 hours 45 minutes from GMT[(437)] and in 2005 there was no daylight saving time throughout the year in Nepal.[(438)] On 2 October 2005, the latest time for praying shacharit under normal conditions was 9.42, and in an emergency at midday which was at 11.42.[(439)]

PA does not state the time he prayed Shacharit that day. However, he states that he arrived in Sunauli at eight o'clock in the morning. He then had to reach the border, cross it, take a rickshaw to Bhairawa, find a hotel, register in the hotel and wait for Ari to arrive. It would thus seem unlikely that PA and Ari prayed Shacharit before 9.42, although noon seems possible.

When praying shacharit one puts on a tallit and tefillin.[(440)] However, the book makes no mention of this, although it is almost certain that Ari had a tallit and tefillin with him when he came to Bhairawa. PA did not manage to bring his tallit and tefillin with him when he escaped.

[Ari told PA that they would] *leave the country* [Nepal] *as soon as possible. 'Maybe we we will even make it to Uman.' ... I knew it wasn't possible. It was Sunday and Rosh Hashanah was the following night. (p.368)*

During his lifetime, Rebbe Nachman of Breslov encouraged his followers to spend each Rosh Hashanah with him. Hundreds of his followers would come to him for the Rosh Hashanah prayers, festive meals and the special Torah lessons which he delivered. He died in 1810 and was buried in Uman which is now in the

Ukraine. The following year, his main disciple, Rebbe Noson, started to organise a pilgrimage to his grave for Rosh Hashanah. From then on, every year, hundreds of Chasidim would come from the Ukraine, Belarus, Lithuania, and Poland to visit his grave on Rosh Hashanah. However, this pilgrimage came to a halt with the Bolshevik Revolution of 1917, which sealed the border between Russia and Poland, and Uman became a closed city and foreigners were strictly prohibited from entering it. However, during the 1920s and 1930s, Breslover Chasidim in Russia continued to go every Rosh Hashanah clandestinely to Uman. The Second World War seems to have put a stop to these pilgrimages and they resumed on a small scale in 1948 when eleven Breslover Chasidim managed to travel from various cities within Russia to Uman, and until the 1970s a similar number went there. In addition, from the 1960s until the fall of Communism in 1989, several hundred Israeli and American Jews would annually make their way to Uman, both legally and illegally. After the fall of Communism, there were no bars to going to Uman and from year to year the numbers going each Rosh Hashanah dramatically increased. In the year 2005, the year of PA's escape, about 20,000 men and boys from all countries and all backgrounds arrived in Uman for Rosh Hashanah.[441]

Uman, (which is a four-hour bus ride from Kiev, the capital of Ukraine), rests on the banks of the Umanka River and it serves as the administrative centre of the Umanskyi Raion (district). Its history goes back to the year 1616, when it was a defensive fort built against Tatar raids and a Cossack regiment was stationed in that town. Amongst the famous landmarks in Uman is the park complex Sofiyivka, which was founded in 1796 by Count Stanisław Szczęsny Potocki, who named it for his wife Sofia. The park features a number of waterfalls and narrow, arching stone bridges crossing the streams and scenic ravines. Of this park Rebbe Nachmann would say: "To be in Uman and not go there?" and it has been suggested that the bridges in this park may have inspired him for his famous quote: "All the world is just a narrow bridge, but the main thing is not to fear." These words in Hebrew have been set to music, and it is sung by Jews around the world.[442]

There was a large Jewish community in Uman in the 18th and 19th centuries. However, during the Second World War, the Nazis deported and murdered the Jews living there. They also completely destroyed the large Jewish cemetery, which included the grave of Rebbe Nachman. After the war, a Breslov Chasid located the grave by finding two metal poles which had been at the head and the foot of the grave. Since the fall of the Soviet Union, the Breslovs have completely refurbished the area of the grave and have built a number of buildings in the area which include a large Synagogue, a number of mikvahs (ritual baths) and a nine floor hotel called Shaarei Zion to accommodate at least some of the Jews visiting Uman.[(443)]

[Ari said to PA] *There are two options* [to get to Kathmandu]. *The first is we travel by car or train; it's a ten hour trip, there are a lot of checkpoints along the way, and I don't think it's worth the risk. (p.368)*

Actually there are no trains in Nepal, other than an obscure branch line from India of limited interest to travellers, the reason being that the landscape is so mountainous.[(444)]

One can however travel between Bhairawa and Kathmandu by car or bus. In 2012, "Google Maps" suggested a route for cars which was of distance of about 280 kilometres. It went via Bharatpur and Benighat, and took just over 6 hours.[(445)]

Buses from Bhairawa to Kathmandu take about 9 to 12 hours, and cost about 120 Nepalese Rupees (as at 2010). There are many buses every day, the daytime ones leaving regularly until about eleven o'clock in the morning and the overnight ones leaving regularly from about four o'clock until seven o'clock in the afternoon.[(446)]

As stated above, at the period of PA's escape, there was a Maoist insurgence in Nepal. The terrorists were attacking the vehicles on the road.[(447)] Thus there were a lot of police checks on the roads.

The second option is to take a flight. The airport is fifteen minutes away from here, and it's an hour and a half flight. ... We immediately hailed a taxi and after fifteen minutes arrived at the small primitive airport. (p.368)

Bhairawa has its own airport, operated by the Nepalese government. It is one of Nepal's busiest airports and its official name is Gautam Buddha Airport, being named after Buddha who was born in nearby Lumbini. The airport is about three kilometres to the west of the hotels in Bank Road.[448] It is a small airport since it only has one runway which is of length of about one and a half kilometres. The airport does not offer the type of amenities which tourists are used to in larger places.[449]

The inadequacy of the water at this airport was described in an article in "The Kathmandu Post" in May 2008. The article is by Madhav Dhungana (who often wrote for this newspaper) and is headed "Bhairahawa airport sans water." Dhungana writes: "If you happen to visit Bhairahawa Airport, you might as well equip yourself with a bottle of mineral water. Water supply in the restroom inside this airport runs intermittently, and no one really enjoys the idea of dry coughing faucets inside public toilets, especially when it belongs to an airport... This problem has persisted for years but the airport administration has not tended to it... The so-called water tanks inside the airport are infested with insects and foul-smelling scum. Even the complaint box, which is stiffed full of complaints and suggestions, has not been opened since years."[450]

As we crossed the threshold [of the airport] *four policemen approached us 'Passport please'. (p.368)*

Since this was just an internal flight within Nepal, it was unexpected that there would be passport inspection. Perhaps this was due the political situation in Nepal.

I took out my passport and gave it to the officer. ... [In the same pocket as the passport were almonds which Eliezer's wife had given PA in Varanasi.] *I reached into the bag of almonds, made a blessing and ate an almond. (p.369)*

According to Jewish Law, it is forbidden to benefit from anything in this world, without giving thanks to the Almighty, and this is done by reciting a blessing. Not to do so would be regarded as stealing from the Almighty.[451] The Rabbis therefore formulated six blessings to be recited before eating or drinking any kind of food, the particular blessing to be recited is determined by the nature of the food being consumed.[452]

The blessing recited before eating almonds is the blessing recited before eating products of trees, namely fruits, and is "who creates the fruit of the tree."[453] This was obviously the blessing recited by PA at the airport.

The almond tree (Prunus dulcis) is a small deciduous tree growing to between 4 and 10 meters in height, with a trunk of up to 30 centimetres in diameter. These trees begin to bear an economic crop in the third year after planting but the trees only reach a full bearing between five to six years after planting. The fruit is mature in the autumn, 7–8 months after flowering. In botanical terms, the fruit of an almond tree is in fact not a true nut but a drupe, which consists of an outer hull over a hard shell with the almond "nut" inside. This tree is to be found, amongst other places, in the Middle East and Far East, which would include India and Nepal.[454]

[The officer asked what these almonds were] *There are no almonds in Nepal and apparently they had never seen them in their life. ... I generously gave them the entire bag* [of almonds], *and took my passport from the officer's hand, which he didn't even inspect ... and got out of there as fast as we could. (p.369)*

It is incorrect to say that "there are no almonds in Nepal." In an undated report (probably about 1998-99) entitled "Deciduous

Fruit Production in Nepal" written by Lok Nath Devkota, the Chief of the Fruit Development Division, Department of Agriculture, in Nepal, the writer states that in 1997 there were 900 "government nurseries" for almonds, but no private nurseries. However, it should be added that this was far fewer than the "nurseries" (government and private) for apples, pears, peaches, plums and walnuts. This report also states that the areas where these almonds were grown were in the high mountain region of Nepal.[455]

A more relevant point could be the market availability of these almonds to the general public. A tourist in September 2007 reports on his travels in Nepal: "As it was our last day we wandered around town [Kathmandu] looking for snacks for our trip, we ended up buying 2 kilos of almonds and raisens (sic) for a homemade trail mix, after much haggling, apparently almonds come from India which explains why they are so expensive in Nepal."[456]

Due to the price and also probably limited availability of almonds in Nepal, it is plausible that these policemen had never seen them, and they were thus delighted to receive them from PA.

As is customary in this part of the world, a little baksheesh can go a long way!

After a short wait, we boarded a small twenty-passenger plane and took off in the direction of Kathmandu. (p.369)

The book does not give any further details about which airplane PA and Ari travelled on. One of the carriers using this airport in Bhairawa is Buddha Air. It is based in Kathmandu and started its operations in 1997. This carrier used the aircraft American Beech 1900D which has 19 seats. This airplane was built by the Beech Aircraft Corporation which was founded in 1932 by Walter and Olive Beech. During the Second World War and the following decades it built numerous civilian and military aircraft, and in March 1991 it was awarded a type certificate for the 1900D aircraft.[457] Another of the carriers using this airport is Yeti Airlines. It started its operations in 1998, and together with its subsidiary forms the largest domestic airline in Nepal. The aircraft it used was the DHC-6 Twin Otter, which also has 19 seats. This airplane is a Canadian "Short Takeoff and Landing" utility aircraft which was developed by de Havilland Canada – (hence the letters "DHC"), a company founded in 1928 by the British de Havilland Aircraft Company.[458] It is quite possible that PA and Ari travelled on one of these aircraft, and this is confirmed by the fact that PA wrote that the airplane was a "twenty-passenger plane."

In February 2008, flights from Bhairawa to Kathmandu took about 45 minutes and cost about $200 for foreigners and $115 for nationals.[459]

The plane landed in Kathmandu and Ari took me to the hotel in which he stayed the night before. Opposite the hotel I saw a large sign in Hebrew 'Beit Chabad, Strictly Kosher Restaurant, Synagogue, Torah Classes and More'. (pp.370-71)

Kathmandu is the capital city of Nepal and is also the largest metropolitan city in that country. The city is the urban core of the Kathmandu Valley in the Himalayas. Its population in 2005 (the period of PA's escape) was approaching 800,000 inhabitants. The history of the city goes back about two thousand years, as is inferred from an inscription in the Kathmandu Valley. However, the name "Kathmandu" is named after a structure in "Durbar Square" called Kasthamandap which is the Sanskrit for "wood covered shelter" and refers to a two-story pagoda built in 1596 by King Laxmi Narsingh Malla, and it is made entirely of wood with no nails nor supports; a legend states that it was made from a single tree. The term "Dunbar Square" literally means a place of palaces and there are three of them in Kathmandu.[460]

Tourism is an important industry in Nepal and in Kathmandu. The neighborhood of Thamel, which is on the north-western side of the city, is the primary area for tourists. In that area there are numerous hotels, guest houses and restaurants.[461] However, from the comments made by various tourists who were in Kathmandu, it can be seen that even the very basic amenities are not up to western standards. Mary Ogilvie who was there in November 2008, wrote regarding the water: "You have to use bottled water for even brushing your teeth, and are advised not to open your mouth in the shower.... Beer is a pretty good alternative." She added that in contrast, the plumbing (presumably at the place where she stayed) was "in good working order."[462] However, at a similar period, two other tourists, Sandra and Betty, did not concur and commented that "sewer drainage is also very bad." They also mentioned the serious problems with the electricity in the city and that for only eight hours a day there was electricity.[463]

Kathmandu's narrow streets are lined with numerous small shops selling almost everything one could want, which includes food, clothes, handicrafts, DVDs which are mostly pirated, and there are also travel agents there.[464] The principal languages spoken in Kathmandu include Nepali, Newari, English and even Hebrew.[465]

The main religions in Kathmandu are Hinduism and Buddhism, and there are a lot of Hindu temples and Buddhist monasteries in this city. Many of the Buddhists there are Tibetan refugees. There seems to be a good relationship between these two religions in the city, since there are many places where the two religions share a shrine.[466] Two hundred years ago, a Western tourist to the city wrote that there were as many temples as there were houses and as many idols as there were people.[467] An encyclopedic article on this city, lists adherents to other religions found there, (but a smaller number than Hindus and Buddhists), and these include Jains, Sikhs, Muslims and Christians.[468] Jews are not listed amongst them, since the permanent Jewish community in Nepal is very small and consists largely of diplomatic officials and staff at the local Chabad House. Nepal is however the most popular place for Israeli backpackers.[469]

As with a very large number of locations all over the world, there is a Chabad House in Kathmandu. It is situated in the

Thamel district of Kathmandu and its address is Gha-2-516-4 Thamel.[(470)] (The term "Gha" means a side-street.[(471)]) One can immediately see that no street name is given for the Chabad House. This is because the minor streets in this city do not have names – just numbers and the area where they are situated.

The Directors of the Kathmandu Chabad House are Rabbi Chezky Lifshitz and his wife Chani, and they have been there since the year 2000.[(472)] Hanging across the street is a board which has on its top line "Bet Chabad Kathmandu" in Hebrew, and on the next line in English "Chabad House." The bottom line is not clear in the photograph but it could be "Chabad House" written in Nepalese script.[(473)] Chabad House in Kathmandu has many activities and according to its published list these include Shabbat Hospitality, Synagogue, Library, Adult Education, and Hospital and Prison Visitation.[(474)]

A traveller who was there in December 2004 described this Chabad House: "At first you notice the small sign pointing to the stairs, then the painted wall on the way to the second floor 'Glatmandu Restaurant' 'Bet Chabad' etc. the door has a big 'Welcome' painted on and swings both ways. After walking in, you notice the myriad of different things going on ... from people eating kosher Schnitzel and Humus, playing on the guitar that is always somewhere here, reading the different notes on the board, travel books and reports or just books. Walking in deeper you notice the small synagogue area and the Internet right next to it, people uploading photos and chatting with family."[(475)]

The Chabad House Kathmandu website states that it is located opposite a certain named hotel. This hotel is a building 5 stories high and it was opened in 1990. According to its prospectus, in addition to the standard rooms, the hotel has 50 de luxe rooms, 5 mini-suites and also an annex which has 40 standard rooms; it has a restaurant and cafe which serve a variety of cuisines which include Chinese, Continental, Indian or Nepalese; there is also a conference room which can accommodate 120 people for a conference and 300 for a cocktail dinner.[(476)] The reviews of those who had stayed at this hotel in 2011 were mixed. Some summaries by "TripAdvisor" include "Clean, comfortable and great location," "Horrible Hotel with even worse service," "Simple but good," and "Worst Place."[(477)]

The book does not state the name of the hotel that Ari stayed in except that it was opposite Chabad House, and it is thus possible that it was this hotel. Alternatively, there are many other hotels in the area of Chabad House[(478)] and the reason that they state they are opposite this particular hotel is that it is prominent as a landmark, even though there is another hotel in the immediate area which is larger or at least of similar size.[(479)]

Many of the stores in the area in the area had Hebrew signs, and the streets were filled with Israelis. (p.371)

The book "Israeli Backpackers" writes on this, "... backpacker ghettos in ... Kathmandu .... contain visible 'sections' that Israelis frequent. Such sections include special guest houses, restaurants, bookstores, and travel agencies catering to Israelis, with Hebrew signs, Hebrew menus, Hebrew fonts in the internet cafes.... Since no one but Israelis can read them, Hebrew signs and notes on bulletin boards around ... Kathmandu give other Israelis encoded information about recommended restaurants, hotels and services."[(480)]

Furthermore, trekkers in Kathmandu have reported on the Hebrew signs. One of them wrote: "Trekking in Nepal is fashionable among young Israelis. So much so that many shops in Kathmandu and Pokhara have signs in Hebrew."[(481)] Another one wrote: "Quite a few Israelis in Kathmandu, lots of signs in Ivrit [Hebrew]."[(482)] Yet another wrote: "Lakeside in Pokhara and Thamel in Kathmandu are constructs for tourists and hardly count as Nepali at all. Signs are usually only in English, occasionally in Hebrew too. The Nepali script is nowhere to be seen."[(483)]

As will been seen later, around the period of Rosh Hashanah (the period when PA was in Kathmandu) and even more so for Pesach, there are hundreds or even thousands of Israelis in this area of Kathmandu.

Even though countries like foreign tourists since it brings them in money, it would seem from the very critical words of one trekker that this was not the case with the Israeli backpackers in Nepal. He described them as "rude, arrogant, and argue over trifling amounts of money." He even went as far as writing that "many guesthouses in this poor country [Nepal] will even tell Israeli trekking groups that they are full rather than accept them."[(484)]

[Because PA was afraid that an Israeli in the area of Thamel might recognise him and immediately it would become public knowledge] *I asked Ari to switch to a hotel in a less Israeli area* [which Ari then did]. *(p.371)*

The book does not state the name of the hotel they moved to, or even the area of Kathmandu where it was located. There are about 112 hotels in Kathmandu with the largest concentration of them being located in Thamel (about 36 hotels) or the adjoining areas of Paknajol (about 11 hotels).[(485)] The new hotel was obviously not a hotel in these areas, nor probably in the adjoining areas, such as Jyatha or Chhetrapati.[(486)] Because riding is forbidden on Shabbat and Festivals, PA and Ari had to walk to the prayer services on Rosh Hashanah. Therefore, presumably the hotel they stayed at was not too far away from Thamel (or from the place where the prayer services were held). This still leaves a lot of possible hotels, but no further conclusion can be arrived at as to the actual hotel.

[Unknown to PA, his father had died 7 months earlier and on erev Rosh Hashanah] *Ari came over to me and tore my shirt* [telling PA that his father had died adding] *We asked Rabbi Ovadia Yosef and he told us not to tell you since you were in so much pain already and he was afraid it would break you completely. (p.372)*

One of the laws of mourning on the death of a close relative is the ceremonial tearing of one's garments. For a parent this tearing is done on all the garments on the left side "to expose the heart" and for a different close relative it is done on just one garment on the right side.[487] If one hears of the death of a close relative within 30 days of the burial, one has the full mourning rites, namely firstly the shiva period for a week, then the shloshim period for a further 23 days.[488] For a parent there is a total period of mourning for 12 months. If however, one hears of the death only after 30 days from the date of the burial, one only has a period of "one hour" of mourning and for a parent the remainder, if any, of the 12 months.[489] Since it was then over 30 days but within 12 months of the date that PA's father had died, he just had to tear his garments, observe "one hour" of more intense mourning, together with just 5 months observance of the mourning regulations which apply during the 12 month mourning period for parents.

If by informing a person of the death of a relative it could affect his health in some way, then one may not inform him.[490] For this reason PA was not informed at the time of his father's death.

🕊 🕊 🕊 🕊 🕊 🕊 🕊 🕊 🕊 🕊 🕊

The Chabad messengers rented a large hall for the Rosh Hashanah meals. There were approximately one thousand five hundred Israelis of all colors and types. The prayers were amazing, the meals excellent and an ambience of joy pervaded the room. (p.373)

The location of the large hall is not stated, but on the following Pesach, (another occasion in the year when there is a large visitation of Israelis in Kathmandu), Chabad rented a hall in a hotel which was in the Lazimput district of Kathmandu,[491] about 1.4 kilometres (by road) from Chabad House.[492]

It is possible that they rented the same large hall for that Rosh Hashanah. This Festival which is of duration two days is the Jewish New Year and occurs in September or October – in 2005 it occurred on Tuesday–Wednesday, 4–5 October.[493] The Synagogue services are considerably longer than those of other Festival[494] and the shofar is blown, customarily 100 blasts, during the service.[495] There are special foods at the meal which include apple which is dipped in honey, pomegranate and various other fruits and vegetables. Over each of these foods, one says a special prayer of hope for the New Year.[496]

Rosh Hashanah in Chabad House in Kathmandu "has been dubbed as the biggest Rosh Hashana meal in the world." One of the Israeli hikers who was there for Rosh Hashanah in 2008 reported on how the various hikers co-operated in the preparations. He wrote: "The atmosphere is amazing, everyone joined together to help the Chabad House. Not one hiker has remained indifferent, everyone has rolled up their sleeves and are helping out."[497]

A number of people who have spent a Rosh Hashanah at the Chabad House in Kathmandu have recorded their comments and reminiscences. Here are some of them:

> "I participated in the Rosh Hashana meals at the Chabad House in Nepal three years ago [2002 or 2003] and I was one of 1500 Israelis who experience this special feeling. Rabbi Chezki who is a hiker himself (he knows all the places in Nepal) is marvelous, he knows everything and is always there for you for whatever you need ..." (signed by a girl calling herself "Complete secular girl").[498]

"Every Rosh Hashana you get hundreds of secular, young Israelis flocking to Kathmandu's Chabad House to dine together. It's not a matter of religious or secular. It's linked to wanting to feel connected to something for a few hours." (Boaz Albaranes, a student at the Haifa Technion.)[499]

" ...I came in from celebrating the Jewish New Year ... with the Israelis in Kathmandu, a contingent of 300+ young people, mostly traveling through Nepal, at one of the city's ubiquitous 'party palaces' [a place hired by Chabad of Kathmandu for Rosh Hashanah] .... I doubt, however, that many bar mitzvahs, Pesach seders or Rosh Hashonah celebrations have rattled these walls, much less seen bearded, impish Reb Kresky once again up on his make-shift chair singing to his heart's delight, black suit & black hat swaying to his own tune, to usher in the joyful fragrance of a new year.... we sat at the long table covered with plates of humus, challah bread, honey, pomegranate and salads with vivacious young Jews of all varieties." (Posted by Keith D. Leslie)[500]

"Even though I spent too much time in Kathmandu and it started to bore me, I had to wait a little longer to the main event. The Jewish new year [Rosh Hashanah] is celebrated each year in Kathmandu in a huge forum of more than 600 people, being led by Chabad House. It is always in the peak season of tourism in Nepal, and for that reason the celebration is very popular. In reality – the event was quite disappointing, though a happy one. The Rabbi decided that he doesn't want the people celebrating new-year to envy the people celebrating Passover (which also falls in the peak tourist season of April), so he asked everybody to sing the popular Passover song "ECHAD MI YODEA", after explaining that nowhere it is stated that the song is only for Passover! I found myself singing "ECHAD MI YODEA," a Passover song during ROSH HASHANA (new year's day) and looking for the candid camera..." (R. Eldar)[501]

This last reminisce was from Rosh Hashanah 2005, the Rosh Hashanah that PA was in the Chabad House in Kathmandu.

One might mention that although there is a large attendance of Israelis at the Kathmandu Chabad activities on Rosh Hashanah, the numbers are even larger for the Pesach Seder. The first Seder for Israelis in Kathmandu was organised by the Israeli Embassy in 1989 and took place in a local bakery. Some years later, the Seders were organised by Chabad and the numbers radically increased that by 2005 there were 2000 participants.[502]

[A new Israeli passport with PA's name had been ordered and had arrived from Israel, but it had no entrance stamp to Nepal nor a Nepali visa stamped in it. Great efforts were made to get these necessary stamps] *and in the end we found someone who could obtain the stamp we needed. He operates with a border policeman, who in exchange for money stamps passports with real visas. (p.373)*

Nepal is very strict on having entrance stamps and visas to enter the country and a failure to do so can lead to severe penalties.

In an information leaflet brought out by the United States Embassy in Nepal it states under the heading "Arrest and detention Procedures"; "IMMIGRATION VIOLATIONS: Violation of immigration regulations can result in lengthy prison sentences and/or deportation. In the case of visa overstays, if the violator is unable to pay owed visa fees and fines, the person will be imprisoned until the fees are paid or 'served off' at the rate of 25 rupees served off per day."[503]

A 36-year-old journalist Jonathan Mitchell, who had been born in Newcastle in England, described what happened to him in connection with visas in Nepal. He wrote: "The Nepalese government 'lost' my passport and destroyed any files relating to my press visa, denying it ever existed ... I was locked up for three weeks in Immigration Detention and they demanded and were paid US$ 10,000 in 'visa fines'! If I had not raised the money ... then I was facing being charged and tried under Nepali law and would have had to await the trial and outcome from Kathmandu Central Jail."[504] According to a report in "The Sentinel", a Staffordshire newspaper, Mitchell claims that all he did was to overstay his tourist visa "a month or so" and the Nepalese authorities had told him that if he did not pay this fine he could "face 10 years behind bars." It was an internet campaign, highlighting his plight which enabled him to raise most of the money to pay the fine.[505]

Even the absence of just an entrance stamp in one's passport can make problems for the visitor. A visitor wrote: "I can't believe they're making us pay a fine. We have our visa and receipts to prove our transportation and hotel stay in Nepal. Why didn't the guy stamp our passports at the border?"[506]

In addition to a visa, if people want to go on "most of Nepal's popular trekking areas [they] require separate permits which can be bought in Kathmandu or through trekking companies.

If you get caught in a park without a permit, you will be heavily fined."[507]

It can therefore be seen why every effort was made to secure the necessary stamps in PA's Israeli passport. Any punishment could have easily disclosed that he had escaped from prison in India and could have had led to very unpleasant consequences.

We spent Shabbat in the Chabad House. (p.374)

That year Rosh Hashanah had been on Tuesday and Wednesday. The following Shabbat, namely, the Shabbat between Rosh Hashanah and Yom Kippur, is known as Shabbat Shuva the Sabbath of Repentance. The haftarah (reading from the Prophets) on that Shabbat begins with the words "Shuva Yisrael" – Return O Israel to the Almighty.[508]

One of the many activities of the Chabad House in Kathmandu in their list of advertised activities is "Shabbat Hospitality."[509] It is on Shabbat that the kosher restaurant on the premises doubles up as a large dining hall where open Shabbat meals for tourist are held.[510]

One of the visitors to this Chabad House in November 2004 wrote on this that, "Shabbat and Holidays are of course the highlights of Bet Chabad activity with Kiddush and Candle Lighting, meals, conversations and explanations about religion and other things. After the first meal Friday night there is 'story time' where around the table people tell stories or remarks, sometimes about Bet Chabad, sometimes about religion and sometimes just funny anecdotes. It's a special feeling in the air, and almost every time someone says something moving or just amazing."[511]

A visitor in June 2008 wrote: "Shabbat in Kathmandu was really nice. We went to Chabad for both meals (strange that our first food here tasted like it was straight from Brooklyn) - was very pleasant."[512]

Another group who had been trekking around Mount Everest, finished their two week sojourn in Nepal with a Shabbat in the Chabad House in Kathmandu and : "Our trek ends with Shabbat in Kathmandu, including davening and meals at Chabad House - Beit Knesset (synagogue), Kosher restaurant, meeting place and home away from home for many Jewish travellers."[513] Both on the Friday night and Shabbat day this group ate their meals at the Chabad House.[514]

We left Kathmandu at seven o'clock in the [Sunday] *morning and were scheduled to land in Israel on Monday at four o'clock in the morning, after a stopover in Thailand. It would be one day before Yom Kippur. (p.374)*

Actually, Yom Kippur that year was on Thursday and so it is inaccurate to write that they were scheduled to arrive in Israel "one day before Yom Kippur."

The airport at which PA and Ari, began this last stage of their journey was almost certainly Tribhuvan International Airport, which is the sole international airport in Kathmandu. It was originally known as Gaucher Airport, named after the area of Kathmandu where it is situated. It was renamed Tribhuvan Airport in 1955, after the father of the then King of Nepal. The airport is situated about six kilometres from the city center in the Kathmandu valley. It has two terminals, one for domestic flights and one for international flights and there is an executive lounge for First Class passengers and Business Class passengers. Today about 30 international airlines use this airport.[515]

There are no El Al flights from Kathmandu. One needs to go to Bangkok to get a flight to Israel. The name of the airline on which PA travelled is not mentioned in the book but there are only two airlines which have as one of their routes Kathmandu to Bangkok (although there might have been others in 2005).[516]

One of these airlines is Nepal Airlines and it was established in 1958 as a government owned national flag-carrier airline.

It originally had the word "Royal" in its name – this was the period of the monarchy in Nepal and hence the word "Royal." Over the years it acquired a number of airplanes including several Boeings. It originally had a number of domestic routes and also international routes which included Europe and the Far East. However, in later years, the airline terminated its services to Europe and to some of those to the Far East.[517]

The other airline is Thai Airways International. It is the national flag carrier and largest airline of Thailand and was formed in 1988, although its origins date back to 1960. It is the largest airline in Thailand. It was the first Asia-Pacific airline to serve London Heathrow Airport and among East Asian airlines it has one of the largest passenger operations in Europe. As at 2011, it flies to 72 destinations in 35 countries using a fleet of 89 aircraft, and has destinations which include Europe, Asia, Africa, North America and Oceania. Like Nepal Airlines, it has also curtailed a number of its international flights.[518]

☥ ☥ ☥ ☥ ☥ ☥ ☥ ☥ ☥ ☥ ☥

[When PA handed his passport to the clerk at the Kathmandu airport, the clerk] *looked at it and began to act in a very strange way. ... beads of sweat dripped down his forehead ... fiddled with papers on his desk ... licked his lips a few times. ...* [Finally he] *stamped 'exit' on my passport. (p.374)*

When entering or exiting any country, one has to go through passport control. There, a passport stamp, which is almost always a rubber stamp inked impression, is stamped in one's passport, together with the date, both when entering and exiting a country. Countries also often have a different shape of the stamp or a different colour ink for entries and exits. Such stamps enable a country to know which foreign nationals are present in a country, and whether they are there illegally, either without any visa or whether they have overstayed their visit to that country.[519]

Even a person who has legally entered a country might not always be safe in that country. An example could be the case of a person who has been convicted of a crime in one country or even suspected of committing a crime but succeeds in fleeing to another country. For such a person, there is a process known as extradition whereby one nation or state surrenders a suspected or convicted criminal to another nation or state. However, this process is not automatic but is governed by a treaty between two such countries. Even in such treaties there are often many exceptions as to who can be extradited. Such reasons could be that the crime is of a political nature, or if extradited he might receive cruel, inhumane or degrading treatment or that the death penalty may be imposed on that person, or that they might not be given a fair trial. There are some nations who refuse to extradite their own citizens, preferring to put on them on trial themselves.[520]

There have been extradition treaties in the past between India and Nepal. The first treaty was signed in 1855, and it was revised in 1953.[521] The latter was the treaty which was in force when PA escaped from India to Nepal in 2005.

However, according to Article 2 of this 1953 extradition treaty: "Neither Government [i.e. India and Nepal] shall be bound in any case to surrender any person who is not a national of the country by the Government of which the requisition has been made."[522] In other words this treaty does not have provisions for the extradition of third-country nationals.

At the beginning of 2005, there were negotiations to amend the extradition treaty between India and Nepal, and it was then even reported that they were close to signing. However, there were differences of opinion between these two countries on the extradition of third country nationals which prevented its signing. The "Nepali Times" at that period wrote: "Foreign and Home Ministry officials in Kathmandu were tight-lipped about whether Nepal had finally given in to Indian demands that it hand over third country nationals caught in Nepal to India."[523] According to "The Times of India" of January 2010, due to the "political instability" in Nepal, this revised extradition treaty had still not yet been signed.[524]

PA was a national of Israel and not of India nor Nepal, and was thus a "third-country national" and was therefore not covered by the Indo-Nepal extradition treaty in force in October 2005.

It is thus not clear why there was this initial hesitation on the part of the clerk at the airport to stamp "exit" in PA's passport. Had he been informed that there was an escaped prisoner who might have reached Nepal? In any case, the extradition of a third-country national from Nepal to India was not covered in the treaty. What made the clerk after this hesitation finally stamp PA's passport? Could it be that the delay by the clerk was due to something else completely, but the nervous state of PA made him attribute the apparent hesitation to something connected to himself?

The flight to Thailand was short, but we had to wait ten hours there for our El-Al flight there to Tel Aviv. (p.374)

In 2010, the time to fly from Kathmandu to Bangkok nonstop was about three and a quarter hours.[525] In Bangkok, PA and Ari had to wait for the El Al flight.

El Al Israel Airlines, the flag-carrier of the State of Israel, was established in 1948 soon after the establishment of the State of Israel. The Hebrew words "El Al" translated into English are "To the Skies." It operates international passenger and cargo flights, between Israel and destinations in Europe, Asia, America, Africa, and the Far East and these destinations include Bangkok. However, some of El Al's routes have during the last decade been transferred to the Israel's two private airlines. Throughout the decades El Al has purchased more modern aircraft and today its fleet consists of Boeing aircraft. Its head office is located in the grounds of Ben-Gurion Airport. During its history, El Al has airlifted Jews to Israel in countries where they were at risk, such as Ethiopia and Yemen. In order to foil any terrorist attacks and hijacking, El Al has incorporated numerous security measures in its operations and is acknowledged to be the world's more secure airline.[526]

It was a long and emotional flight [to Israel]. *The plane flew on and on. ... Suddenly I saw the lights of my beloved Israel from above. (p.375)*

Theoretically the shortest way to fly from Bangkok to Tel Aviv would be to fly over Myanmar (Burma), India, Pakistan, Iran, Iraq, Saudi Arabia and Jordan. However, most of these countries are not at all friendly to Israel and one cannot fly over their airspace.

Airspace is the portion of the atmosphere controlled by a country above its territory, including its territorial waters. There is no international agreement on the vertical extent of sovereign airspace; there are only suggestions which range from about 30 kilometres (the extent of the highest aircraft and balloons) to about 160 kilometres (the lowest extent of short-term stable orbits).[527]

It can be dangerous, even fatal, to fly over airspace of a country without its consent. This occurred with an El Al passenger plane which went off route over Bulgaria due to bad weather in July 1955. Bulgaria shot down the airplane, which then burst apart and crashed in flames, killing all the 51 passengers and the 7 crew members. Bulgaria belatedly issued a formal apology, stating that their fighter pilots had been too hasty in shooting down the airplane and agreed to pay compensation to the victims' families.[528]

As a result of these non-friendly countries, El-Al has to take a more indirect route when flying between Bangkok and Tel-Aviv. Since Israel has good relations with Myanmar, it can fly over that country. It also has overflight rights for India. The flight continues over the Indian Ocean until it reaches the Gulf of Aden taking care to avoid Somali and Yemeni airspace. It then makes an almost 90 degree turn to the north and continues over the Djiboutian and Eritrean side of Bab-el-Mandeb. It then continues over the Egyptian side of the Red Sea (Egypt and Israel have given each other mutual overflight rights) taking care to avoid Saudi airspace. Finally it flies over the Gulf of Aqaba, Eilat and continues northwards to Tel-Aviv.[529] The shortest time for such a flight is about 11 hours.[530]

This indirect route resulted in an exchange of comments by users in February 2002, on "The Wings of the Web" following the death of a man on this Bangkok to Tel-Aviv route.

The news item was: "A 75 years old man collapsed yesterday 4 hours into an El-Al flight from Thailand to Israel. Doctors on the plane tried to give him a treatment but he died. The B777 with 250 pax [passengers] on board continued to Tel-Aviv."

There was immediately a comment by "Iain": "Pretty much every other airline apart from El Al would have landed ASAP! [as soon as possible]." To this, a person calling himself "LY744" wrote in a sarcastic manner: "Yeah, I'm sure LY's Arab friends would be glad to help them ... I'm talking about such friendly nations as Yemen, Saudi Arabia, Somalia, Sudan etc." In a similar vein "Pete" wrote: "I'm with LY744.... don't put this guilt trip on Israel, too. El Al flights in that region have to take extremely circuitous routes to avoid the 'friendly skies' of our Muslim friends."[(531)]

Finally, this flight approached the shores of Israel. PA writes that he saw "the lights of my beloved Israel" and earlier he stated that he was scheduled to arrive in Israel at 4 o'clock in the morning. The date was Monday, 10 October 2005 and sunrise in Tel Aviv was 5.40 a.m.[(532)] (Israel Standard Time - Daylight Saving Time ended that year in Israel on the previous day.[(533)]) Thus at 4 o'clock in the morning, it would be pitch dark and a mass of street lights in the cities would be seen through the windows of the airplane.

When I left Israel a year and a half before the new terminal was under construction, and upon my return an unfamiliar terminal greeted me. (p.375)

Ben-Gurion International Airport has its origins from 1936, the days of the British Mandate when it was called Wilhelma Airport and in 1943 it was renamed RAF Lydda, due to its proximity to the city of Lod, which in Greco-Latin is Lydda. On the establishment of the State of Israel, its name was changed to Lod Airport. In 1973 it was named Ben-Gurion International Airport, after David Ben-Gurion, the first prime minister of Israel.[534]

The airport is operated by the Israel Airports Authority which is a government-owned corporation that manages all public airports and border crossings in the State of Israel. It has three runways and is used by commercial, private and military aircraft. This airport is regarded as one of the world's most secure airports with a security fence that includes both police officers and soldiers. In 2005, when PA returned about nine million passengers passed through this airport.[535]

Originally, all the flights departed from what is today known as "Terminal 1" but as time when on and more and more passengers used this terminal, it became completely inadequate, and in 1994 it was decided to build a much larger terminal. However, it was not until October 2004 that this new building known as "Terminal 3" was opened. (From 1969 there was also a "Terminal 2" to serve domestic flights.)[536] Thus, when PA left for India in mid-2004, only "Terminal 1" was in use, but when he returned in October 2005, he disembarked to "Terminal 3." After "Terminal 3" had been built, in an article in "Architectural Record", Andrea Dean described "Terminal 1" as "an outmoded remnant from the 1930s British Mandate over Palestine."[537]

The old terminal [Terminal 1] *was small, but the new one* [Terminal 3] *was huge. I found myself walking endlessly. (p.375)*

"Terminal 3", which cost about one billion US dollars to build, replaced "Terminal 1" as the main international gateway to and from Israel. The overall layout is similar to that of airports in Europe and North America, with multiple levels and considerable distances to walk after disembarking from the aircraft, but such a walk is assisted by escalators and moving walkways. Hence PA's comments: "I found myself walking endlessly." The ground floor departures hall has 110 check-in-counters and is of size of over

10,000 square metres. This terminal also has a small shopping mall, which includes shops, restaurants, a post-office and the airport also has two Synagogues. Airplanes which take off and land can be viewed from a distinctive tilted glass wall. At the lower level of this terminal there is a railway station with trains to Tel Aviv, Haifa and Modi'in. The airport is also accessible by public buses and cars.[538]

Security at this airport is naturally tight, and this includes questioning travelers, but unfortunately in today's world, one has to be one step ahead of the terrorists. It is natural that most of the comments on this airport which are posted on the internet will refer to this security and most see it in a positive way.

Here are some extracts of examples of these comments made towards the end of 2009: "Ben Gurion Airport is incredible! I have travelled through a few times in the past year, and have been out of the terminal within 30 minutes including picking up luggage! That is incredible. Security is tight but there are no long queues and it is efficient." Another supportive comment: "Great airport! Modern clean terminal is a pleasure to travel through. Staff are all helpful and assertive and security seems excellent. Queues were not too bad for anything, whilst duty free selection has improved. Terminal design makes travelling relaxing and at some times, almost like being in a lounge."[539]

However, there are also non-complimentary comments arising mainly from the strict security checks: "Was made to go thru the security drama. Stand in a line and are asked questions regarding who I visited, why I was there etc... my sister being questioned - is she a Jew, who is she married to, how long has she lived here ... Off to a long bench. Unpack EVERYTHING that took me 4hrs the night before.... Went thru two more checks after booking in. Staff very arrogant and don't care attitude. Would it help to be friendly??? They have all the power...."[540]

PA's family was at the airport to meet him and this included his second daughter who had been born whilst he was jail in India.

He returned to his home in Safed, a city in northern Israel. As to be expected, after such a traumatic experience in an Indian jail, it took PA some time to undergo a full physical and emotional rehabilitation.

REFERENCES

(1) Mumbai online: Hospitals (www.mumbaionline.in/EmergencyServices/Hospitals/ - accessed 21 December 2009); 95 Private Hospitals in Mumbai (www.karmayog.com/lists/mumpvthospitals.htm - accessed 21 December 2009).

(2) Mumbai City Map, (Eicher Goodearth: New Delhi, 2009) [henceforth: Mumbai Map], p.17.

(3) Grant Medical College & Sir J.J. Group of Hospitals (www.grantmedicalcollege-*jjhospital.org/history.htm*); Wikipedia: Grant Medical College and Sir James Jamshedjee Jeejeebhoy Group of Hospitals. (accessed 18 May 2010); Grant Medical College: A Fragile Heritage (www.grantmedicalfriends.com/Images/pdf/CONSERVATION_ARCHITECT_REPORT_AND_ESTIMATES.pdf - accessed 25 December 2011).

(4) Grant Medical College & Sir J.J. Group of Hospitals (www.grantmedicalcollege-*jjhospital.org/present.htm*)

(5) Wikipedia: Urinalysis - accessed 25 December 2011.

(6) "Quantitative detection of Plasmodium falciparum DNA in saliva, blood and urine", Journal of Infectious Diseases, 2009 Jun 1, 199 (11):1567.

(7) Wikipedia: Malaria – accessed 25 December 2011.

(8) "Detection of antigens and antibodies in the urine of humans with Plasmodium falciparum malaria". Journal of Clinical Microbiology 1991 Jun; 29(6):1236-42.

(9) Letter to Editor, Saudi Journal of Kidney Diseases and Transplantation, 2000, 11(2) pp. 208-09.

(10) "Burden of Malaria in India: Retrospective and Prospective View", American Journal of Tropical Medicine and Hygiene, 77 (6 suppl.) 2007 p.69.

(11) "Dengue Danger", The Times of India, 3 October 2006.

(12) "Millions suffer in Indian monsoon", BBC News, 1 August 2005; "Indian monsoon death toll soars", BBC News, 28 July 2005.

(13) "Malaria outbreak in Mumbai" SiliconIndia, 14 October 2002.

(14) Dengue Danger, op. cit.

(15) Travel Medicine, India, 2008, (www.travmed.com/guide/country.php?c=India – accessed 1 August 2010).

(16) Wikipedia: Squat toilet – accessed 19 May 2011.

(17) "Squat toilets in Rochdale shopping centre", BBC News Manchester, 15 July 2010.

(18) Wikipedia: Squat toilet, op. cit.

(19) Squat Toilet: (www.docstoc.com/docs/6244425/Squat_toilet - accessed14 December 2011).

(20) Christopher W. London, *Bombay Gothic*, (India Book House: Mumbai, 2002), p.15.

(21) Grant Medical College: A Fragile Heritage, op. cit.

(22) Wikipedia: Rust – accessed 3 July 2011.

(23) Mumbai Map, p.17.

(24) "Israeli arrested in drug case flees", The Times of India, 28 September 2005.

(25) "Israeli drug peddler flees JJ Hospital", DNA (Daily News and Analysis), 28 September 2005.

(26) Grant Medical College: A Fragile Heritage, op. cit.

(27) Wikipedia: Grant Medical College..., op. cit.

(28) m.sulekha.com/mumbai/***chinch-bunder_contact-address/379924.htm – accessed 25 December 2011.

(29) 70.86.139.42/mumbai/listing/travel-and-transportation/accommodation/hotel***- 4c93639b84c57.html - accessed 25 December 2011.

(30) "CCTVs to keep an eye on J.J. Hospital", DNA (Daily News and Analysis), 3 March 2010.

(31) Mumbai Map, p.17. [Henceforth, if the original names of the roads are known, they will be added in brackets after the current name.]

(32) "Censorship battle rages in India over Mistry novel", The Globe and Mail (Toronto, Canada) 15 October 2010.

(33) Samuel T. Sheppard, *Bombay Place-Names and Street-Names: Excursion into the By-ways of the History of Bombay City,* (Bombay: The Times Press, 1917), 23 - Bombay Place Names.

(34) via google – Rachmandra Bhatt Marg and /or Babula Tank Road.

(35) The Sunnis and Shia Moharam, (www.flickr.com/photos/firozeshakir/557183524/ - accessed 4 August 2010).

(36) Wikipedia: Shi'a-Sunni relations – accessed 25 December 2011.

(37) Mumbai Map, p.17.

(38) Ibid.

(39) Ibid; List of Schools I.J.K.L. (as at 10.11.02), Municipal Schools I.J.K.L., (www.karmayog.com/lists/sch-ijkl.htm - accessed 25 December 2011).

(40) Mumbai Map, p.17; Google Maps.

(41) Muharram in Mumbai, (mumbai.metblogs.com/2006/02/11/muharram-in-mumbai/ - accessed 20 May 2011).

(42) Mumbai Map, p.17; Google Maps.

(43) Wikipedia: Tanks of Bombay – accessed 20 May 2011.

(44) Samuel T. Sheppard, op. cit.

(45) Mumbai Map, p.17.

(46) Wikipedia (as at 17 September 2010): Taxis in India – accessed 22 May 2011.

(47) Ibid.

(48) IndiaMike, fatal_error, (www.indiamike.com/india/mumbai-(www.indiamike.com/india/mumbai-bombay-f22/some-questions-about-mumbai-t91432/2 - accessed 5 August 2010).

(49) IndiaMike, Taxis in Mumbai, (www.indiamike.com/photopost/showphoto.php/photo/546/size/big/ppuser/external.php?type=RSS2 – accessed 5 August 2010).
(50) IndiaMike, **Scam Warning - Bombay Autos/Taxis - Non Working Meters.** - accessed 5 August 2010).
(51) Ibid.
(52) Ibid.
(53) IndiaMike, Taxi rip off at Mumbai, - accessed 5 August 2010).
(54) India's Leading Business Directory Service, (www.askme.com/mumbai/cuffe-parade-restaurants-bars-***-restaurant/listing-print/14771085331 - accessed 22 May 2011).
(55) Hotelier Caterer, (www.expresshospitality.com/20040112/foodbeverage01.shtml - accessed 5 August 2010).
(56) Short video film on the restaurant (www.concierge.com/video/asia/mumbai/mumbairestaurants/1825938935/***-restaurant-mumbai/1832211723 - accessed 26 December 2011).
(57) Restaurant Reviews from the Moon, (bluesviews.bluesmoon.info/2005/12/***-cuffe-parade-mumbai.html - accessed 26 December 2011).
(58) India's First Signature Chef, (yourstory.in/2009/04/***-indias-first-signature-chef/ - accessed 26 December 2011).
(59) Hotelier Caterer, op. cit.
(60) Restaurant Reviews from the Moon, op. cit.
(61) Leviticus 11:10; Deuteronomy 14:10; Shulchan Aruch, Yoreh Deah, 83.
(62) Simply beautiful, (mumbai.burrp.com/listing/***_cuffe parade_mumbai_restaurants/153130356__UR__reviews?page=2 – accessed 26 December 2011).
(63) Shulchan Aruch, Yoreh Deah, 89:1.
(64) Rainrays, (www.rainrays.com/hotels/profile/33 - accessed 22 May 2011); India's Leading Business Directory Service, op. cit.
(65) www.***.in/ - accessed 26 December 2011.
(66) www.hospitalitybizindia.com/detailNews.aspx?aid=1281&sid=23 – accessed 22 May 2011.
(67) Mumbai Map, pp.13, 17.
(68) Ibid., p.17.
(69) Ibid., p.13.
(70) Ibid.
(71) "'Bridges to wealth' are in poor health", The Times of India, 29 December 2004.
(72) Ibid.
(73) "Carnac Bridge not fit for trains", The Times of India, 8 August 2001.
(74) Wikipedia: James Rivett-Carnac – accessed 26 December 2011.
(75) Wikipedia: Colaba – accessed 22 May 2011.
(76) Ibid; Top 5 Mumbai Markets (goindia.about.com/od/shopping/tp/best-mumbai-markets.htm – accessed 23 May 2011) ; Colaba Causeway, (www.famous-india.com/markets/colaba-causeway.html - accessed 23 May 2011) ; About Colaba Mumbai (www.hotelsincolaba.net/ - accessed 10 August 2010).
(77) Wikipedia: Colaba, op. cit.

(78) IndiaMike, www.indiamike.com/india-hotels/mumbai-bombay-hotels-c58/?sort=rating&pag=4&dir=next – accessed 26 December 2011.

(79) Frommer's India, (Wiley Publishing, Hoboken, New Jersey 2010) p.123; via Google – Shahid Bhagat Singh Marg.

(80) Mumbai Map, p.17.

(81) Ibid., pp.17, 13, 10.

(82) Wikipedia: Bombay High Court – accessed 27 December2011.

(83) Mumbai High Court (www.mumbaionline.in/Administration/courts.asp - accessed 10 August 2010).

(84) This was stated in the various lectures given by PA.

(85) "Yosef was forgotten in prison, but not me", Beis Moshiach, (Brooklyn, New York: 29 Kislev 5769 (2008)), issue 676, pp.10-11; "Escape from India", L'Chaim (Lubavitch Youth Organization, Brooklyn New York: 8 May 2009), issue 1069.

(86) Mumbai Map, p.10.

(87) Is Shelleys Hotel closed? (www.tripadvisor.com/ShowTopic-g304554-i4228-k1695732-Is_Shelleys_Hotel_closed-Mumbai_Bombay_Maharashtra.html - accessed 25 May 2011).

(88) Mumbai Map, pp.9-10.

(89) Shelleys Hotel Mumbai (indoexpedition.com/shelleys-hotel-mumbai.html - accessed 10 January 2010).

(90) Hotels Mumbai India (www.hotelsmumbaiindia.com/hotel-shelleys.html - accessed 25 May 2011) ; Shelleys Hotel Mumbai (www.indiahotel andresort.com/hotels-in-maharashtra/hotels-in-mumbai/budget-hotels/shelleys-hotel.html - accessed 25 May 2011).

(91) IndiaMike: Hotel Shelleys Mumbai (Bombay) – accessed 10 August 2010.

(92) Wikipedia: Nariman House – accessed 22 December 2009; New York News & Features, G-d's Work (nymag.com/news/features/56001/index2. html - accessed 22 December 2009).

(93) Chabad.org. Centers, Chabad-Lubavitch of Mumbai (www.chabad.org/centers/default_cdo/aid/118651/jewish/Chabad-Lubavitch-of-Mumbai.htm - accessed 24 January 2012).

(94) "Murderers in my Prison Cell", Mishpacha, English edition, 12 October 2008, pp.56-57.

(95) Wikipedia: Nariman House, op. cit.

(96) Wikipedia: Chabad – accessed 24 January 2012; Wikipedia: Chabad house – accessed 24 January 2012.

(97) Chabad.org, Centers (www.chabad.org/centers/default_cdo/jewish/Centers.htm - accessed 24 January 2012).

(98) Wikipedia: Chabad, op. cit.; Wikipedia: 770 Eastern Parkway – accessed 24 January 2012.

(99) "Yosef was forgotten in prison, but not me", op. cit.

(100) "Murderers in My Prison Cell", Mishpacha, English edition, 10 December 2008, p.57.

(101) "Yisraeli barach mehakele hahodi", Yediot Acharonot, 29 September 2005, p.13; Ezrach Yisraeli nimlat mimatzar behodu", Ma'ariv, 29 September 2005, p.16.

(102) Acknowledgements to "Ghmyrtle' via Wikipedia Reference desk – Humanities, 31 January 2010 for this information.

(103) Wikipedia: Breach Candy – accessed 26 May 2011.

(104) Breach Candy Hospital Mumbai (www.indianhealthguru.com/breach-candy-hospital-mumbai.htm - accessed 26 May 2011); Wikipedia: Breach Candy Hospital – accessed 26 May 2011.

(105) Google Maps – get directions.

(106) For route see Mumbai Map, pp. 10, 13, 12, 16, 12, 11, 15, 16.

(107) Wikipedia: History of the telephone – accessed 25 January 2012.

(108) Wikipedia: Telephone exchange – accessed 25 January 2012.

(109) Wikipedia: Trunk vs. Toll – accessed 25 January 2012.

(110) BBC News: 50th anniversary of historic call (news.bbc.co.uk/2/hi/uk_news/7766631.stm - accessed 25 January 2012).

(111) Google Maps – get directions.

(112) BBC News: 50th anniversary of historic call, op. cit., text of Queen's speech.

(113) Yahoo Answers: What does std stand for in phone terms? (uk.answers.yahoo.com/question/index?qid=20080726054911AAg87Pe – accessed 25 January 2012).

(114) Wikipedia: International direct dialing – accessed 25 January 2012.

(115) Wikipedia: List of country calling codes – accessed 25 January 2012.

(116) Wikipedia: Telephone numbers in Israel – accessed 25 January 2012.

(117) Yahoo Answers: What does std stand for in phone terms? op. cit.

(118) Google Maps – get directions.

(119) Ibid.

(120) India Railway Atlas, & Time Table ed. R.P.Arya   (India Map Service: Jodhpur, 2003) pp.34-35; Mumbai Suburban Railway (www.search.com/reference/Mumbai_Suburban_Railway - accessed 26 May 2011).

(121) Gujarat Mail (indiarailinfo.com/train/570/297/60 – accessed 27 May 2011).

(122) Wikipedia: Gujarat Mail (as at 29 March 2006) – accessed 27 May 2011; Gujarat Mail/12901 (indiarailinfo.com/train/570/298/60 – accessed 27 May 2011).

(123) Mumbai Jaipur SF Special/0237 (indiarailinfo.com/train/7713/297/272 – accessed 27 May 2011).

(124) Wikipedia: India – accessed 27 May 2011; Wikipedia: Government of India – accessed 27 May 2011; Our Parliament (parliamentofindia.nic.in/ls/intro/p1.htm – accessed 1 February 2012); Supreme Court of India (supremecourtofindia.nic.in/jurisdiction.htm – accessed 1 February 2012).

(125) Dadar (www.search.com/refernce/Dadar - accessed 26 May 2011); Mumbai Suburban Railway, op. cit., Wikipedia - Mumbai Suburban Railway – accessed 29 May 2011.

(126) Mumbai Map, p.7.

(127) WikiAnswers (wiki.answers.com/Q/What_days_is_the_manish_market_of_dadar_open –accessed 29 May 2011)

(128) Via Google – Manish market – clothing.

(129) www.asklaila.com/listing/Mumbai/Dadar+West/RR+Enterprises/14fUXWsl/ - accessed 28 December 2011.
(130) Dadar Manish Market 26 April 2011 (akhtarissak.blogspot.com/2011/04/dadar-manish-market-26th-april-2011.html – accessed 29 May 2011).
(131) Ibid.
(132) Frommer's India, op. cit., p.130.
(133) Shopping in Mumbai (www.mumbaispider.com/resources/2160-Shopping-Mumbai.aspx - accessed 28 December 2011).
(134) www.buzzintown.com/mumbai/restaurant-*** -snacks-bar/id--35710. html - accessed 30 May 2011.
(135) Mumbai Map, p.7.
(136) Wikipedia: Mumbai Police – accessed 23 February 2010.
(137) Mumbai Map, p.7.
(138) Google Maps.
(139) khojguru.com/mumbai/*** -restaurant-restaurant-in-dadar-w-mumbai_ uqs3y - accessed 30 May 2011; www.indianexpress.com/news/in-100th-year-mama-kanes-in-for-a-menu-cha/577236/ - accessed 30 May 2011.
(140) Google Maps.
(141) Wikipedia: Pathare Prabhu – accessed 31 May 2011.
(142) via Google – Mumbai - D'Silva Road and Jawge Marg.
(143) "For those in Dadar, hawkers are a perpetual menace", The Times of India, 10 August 2005; "Merchants asks BMC to remove D'Silva Road hawkers", The Times of India, 19 January 2002.
(144) Mumbai Map, p.24.
(145) Indian Railway Atlas, op. cit., p.35; Mumbai Suburban Railway, op. cit.
(146) Mumbai Map, pp.24, 25, 33.
(147) Ibid., p.41.
(148) www.askme.com/mumbai/bandra-east-travel-tours-*** -tours-travels/listing/70142859918 - accessed 28 December 2011.
(149) Mumbai to Goa Bus Tickets Booking (www.makemytrip.com/bus-tickets/mumbai-goa-booking.html - accessed 31 May 2011); Travel to Goa by Air-Conditioned Luxury Volvo make coaches (www.amchogoa.com/volvo-bus-service-from-mumbai-to-goa.htm - accessed 28 December 2011).
(150) Wikipedia: Goa – accessed 31 May 2011.
(151) Wikipedia: Nariman House – accessed 27 January 2012.
(152) Google Maps - get directions.
(153) Ibid.; Mumbai Map, pp.25, 33, 41.
(154) Ibid.; Ibid. pp.41, 42, 49, 42.
(155) Google Maps – get directions.
(156) Ibid.
(157) via Google – travel agents in Sion Mumbai.
(158) Mumbai.justdial.com/*** -travels_sion_Mumbai_kyvivelFPrsq.htm – accessed 1 June 2011.
(159) www.justdial.com/Mumbai/*** -travels-and-cargo-%3Cnear%3E-Sion/022PXX22-XX22-000352335757-G3X5 - accessed 28 December 2011.

(160) via Google – Mumbai to Ahmedabad – bus.
(161) Mumbai Map, p.34.
(162) via Google – Sion circle – shops.
(163) via Google – Sion circle – restaurants.
(164) www.mouthshut.com/review/Central-Peninsula-Sion-Bombay-Mumbai-review-susqstsnp - accessed 2 June 2011.
(165) www.onyomo.com/mumbai/200135827-durga-restaurant-sion - accessed 2 June 2011.
(166) Mumbai Map, p.34.
(167) Ibid.; www.asklaila.com/listing/Mumbai/Sion+East/***+Bazaar+Co-operative+Departmental+Store/5a6HjTB2/ - accessed 2 June 2011.
(168) Gujarat to Mumbai by road (www.indiatransit.com/india_bus_routes/luxury-bus-gujarat-mumbai.html - accessed 2 June 2011).
(169) via Google – Mumbai to Ahmedabad – bus.
(170) Shulchan Aruch, Orach Chaim 110:4, 5, 7.
(171) Acknowledgements to "nycank" via IndiaMike for the information.
(172) Acknowledgements to "obione980" via IndiaMike for the information.
(173) Acknowledgments to Wikipedia Reference Desk – Humanities for information.
(174) Drinking in Ahmedabad (travel.myyog.com/question/42701943-Drinking-in-Ahmedabad - accessed 29 December 2011).
(175) Prohibition – Gujarat's worst kept secret. (www.rediff.com/election/2002/dec/11guj4.htm - accessed 5 June 2011).
(176) Not so dry in dry Gujarat (www.merinews.com/article/not-so-dry-in-dry-gujarat/206.shtml - accessed 5 June 2011).
(177) Wikipedia: Bhilad – accessed 3 June 2011.
(178) Wikipedia: National Highway 8 (India) – accessed 5 June 2011; Google Maps – get directions.
(179) National Highway No. 8 (www.mapsofindia.com/driving-directions-maps/nh8-driving-directions-map. html - 3 June 2011).
(180) Google Maps – get directions.
(181) ikipedia: List of National Highways in India – accessed 5 June 2011.
(182) Wikipedia: Ahmedabad Vadodara Expressway – accessed 4 February 2012.
(183) A4 District Wise Forest Cover (*vfor.nic.in/fsi/sfr97/A4.html – accessed 10 March 2011*).
(184) Online bus ticket booking _ Mumbai to Ahmedabad. (bustickets. makemytrip.com/BusIntegration/bus/booking?execution=e1345350s2 – accessed 1 June 2011).
(185) Rabbi Meir Posen, *Ohr Meir*, (London, 1973), Hebrew text p.327 and Tables p.123.
(186) Map of Ahmadabad, (TTK Healthcare, Tamil Nadu, India).
(187) Ibid.
(188) A Road Guide to Ahmadabad, (TTK Healthcare, 2009), pp.4, 6, 8; Gujarat Road Atlas (Indian Map Service, Jodhpur, 2007) p.4; Wikipedia: Ahmedabad – accessed 20 June 2011.

(189) Wikipedia: Demographics and culture of Ahmedabad, op. cit. - accessed 20 June 2011.

(190) "Ahmedabad's ghettos", Frontline, (India's National Magazine from the publishers of "The Hindu") vol.20, issue 20, 27 September – 10 October 2003.

(191) "A polarised society that is Gujarat", Business Line (Financial daily from "The Hindu" group of publications) 20 May 2002.

(192) "Ahmedabad elects India's 1st Muslim woman Mayor" Indian Express, 17 April 2003.

(193) Definition of Hijab for Muslim Men. (maria-zain.suite101.com/definition-of-hijab-for-muslim-men-a44107 - accessed 30 December 2011); Islamic Clothing Requirements (islam.about.com/od/dress/p/clothing_reqs.htm – accessed 22 June 2011).

(194) Wikipedia: Thaub – accessed 21 June 2011.

(195) Ahmadabad Local Transport (www.ahmedabad.org.uk/travel-tips/local-transport.html - accessed 21 June 2011; Road Guide of Ahmadabad, op. cit., pp.40-43.

(196) Wikipedia: Rickshaw – accessed 21 June 2011.

(197) Wikipedia: Cycle rickshaw – accessed 21 June 2011.

(198) Wikipedia: Auto rickshaw – accessed 21 June 2011.

(199) Ahmadabad Local transport, op. cit.

(200) Acknowledgements to "ianscott", a resident of Ahmedabad, via IndiaMike for the information.

(201) via Google - Manek Chowk – clothing.

(202) Road Guide to Ahmadabad, op. cit. p.26, Jama Masjid Ahmedabad. (www.ahmedabad.org.uk/religious-places/jama-masjid.html - accessed 1 January 2012); Jamar Masjid in Ahmedabad (www.asiarooms.com/en/travel-guide/india/ahmedabad/sightseeing-in-ahmedabad/jama-masjid-in-ahmedabad.html - accessed 1 January 2012).

(203) Wikipedia: Jaipur – accessed 22 June 2011.

(204) India Railway Atlas, Railway Time Table, op. cit., pp.22, 23.

(205) Ashram Express (12915), (www.mustseeindia.com/trains/Ashram-Express-12915 - accessed 23 June 2011.

(206) Samit Roychoudhury, The Great Indian Railway Atlas, (Calcutta Art Studies: India, 2005), p,19; Wikipedia: Udaipur (Rail) – accessed 20 June 2011.

(207) Wikipedia: Track gauge – accessed 22 June 2011.

(208) Wikipedia: Indian Gauge – accessed 22 June 2011.

(209) Wikipedia: Udaipur, op. cit.

(210) Great Indian Railway Atlas, op. cit., p.86.

(211) Wikipedia: Udaipur, op. cit.

(212) Great Indian Railway Atlas, op. cit., p.2.

(213) IndiaMike: A Guide to the India Railway System and the Indian Train.

(214) Ibid.

(215) IndiaMike: Train - RT CLS Suspended before booking opens!!, "vsp27759".

(216) Ibid.
(217) Wikipedia: Himatnagar – accessed 20 June 2011.
(218) Great Indian Railway Atlas, op. cit., p.29.
(219) e.g. Himmatnagar Ahmedabad Passenge/ 52919 (www.onefivenine.com/india/Rail/RailDetails/52919 - accessed 1 January 2012); Nandol Dehegam Ahmedabad Passenger / 52915 (www.onefivenine.com/india/Rail/RailDetails/52915 - accessed 1 January 2012).
(220) Great Indian Railway Atlas, op. cit., p.30.
(221) Ahmadabad-Delhi Mail (as at 1 December 2005) (www.india9.com/i9show/Ahmedabad-Delhi-Mail-60025.htm - accessed 23 June 2011); Ashram Express (as at 7 June 2005), (www.india9.com/i9show/Ashram-Express-52282.htm - accessed 23 June 2011); India Railway Atlas, op. cit., Railway Time Table (2003-2004), p.22, 23.
(222) India Railway Atlas, Railway Time Table, op. cit., pp.23, 29.
(223) Ibid., pp.23, 24.
(224) via Google – Indian trains – late.
(225) Chetak Express (as at 7 June 2005), (www.india9.com/i9show/Chetak-Express-54874.htm - accessed 24 June 2011); India Railway Atlas, Railway Time Table, op. cit., p.11.
(226) Lake City Express (as at 7 June 2005), (www.india9.com/i9show/Lake-City-Express-59707.htm - accessed 25 June 2011); India Railway Atlas, Railway Time Table, op. cit., p.11.
(227) Rajasthan Tourist Road Atlas (Indian Map Service: Jodhpur, 2008), p.16; Wikipedia: Udaipur – accessed 26 June 2011; Wikipedia: City Palace, Udaipur – accessed 26 June 2011.
(228) The Times of India, op. cit.; DNA, op. cit. – contents of articles have been given above.
(229) Yediot Acharonot, op. cit.
(230) Ma'ariv, op. cit.
(231) Tourist Map Rajasthan (Indian Map Service: Jodhpur, 2008); a TTK map Uttar Pradesh (TTK Healthcare: Tamilnadu, 2009); Google map – get directions.
(232) Tourist Map Rajasthan, op. cit.; TTK map Uttar Pradesh, op. cit.; Google Maps – get directions.
(233) Google Maps – get directions.
(234) Wikipedia: Western Union (as of 1 February 2006 and 11 June 2010) – accessed 27 June 2011.
(235) via Google – Western Union – Rajasthan.
(236) Wikipedia: Thar Desert –accessed 27 June 2011.
(237) IndiaMike, "Wealthy village in Rajasthan" – question submitted on 25 April 2010.
(238) Phasor, "Wealthy village in Rajasthan" – question submitted on 30 April 2010.
(239) Wikipedia: Shekhawati – accessed 26 June 2011.
(240) History [of Jhunjhunu] (www.myjhunjhunu.com/jhunjhunu/History%20of%20District%20Jhunjhunu.htm – accessed 8 January 2012).

(241) Wikipedia: Shekhawati, op. cit.; History [of Jhunhunu], op. cit.; Heritage Hotels in Mukundgarh (www.india-heritage-hotels.com/hotels-in-india/heritage-hotels-in-india/heritage-hotels-in-mukundgarh-india.html - accessed 28 June 2011).

(242) History [of Jhunhunu], op. cit.

(243) Tourisum Places – Mandawa-Jaipur (webtourisum.blogspot.com/2011/06/mandawa-jaipur.html - accessed 8 January 2012).

(244) Google Maps – get directions.

(245) Western Union in Sikandra, India (www.wu-store.com/western-union-india-sikandra.php - accessed 8 January 2012); Western Union in Jhunjhunu, India (www.wu-store.com/western-union-india-jhunjhunu.php - accessed 8 January 2012); via google – westernunion – infonow.net – select country, India – enter city, Jhunjhunu and Sikar.

(246) Google Maps – get directions.

(247) Wikipedia: Taj Mahal – accessed 29 June 2011; Wikipedia: New Seven Wonders of the World – accessed 29 June 2011.

(248) Google Maps – get directions.

(249) Wikipedia: Varanasi – accessed 29 June 2011; Varanasi (sankatmochan.tripod.com/Varanasi.htm – accessed 29 June 2011); A Road Guide to Uttar Pradesh (TTK Healthcare: Kanchipuram, 2009), p.4.

(250) The Ghats of Varanasi (hinduism.about.com/od/temples/a/varanasi_ghats.htm – accessed 29 June 2011); Tourist Guide & Map Varanasi ((Indian Map Service: Jodhpur [n.y.], p.4.

(251) Wikipedia: Varanasi, op. cit.; Tourist Guide & Map Varanasi, op. cit., p.2; Varanasi, op. cit.

(252) Wikipedia: Varanasi, op. cit.

(253) Varanasi – old city alleys (www.angelfire.com/indie/widowshome/varanasialleys.html - accessed 9 January 2012).

(254) Varanasi traffic and people (www.angelfire.com/indie/widowshome/traffic.html - accessed 9 January 2012); Varanasi – old city alleys, op. cit.

(255) Varanasi – old city alleys, op. cit.

(256) Varanasi – the old city (www.angelfire.com/indie/widowshome2/varanasi.html - accessed 9 January 2012).

(257) "Awesome hotel, but get all rates in writing" (www.tripadvisor.com/ShowUserReviews-g297685-d307314-r47924296-Hotel_Ganges_View-Varanasi_Uttar_Pradesh.html - accessed 9 January 2012).

(258) Wikipedia: Varanasi, op. cit.

(259) "From Goa to Gemara", Mishpacha, English edition, 23 September 2009, p.38.

(260) Telephone conversations with Rabbi Oded David 3 February 2010 and Rabbi Eliezer Botzer, 10 February 2010.

(261) Telephone conversation with Rabbi Eliezer Botzer, op. cit.

(262) Tourist Guide Map Varanasi (Indian Map Service: Jodhpur, 2005).

(263) Telephone conversations wwith Cannu, a resident of Varanasi, 17 & 18 February 2010.

(264) Ministry of Tourism India, Executive Summary – Collection of Tourism Statistics for the State of Uttar Pradesh (April 2005 – March 2006), (ACNielsen.Org.Marg), Survey of Tourist Accommodation Unit, Varanasi hotel no. 107, (tourism.gov.in/CMSPagePicture/file/marketresearch/ statisticalsurveys/06%20up.pdf – accessed 10 January 2012).

(265) Tourist Guide & Map Varanasi, op. cit., p.4.

(266) Paying Guest Varanasi, (www.varanasi-ganges.com/paying-guest-varanasi.html -accessed 30 June 2011).

(267) Ministry of Tourism – Tourism Statistics, op. cit.

(268) Telephone conversations with Cannu, Rabbi Eliezer Botzer, Rabbi Oded David, op. cit.

(269) Happy 24th birthday in Varanasi India (www.travelblog.org/Asia/India/ Uttar-Pradesh/Varanasi/blog-206289.html - accessed 13 January 2010).

(270) "Where the spirit moves them" Ha'aretz online , 14 September 2004, (www.haaretz.com/where-the-spirit-moves-them-1.134813 - accessed 10 January 2012); Nehama David, (www.yeshmeain.com/47811/abut - accessed 15 January 2010).

(271) Breslever Shabbat Songs, (www.breslev.co.il/articles/judaism/jewish_ culture/breslever_shabbat_songs.aspx?id=18421&language=english – accessed 6 July 2011).

(272) Wikipedia: Nachman of Breslov – accessed 7 July 2011; Rabbi Nachman: Overview II (www.azamra.org/Torah/Introduction/Overview2.htm - accessed 7 July 2011).

(273) Tourist Guide Map Varanasi, op. cit.

(274) Wikipedia: Ovadia Yosef – accessed 26 January 2012; Wikipedia: Shas – accessed 26 January 2012.

(275) Rabbi Yehoshua Neuwirth, *Shemirat Shabbat Kehichata* (Jerusalem, 1979), vol.1, chap.32, par.1.

(276) Ibid., par.7.

(277) Ibid., par.16.

(278) Shulchan Aruch, Orach Chaim 260:1 and Rema; Mishnah Berurah 260:1.

(279) Rabbi Simchah Rabinowitz, *Piskei Teshuvot*, vol.1. 88:1.

(280) Ibid., 88:6.

(281) Ibid.; Shulchan Aruch, Yoreh Deah 201: 2, 6.

(282) Rabbi David Miller, *The Secret of the Jew*, (Oakland, California, 1930), chap.19.

(283) Rabbi David Miller's The Secret of the Jew (www.homemikveh.org/sotj/ sotj.html - accessed 1 July 2011).

(284) Rabbi David Miller, op. cit.

(285) Ibid.

(286) Piskei Teshuvot, op. cit., vol.1 chap. 88 fn.44.

(287) Babylonian Talmud, Shabbat 113a.

(288) Piskei Teshuvot, op. cit., vol.3, 262:4.

(289) Shulchan Aruch, Orach Chaim 262:1 and gloss of Rema; Mishnah Berurah 262:1-2; Biur Halachah on Mishnah Berurah 262 "yesader shulchan".

(290) Ibid., 261:1, 2; Mishnah Berurah 261:19, 23.
(291) Acknowledgements to Rabbi Dr. Eliyahu Simons of Haifa for information.
(292) Wikipedia: Hasidic Judaism - accessed 3 July 2011.
(293) Wikipedia: List of Hasidic dynasties – accessed 11 January 2012.
(294) Wikipedia: Breslov (Hasidic group) – accessed 3 July 2011.
(295) Wikipedia: Ger (Hasidic dynasty) – accessed 3 July 2011.
(296) Wikipedia: Hasidic Judaism, op. cit.
(297) Ibid., The Hats of Borough Park (www.werrnercohen.com/hats.html - accessed 3 July 2011).
(298) Wikipedia: Hasidic Judaism, op. cit.; Wikipedia: Shtreimel – accessed 11 January 2012.
(299) From Goa to Gemara, op. cit.
(300) Karma Kosher Conscripts in New-Age Diaspora Seek Refuge in Goa (www.bloomberg.com/apps/news?pid=newsarchive&sid=a12JnKt1Pwlc – accessed 11 January 2012).
(301) Ayana Shira Haviv, "Next Year in Kathmandu", *Israeli Backpackers and their Society"* ed. Chaim Noy and Erik Cohen, (State University of New York Press New York, 2005), p.64.
(302) Karma Kosher conscripts ..., op. cit.
(303) India as backdrop for Israeli debate, (sepiamutiny.com/blog/2009/04/15/india_as_backdr/ - accessed 11 January 2012).
(304) Bikebrats: Triplogue – Delhi to Agra (www.bikebrats.com/india/trindia1.htm – accessed 25 May 2010).
(305) Karma Kosher Conscripts, op. cit.
(306) India as backdrop for Israeli debate, op. cit.
(307) Karma Kosher Conscripts, op. cit.; Wikipedia: Anjuna – accessed 4 July 2011.
(308) India as backdrop for Israeli debate, op. cit.
(309) Ibid.; A brief introduction to the Vagator Beach, (travelgoa.co.uk/a-brief-introduction-to-the-vagator-beach/ - accessed 4 July 2011).
(310) Siddur – Kabbalat Shabbat service; Piskei Teshuvot, op. cit., 267:3 and footnotes; Wikipedia: Lekhah Dodi – accessed 5 July 2011.
(311) Rebbe Nachman's Lecho Dodi Niggun (www.youtube.com/watch?v=FejkOAED0S8- accessed 5 July 2011).
(312) Ibid.
(313) Breslov eikh she-hu (www.scribd.com/doc/27747171/Breslov-Customs-Weekdays -accessed 28 May 2010).
(314) The Breslov Synagogue (www.safed.co.il/breslov-synagogue.html - accessed 5 July 2011).
(315) Mishnah Berurah 271:1.
(316) Babylonian Talmud, Beitzah 16a; Shulchan Aruch, Orach Chaim 242:1; Mishnah Berurah 242:1, 2, 4.
(317) A Simple Jew – Eating on Shabbos (asimplejew.blogspot.com/2005/09/eating-on-shabbos.html – accessed 11 January 2012).
(318) Wikipedia: Zemirot – accessed 6 July 2011.
(319) Rabbeinu Simchah, *Machzor Vitri* (Ish Hurwitz edition), pp.147-48.

(320) Breslever Shabbat Songs (www.breslev.co.il/articles/judaism/jewish_culture/breslever_shabbat_songs.aspx?id=18421&language=english – accessed 6 July 2011).
(321) Likutei Moharan vol.2, par.104.
(322) Wikipedia: Nachman of Breslov, published works – accessed 7 July 2011.
(323) Likutei Moharan p.54b par.44; p.109a par.181.
(324) Israeli Backpackers, op. cit., p.67.
(325) Ibid., p.68.
(326) Ibid., p.66.
(327) Telephone conversation with Rabbi Eliezer Botzer, op. cit.
(328) Only Mumbai, 29 January 2007, Arthur Road Jail, (onlybombay. blogspot.com/2007/01/arthur-road-jail.html – accessed 12 January 2012); Wikipedia: Arthur Road Jail – accessed 10 January 2011.
(329) Mumbai Map, p.20.
(330) Only Mumbai, op. cit.
(331) My experience in Police custody and Jail (www.ispsquash.com/MCOCA_Jail.HTM – accessed11 July 2011); Wikipedia: Arthur Road Jail, op. cit.; "Indian prisons – rhetoric and reality", The Hindu, online edition 20 April 2004; Only Mumbai, op. cit.
(332) My experience in Police custody and Jail, op. cit.
(333) "HIV stalks Arthur Road jail", Indian Express, 21 November 2004.
(334) Wikipedia: Arthur Road Jail, op. cit; HIV stalks Arthur Road jail, op. cit.; "Free after 5 years", Sunday Mirror (London), 13 May 2007.
(335) My experience in Police custody and Jail, op. cit.
(336) Free after 5 years, op. cit.
(337) Ibid.
(338) "Detainees in Arthur Road Jail in Mumbai", PUCL Bulletin, August 2000, (www.pucl.org/reports/Maharashtra/arthur_road.htm - accessed 12 January 2012).
(339) My experience in Police custody and Jail, op. cit.
(340) Arthur Road jail inmates beaten without provocation: judicial report, (reported in twocircles.net., 28 November 2008), (twocircles. net/2008nov27/arthur_road_jail_inmates_beaten_without_provocation_judicial_report.html – accessed 12 January 2012).
(341) My experience in Police custody and Jail, op. cit.
(342) Wikipedia: Varanasi, op. cit., climate; Climate of Varanasi (www. varanasicity.com/climate-varanasi.html - accessed 11 July 2011).
(343) Historical Weather: Varanasi / Babatpur, September 2005, (www. tutiempo.net/en/Climate/Varanasi_Babatpur/09-2005/424790.htm - accessed 12 July 2011).
(344) October Journal, (www.azothdesign.com/chinaoctober.html - accessed 11 July 2011).
(345) Historical Weather: Gorakhpur, September 2005, (www.tutiempo.net/en/Climate/Gorakhpur/09-2005/423790.htm - accessed 12 July 2011).
(346) Historical Weather: Varanasi / Babatpur, September 1999, (www. tutiempo.net/en/Climate/Varanasi_Babatpur/09-1999/424790.htm - accessed 12 July 2011).

(347) Historical Weather: Bhairawa Airport Nepal, September 1999, (www. tutiempo.net/en/Climate/Bhairawa_Airport/09-1999/444380.htm - accessed 12 July 2011).

(348) Reviews from our community "Grumpy staff, unpleasant bathroom" (www.tripadvisor.com/ShowUserReviews-g297685-d307314-r4985425-Hotel_***-Varanasi_Uttar_Pradesh.html - accessed 12 July 2011).

(349) Reviews from our community "great location and terrace", (www. tripadvisor.com/ShowUserReviews-g297685-d307314-r5019091-Hotel_***-Varanasi_Uttar_Pradesh.html - accessed 12 July 2011).

(350) Rabbi Dovid Ribiat, *The 39 Melochos*, (Feldheim: Jerusalem, 6th ed. 2001), vol.1, p.63.

(351) Rambam. Mishnah Torah, Zemanim, Hilchot Shabbat, chap.6, halachah 2.

(352) Rabbi Ribiat, op. cit., vol.1, pp.70-71.

(353) Shulchan Aruch, Orach Chaim 328:12.

(354) Rabbi Ribiat, op. cit., p.74; Rabbi Neuwirth, op. cit., vol.1, chap.30, par.11.

(355) Rabbi Yitzchak Weiss, *Minchat Yitzchak*, vol.3, responsum 23; Rabbi Ribiat, op. cit., vol.4, p.1231; Rabbi Neuwirth, op. cit., vol.1, chap.13, par.34 and chap.30, par.11.

(356) Based on Shulchan Aruch, Orach Chaim 276:5, which allows a non-Jew to light a fire on Shabbat for *children* when it is cold. (For adults this may be done when it is very cold.)

(357) Siddur – Shabbat services.

(358) Shulchan Aruch, Orach Chaim 282.

(359) Ibid., 289.

(360) Wikipedia: Cholent – accessed 18 July 2011.

(361) Ibid., 291.

(362) Piskei Teshuvot, op. cit. Vol.3. 291:1 and fn,11.

(363) Shulchan Aruch, Orach Chaim 296:1.

(364) Babylonian Talmud, Pesachim 54a.

(365) Acknowledgements to Rabbi Dr. Eliyahu Simons of Haifa for information.

(366) Shulchan Aruch, Orach Chaim 300:1.

(367) Mishnah Berurah 300:3.

(368) Shulchan Aruch, Orach Chaim 295:1 gloss of Rema.

(369) Shulchan Aruch, Orach Chaim 338:1; Mishnah Berurah 338:1

(370) Breslov Melave Malka (www.breslov.com/music/).

(371) Google Maps – get directions.

(372) Ibid.; TTK map Utter Pradesh, op. cit.

(373) Short and Sweet-WOW, I'm in Nepal, (blog.travelpod.com/travel-blog-entries/lucinate/whatwedid/1132357500/tpod.html – accessed 18 July 2011).

(374) IndiaMike - India to Nepal simple best route.

(375) Welcome to the district Mahrajganj, (maharajganj.nic.in/ - accessed 22 July 2011).

(376) Wikipedia: Passport – accessed 20 July 2011.

(377) Ibid., Passport message.

(378) Biblical Nehemiah 2:7
(379) UKBA Photograph Guidance; (www.ukba.homeoffice.gov.uk/sitecontent/ applicationforms/ecaa/photo-guidance.pdf - 20 July 2011); smarttraveller, General photograph guidelines (www.passports.gov.au/web/requirements/ photos.aspx - accessed 20 July 2011).
(380) Systemic Failure: Nexus between Netas and Naukars (www.iipm.edu/ iipm-old/systemic-failure.html - accessed 20 July 2011).
(381) India Report 2009 (secure.traceinternational.org/data/public/documents/ IndiaReportPressKit011009-64642-1.pdf – accessed 20 July 2011).
(382) Wikipedia: Sonauli – accessed 20 July 2011; Wikitravel: Sunauli – 20 July 2011; Tours to Sunauli (www.indianholiday.com/uttar-pradesh/cities-in-uttar-pradesh/tours-to-sunauli.html - accessed 20 July 2011).
(383) Tours to Sunauli, op. cit.
(384) Ibid.
(385) Spiritual Guides: Natural Nirvana Vegetarian & Spiritual Shopping (www.naturalnirvana.com/Nepal/Nepal-Others/Sunauli-Bhairawa.htm - 21 December 2009).
(386) India Mike: Crossing overland at Sonauli into Nepal - accessed 20 July 2011.
(387) Wikitravel: Sunauli, op. cit.
(388) Tours to Sunauli, op.cit.
(389) Bradley Mayhew, Joe Bindloss and Stan Armington, Nepal Lonely Planet, (Lonely Planet Publications, 7th edition 2006), p.289.
(390) itravelabout: Sunauli, the border crossing between India and Nepal (www. itravelabout.com/sunauli-the-border-crossing-between-india-and-nepal - accessed 22 July 2011).
(391) numerous photographs via Google e.g. Sonauli - India-Nepal border.
(392) Border signpost, (www.mattandbeckysminiadventure.co.uk/wp-content/ uploads/2009/01/border-cossing-011208.jpg - 20 July 2011).
(393) Border signpost (farm4.static.flickr.com/3577/3657312917_b9f3c5cd38. jpg?v=0 – 20 July 2011).
(394) Border signpost (www.myphotographs.net/nepal/picture1.html -accessed 20 July 2011).
(395) Border signpost (www.pbase.com/image/37166883 - accessed 20 July 2011).
(396) Ibid.
(397) Border barrier e.g. Ibid.; static.panoramio.com/photos/original/19918323. jpg – accessed 20 July 2011.
(398) Spiritual Guides, op. cit.
(399) IndiaMike: Crossing overland at Sonauli into Nepal, op. cit.
(400) Ibid.
(401) Nepalese Confusion (www.ballofdirt.com/entries/846/5396.html - accessed 20 July 2011).
(402) Tracing Illicit Tobacco Trade in South Asia, section 2: Smoke alarm: Illicit Tobacco and Allied Trade across Indian Borders (Framework Convention Alliance, 2010) p.41. (www.healthbridge.ca/Illicit%20Tobacco%20 Trade%20in%20South%20Asia.pdf – accessed 15 January 2012).

(403) Wikipedia: Visa (document) – accessed 24 July 2011.

(404) India Mike: Visa Roundup: Tourist visa FAQs – accessed 24 July 2011.

(405) Getting Nepal Visas (Legal Issues and Red Tape) (www.moonsuntravel. com/nepal/nepal_visaprocedure.php - accessed 24 July 2011).

(406) Travel.state.gov: A service of the Bureau of Consular Affairs – U.S. Department of State – Nepal: Country Specific Information (travel.state. gov/travel/cis_pa_tw/cis/cis_980.htm - accessed 25 July 2011).

(407) Getting Nepal Visas, op. cit.

(408) Buddhist Studies: Lumbini (www.buddhanet.net/e-learning/pilgrim/pg_17. htm - accessed 24 July 2011).

(409) Spiritual Guides, op. cit.

(410) Ibid.

(411) How to travel by train to and from Kathmandu & Nepal ... (www.seat61. com/Nepal.htm - accessed 23 June 2010).

(412) Travel slang (www.travelslang.com/zTravelGuidesSonauli%20(Belahiya). html - accessed 25 July 2011).

(413) Nepal Getting there & around – Bus & tram (www.lonelyplanet.com/ nepal/transport/getting-around#167016 – accessed 25 July 2011).

(414) Spiritual Guides, op. cit.

(415) How to travel by train to and from Kathmandu & Nepal..., op. cit.

(416) Tom Woodhatch, *Footprint Nepal Handbook* 2nd ed. (Footprint Handbooks: Bath England, 1999), p.401.

(417) Google Maps – get directions.

(418) *Footprint Nepal Handbook*, op. cit., p.401.

(419) Google Maps – get directions.

(420) Bhairawa: Gateway to Lumbini (www.nepal.com/central/bhairawa - accessed 24 June 2010).

(421) Visit Nepal (visitnepal2008today.blogspot.com/2008/01/siddhartha nagarbhairahawa.html - accessed 26 July 2011).

(422) Bhairawa: Gateway to Lumbini, op. cit.

(423) *Footprint Nepal Handbook*, op. cit., p.401.

(424) Wikipedia: Nepalese Civil War – accessed 27 July 2011.

(425) Ibid.

(426) Wikipedia: Armed Police Force Nepal – accessed 27 July 2011; Government of Nepal Armed Police Force: Introduction (www.apf.gov. np/introduction/introduction.php - accessed 27 July 2011), Roles (www. apf.gov.np/role/role.php - accessed 27 July 2011).

(427) Nepal Lonely Planet, op. cit., p.289.

(428) Ibid., pp.290-91.

(429) IndiaMike: Anyone used Cosmic Air? – accessed 16 January 2012.

(430) IndiaMike: Train travel in India – accessed 16 January 2012.

(431) Eye in the Sky: Restless and Stuck in Bhairawa Nepal (eye-in-the-blue- sky.blogspot.com/2009/11/restless-and-stuck-in-bhairawa-nepal.html - accessed 27 July 2011).

(432) Rambam, Mishnah Torah, seder Ahavah, Hilchot Tefillah 1:5, 6, 8.

(433) Ibid., 3:1; Shulchan Aruch, Orach Chaim 89:1.

(434) Vilna Gaon on Shulchan Aruch, Orach Chaim 459:2 "veshiur mil"; Mishnah Berurah 58:4; Aruch Hashulchan, Orach Chaim 58:14.

(435) Rambam, Mishnah Torah, seder Ahavah, Hilchot Tefillah 3:1; Shulchan Aruch, Orach Chaim 89:1.

(436) Wikipedia: Siddharthanagar [Bhairawa] – accessed 16 January 2012.

(437) Timeanddate.com (www.timeanddate.com/worldclock/city.html?n=117 – accessed 16 January 2012).

(438) Timeanddate,com (www.timeanddate.com/worldclock/timezone.html?n =117&syear=2000 – accessed 16 January 2012).

(439) Acknowledgements to Rabbi Dr. Eliyahu Simons of Haifa for information.

(440) Siddur – before shacharit; Shulchan Aruch, Orach Chaim 25:4.

(441) Wikipedia: Rosh Hashana kibbutz – accessed 30 June 2010.

(442) Wikipedia: Uman – accessed 14 August 2011; Uman city, Ukraine (ukrainetrek.com/uman-city – accessed 31 July 2011).

(443) Wikipedia: Uman, op. cit.; Uman! Uman! Rosh Hashanah! (Breslov Research Institute: Jerusalem, 1992) (www.breslov.com/bri/umanrh. html#chapter4 – accessed 17 January 2012); hotel Shaarei Zion, Uman (www.stejka.com/4erkasskaja/uman/hotel/waarey_cion/ - accessed 14 August 2011).

(444) Kathamandu and Nepal... Country information (www.seat61.com/Nepal. htm – accessed 14 August 2011); Nepal Transport (www.nepaltravelplan. co.uk/nepal-transport.htm - accessed 14 August 2011).

(445) Google Maps – get directions.

(446) How to travel by train to and from, op. cit.

(447) Wikipedia: Nepalese Civil War, op. cit.

(448) Google Maps – get directions.

(449) Wikipedia: Gautam Buddha Airport – accessed 15 August 2011; Wikipedia: Bhairahawa – accessed 26 July 2011: Flights to Gautam Buddha Airport (BWA) Bhairawa, (www.bookingwiz.com/Bhairawa/ Flights/9105 - accessed 15 August 2011); Google Maps – get directions.

(450) "Bhairahawa airport sans water", The Kathmandu Post, 4 May 2008.

(451) Babylonian Talmud, Berachot 35a; Rambam, Mishnah Torah, seder Ahavah, Hilchot Berachot 1:2.

(452) Talmudic Encyclopedia, vol.4 (Jerusalem, 1956), col.330.

(453) Rambam, Mishnah Torah, seder Ahavah, Hilchot Berachot 8:1; Shulchan Aruch, Orach Chaim 202:1.

(454) Wikipedia: Almond – accessed 16 August 2011.

(455) Deciduous Fruit Production in Nepal, (www.fao.org/docrep/004/ab985e/ ab985e09.htm accessed 17 January 2012).

(456) TravelPod – And we're off... (blog.travelpod.com/travel-blog-entries/ randommaia/epicworldtour/1190461980/tpod.html – accessed 17 January 2012).

(457) Wikipedia: Buddha Air - accessed 31 August 2011; Ace the Himalaya (www.acethehimalaya.com/tripdetails.php?trip_id=65 accessed 5 July 2010; Hawker Beechcraft, About Us, History (www.hawkerbeechcraft. com/about_us/history/ - accessed 31 August 2011).

(458) Wikipedia: Yeti Airlines – accessed 31 August 2011; Wikipedia: de Havilland Canada – accessed 31 August 2011; Wikipedia: de Havilland Canada DHC-6 Twin Otter – accessed 31 August 2011.

(459) Wikipedia: Bhairahawa (as at February 2008).

(460) Wikipedia: Kathmandu – accessed 1 September 2011.

(461) Ibid., Tourism; Wikipedia: Thamel – accessed 1 September 2011.

(462) Trips abroad: First day of work (marytrip.blogspot.com/2008/11/first-day-of-work.html - accessed 13 July 2010).

(463) My Trip Journal: Kathmandu Nepal... (www.mytripjournal.com/travel-436332-food-preparation-kathmandu-nepal-rabbi-lifshitz-trekking-equipment - accessed 18 January 2012).

(464) Wikipedia: Thamel, op. cit.

(465) Wikipedia: Kathmandu, op. cit.

(466) Trips abroad, op. cit.

(467) Anandar Kumar Maharjan and Ammar Raj Guni, *Attractions in Kathmandu and its Successful Management – A Guide Book*, (Kathmandu, 2005), p.5.

(468) Wikipedia: Kathmandu, op. cit., Religion.

(469) Wikipedia: History of the Jews in Nepal – accessed 8 July 2010.

(470) Chabad House of Kathmandu (www.chabad.org/centers/default_cdo/aid/118561/jewish/Chabad-House-of-Kathmandu.htm - accessed 7 July 2010).

(471) Acknowledements to Wikipedia Reference desk – Language for the information.

(472) Chabad House of Kathmandu, op. cit.; "Israeli backpackers undaunted by Mumbai, Pune", The Times of India, 29 March 2010.

(473) Koshertreks: Everest Panorama Photo Album, Chabad House Kathmandu (www.koshertreks.com/everest_photo.php - accessed 18 January 2012).

(474) Chabad House of Kathmandu, op. cit.

(475) Bet Chabad, Kathmandu, (blog.travelpod.com/travel-blog-entries/tomer/asia2/1101497940/tpod.html - accessed 18 January 2012).

(476) Hotel *** (www.hotel***.com – accessed 5 September 2011).

(477) TripAdvisor, Hotel ***: Traveller Reviews (www.tripadvisor.co.uk/Show UserReviews-g293890-d310331-r116627246-Hotel_***-Kathmandu. html - 19 January 2012).

(478) Mapmandu (www.mapmandu.com/neighborhood_listing/18%2C6 – 19 January 2012).

(479) *** Guest House (www.ktmgh.com/kgh/default.php - accessed 7 September 2011).

(480) Israeli Backpackers and their Society, op. cit., p.64.

(481) Voices from Russia (02varvara.wordpress.com/2009/02/09/ - accessed 19 January 2012).

(482) Clepsydra – Ting-ting... (chat.thevalkyrie.com/clubhouse/oldchat/log-107-10-31.htm - accessed 19 January 2012).

(483) Our Really Big Adventure (www.ourreallybigadventure.com/india_nepal/nepal/randr.html - accessed 19 January 2012).

(484) Voices from Russia, op. cit.
(485) Mapmandu (www.mapmandu.com/hotels - assessed 13 July 2010).
(486) Ibid.; Map of Kathmandu (www.lonelyplanet.com/maps/asia/nepal. kathmandu - accessed 13 July 2010).
(487) Rabbi Yechiel Tukachinski, *Gesher Hachaim*, (Jerusalem, 1960), vol.1, chap.4, par. 11. 14. 15; Rabbi Chaim Goldberg, *Penei Baruch*, (Jerusalem, 1986), chap 1, par.12, 15.
(488) ibid., vol.1, chap, 24, shemua kerovah par.1; ibid., chap.26, par.1.
(489) ibid., vol.1, chap, 24, shemua rechokah par.1, 2, 4; ibid., chap.26, par.19, 24.
(490) ibid., vol.1, chap. 19, section 4, par.11; ibid., chap.26, par.30.
(491) "Passover in the Hindu kingdom", Nepali Times, no.293, 7-13 April 2005, p.4.
(492) Google Maps – get directions.
(493) Hbcal Jewish Calendar, Date Converter (www.hebcal.com/converter/?hd= 1&hm=Tishrei&hy=5766&h2g=Convert+Hebrew+to+Gregorian+date – accessed 20 January 2012).
(494) Machzor for Rosh Hashanah.
(495) Tosafot on Babylonian Talmud, Rosh Hashanah 33b, "shiur"; Mishnah Berurah 596:1.
(496) Shulchan Aruch and Rema, Orach Chaim 583:1.
(497) Preparations in Nepal for Biggest Rosh Hashanah Meal (shturem.org/ index.php?section=news&id=29988 – accessed 26 October 2011).
(498) The Chabad House is a "life-saver" (www.shturem.org/index. php?section=news&id=2872 – accessed 15 July 2010).
(499) Kosher CouchSurfing: Israeli students launch Jewish hospitality scheme, Haaretz (online edition), 26 June 2009.
(500) Bambuddhism in Nepal (lesliechand.blogspot.com/ - accessed 8 July 2010).
(501) TravelBlog , Kathmandu Nepal (www.travelblog.org/Asia/Nepal/blog-41448.html - accessed 7 July 2010).
(502) Passover in the Hindu kingdom, op. cit.
(503) Embassy of the United States, Arrest and Detention Procedures (nepal. usembassy.gov/legal_information.html – accessed 15 July 2010).
(504) Committee to Protect Journalists, Nepal's media brave threats in 'interesting times', Comments (cpj.org/blog/2010/02/nepals-media-brave-threats-in-interesting-times.php – accessed 15 July 2010).
(505) Cash raised to release journalist locked up in Nepal jail (www.ekantipur. com/2010/04/12/headlines/Cash-raised-to-release-journalist-locked-up-in-Nepal-jail/312243/ - accessed 16 July 2010).
(506) Nepal – Entry and Exit points (www.visitnepal.com/travelers_guide/ entry_points.php -accessed 15 July 2010).
(507) Where to stay in Nepal: Visa and Passports (www.hoteltravel.com/nepal/ guides/travel_tips.htm - accessed 15 July 2010).
(508) Biblical Hosea 14:2.
(509) Chabad House of Kathmandu, op. cit.

(510) Finding Judaism in Nepal, Celebrating in Israel (lubavitch.com/news/article/2014613/Finding-Judaism-in-Nepal-Celebrating-in-Israel.html - accessed 22 July 2010).

(511) Bet Chabad Kathmandu, op. cit.

(512) Slow and Steady..., Shabbat in Kathmandu (mostlyslow.blogspot.com/2008/06/shabbat-in-kathmandu.html - accessed 22 July 2010).

(513) Koshertreks: Everest Panorama Photo Album, Chabad House Kathmandu, op. cit.

(514) Koshertreks: Everest Panorama Photo Album, op. cit., Itinery for Everest Panorama.

(515) Wikipedia: Tribhuvan International Airport – accessed 31 October 2011.

(516) Ibid.

(517) Wikipedia: Nepal Airlines – accessed 31 October 2011; Wikipedia: Nepal Airlines destinations – accessed 31 October 2011; Royal Nepal Airlines (www.iloveindia.com/airlines-in-india/international/royal-nepal-airlines.html - accessed 31 October 2011).

(518) Wikipedia: Thai Airways International – accessed 31 October 2011; Wikipedia: Thai Airways International destinations – accessed 31 October 2011.

(519) Wikipedia: Passport stamp – accessed 1 November 2011.

(520) Wikipedia: Extradition – accessed 1 November 2011.

(521) "New Indo-Nepal extradition treaty soon", The Times of India, 26 November 2008.

(522) India-Nepal extradition Treaty (www.oecd.org/dataoecd/22/53/39791430.pdf?contentId=39791431 – accessed 24 July 2010).

(523) "Extradition treaty with India", Nepali Times, #231, 21-27 January 2005, p.5.

(524) "Political instability in Nepal holds up revised extradition treaty", The Times of India, 20 January 2010.

(525) How long is a flight from Kathmandu to Bangkok? – (wiki.answers.com/Q/How_long_is_a_flight_from_Kathmandu_to_Bangkok - accessed 22 July 2010).

(526) Wikipedia: El Al - accessed 14 November 2011; El Al loses routes as Israel begins deregulation (www.flightglobal.com/news/articles/el-al-loses-routes-as-israel-begins-deregulation-148327/ - accessed 14 November 2011).

(527) Wikipedia: Airspace – accessed 15 November 2011.

(528) Wikipedia: El Al Flight 402 – accessed 15 November 2011.

(529) Acknowledgements to "Marco polo" via Wikipedia Reference desk – Miscellaneous for information.

(530) Frequently Asked Questions about flights from Bangkok to Tel-Aviv (www.farecompare.com/flights/Bangkok-BKK/Tel_Aviv-TLV/market.html – accessed 25 July 2010).

(531) The Wings of the Web, Civil Aviation – A 75 Years Old Man Died in Flight (qa.airliners.net/aviation-forums/general_aviation/read.main/733901/ - accessed 25 July 2010).

(532) Rabbi Meir Posen, *Ohr Meir*, op. cit., Tables p.12.
(533) Time zone in Jerusalem (www.timeanddate.com/worldclock/timezone. html?n=110&syear=2000 – accessed 22 January 2012).
(534) Wikipedia: Ben-Gurion International Airport – accessed 16 November 2011.
(535) Ibid.
(536) Ibid.
(537) Architectural Record, Ben-Gurion International Airport, Terminal 3 (archrecord.construction.com/projects/bts/archives/airports/05_ben Gurion/overview.asp - accessed 22 January 2012).
(538) Wikipedia: Ben-Gurion International Airport, op. cit.
(539) Review of Tel Aviv, Ben Gurion International Airport (www.reviewcentre. com/reviews-all-127122.html - accessed 18 November 2011).
(540) Ibid.

BIBLIOGRAPHY

Jewish Religious Literature
Tanach
Babylonian Talmud and commentaries
Rambam, Mishnah Torah
Rabbeinu Simchah, *Machzor Vitri,* (Ish Hurwitz edition)
Shulchan Aruch and commentaries
Mishnah Berurah
Aruch Hashulchan
Goldberg, Rabbi Chaim, *Penei Baruch*, (Jerusalem, 1986)
Miller, Rabbi David, *The Secret of the Jew*, (Oakland, Califonia, 1930
Neuwirth, Rabbi Yehoshua, *Shemirat Shabbat Kehichata*, (Jerusalem, 1979)
Posen, Rabbi Meir, *Ohr Meir*, (London, 1973)
Rabinowitz, Rabbi Simchhah, *Piskei Teshuvot*, (Jerusalem)
Rebbe Nachman of Breslov, *Likutei Moharan*,
Ribiat, Rabbi Dovid, *The 39 Melochos*, (Feldheim: Jerusalem, 6th ed. 2001)
Tukachinski, Rabbi Yechiel, *Gesher Hachaim*, (Jerusalem, 1960)
Weiss, Rabbi Yitzchak, *Minchat Yitzchak*, (Jerusalen, 1993)
Talmudic Encyclopedia, vol.4 (Talmudic Encyclopedia Publishing: Jerusalem, 1956)
Siddur
Machzor for Rosh Hashanah

General Literature
London, Christopher W., *Bombay Gothic*, (India Book House: Mumbai, 2002)
Sheppard, Samuel T., *Bombay Place-Names and Street-Names: Excursion into the By-ways of the History of Bombay City,* (Bombay: The Times Press, 1917)

Israeli Backpackers and their Society, ed. Chaim Noy and Erik Cohen, (State University of New York Press New York, 2005)

Maps and Travel Guides

Frommer's India, (Wiley Publishing, Hoboken, New Jersey, 2010)

Gujarat Road Atlas, (Indian Map Service, Jodhpur, 2007)

India Railway Atlas, & Time Table, ed. R.P. Arya et al., (India Map Service: Jodhpur, 2003)

Maharjan, Anandar Kumar and Ammar Raj Guni, *Attractions in Kathmandu and its Successful Management – A Guide Book*, (Kathmandu, 2005)

Map of Ahmadabad, (TTK Healthcare, Tamil Nadu, India, [n.d.])

Map of Uttar Pradesh. (TTK Healthcare: Tamil Nadu, 2009)

Mayhew, Bradley, and Joe Bindloss and Stan Armington, *Nepal Lonely Planet*, 7th edition, (Lonely Planet Publications: Footscray, Victoria, Australia, 2006)

Mumbai City Map, (Eicher Goodearth: New Delhi, 2009)

Rajasthan Tourist Road Atlas, (Indian Map Service: Jodhpur, 2008)

Road Guide to Ahmadabad, (TTK Healthcare, Tamil Nadu, 2009)

Road Guide to Uttar Pradesh, (TTK Healthcare: Kanchipuram, 2009)

Roychoudhury, Samit, *The Great Indian Railway Atlas*, (Calcutta Art Studies: India, 2005)

Tourist Guide & Map Varanasi, ((Indian Map Service: Jodhpur [n.d.])

Tourist Guide Map Varanasi, (Indian Map Service: Jodhpur, 2005)

Tourist Map Rajasthan, (Indian Map Service: Jodhpur, 2008)

Woodhatch, Tom, *Footprint Nepal Handbook* 2nd ed., (Footprint Handbooks: Bath England, 1999)

Newspapers and Journals

American Journal of Tropical Medicine and Hygiene, (Deerfield, Illinois, USA)

BBC News, (London, England)

Beis Moshiach, (Brooklyn, New York, USA)

Business Line [Financial daily from "The Hindu" group of publications], (Chennai, India)

DNA [Daily News and Analysis], (Mumbai, India)

Frontline, [India's National Magazine from the publishers of "The Hindu"], (Chennai, India)

The Globe and Mail, (Toronto, Canada)

Ha'aretz, (Tel Aviv, Israel)

The Hindu, (Chennai, India)

Indian Express, (New Delhi, India)

Journal of Clinical Microbiology, (Washington D.C., USA)

Journal of Infectious Diseases, (Boston, Massachusetts, USA)

The Kathmandu Post, (Kathmandu, Nepal)

L'Chaim, (Lubavitch Youth Organization, Brooklyn New York, USA)

Ma'ariv, (Tel Aviv, Israel)

Mishpacha (English edition), (Jerusalem, Israel / New York, USA)

Nepali Times, (Kathmandu, Nepal)
Saudi Journal of Kidney Diseases and Transplantation, (Riyadh, Saudi Arabia)
Siliconindia, (India)
Sunday Mirror, (London)
The Times of India, (India)
Yediot Acharonot, (Tel Aviv, Israel)

Internet
For each reference from the internet, the website is given together with the date accessed. However, with the numerous websites for "Wikipedia and "IndiaMike," since in almost every case, it is easy to locate the reference via Google, the website is not given; in the few cases where it is more difficult, the website is given.

Section Two

Amongst
the Six Million

THE ZIELINSKI FAMILY OF PRZEDECZ
THE HISTORY OF A FAMILY WHO PERISHED IN
THE HOLOCAUST

Introduction

Three of my grandparents came over to England with their entire families from Eastern Europe at about the end of the 19th century. However, this was not the case with the family of my maternal grandfather. Only he came over, with the remainder of his family remaining in eastern Europe. As with six million other Jews, almost the entire family perished in the Holocaust. Until about 25 years ago, we knew almost no details of the family, and I therefore thoroughly researched the subject.

During the following years I wrote several papers on this research and in this paper, I am combining and editing into one paper the results of my research.

This paper is divided into three sections:

1) The history and description of the city Przedecz Poland where the Zielinski family lived.
2) A report on how I performed my research to ascertain details of the family history of the Zielinski family.
3) The results of this research.

Apart from my family and those whose ancestors came from Przedecz, this paper may well be of interest to historians who are writing about the period of the Holocaust. Furthermore, the methods I used to obtain the information could assist others who wish to document the history of their families who perished in the Holocaust.

The name of the family is sometimes spelled as Zielinski and other times as Zelinski. Throughout this paper I have used the spelling Zielinski.

On a number of occasions there was conflicting information on details of the Zielinski family, which is quite normal when people are recollecting what occurred several decades earlier. In such cases I had to try to decide which information was the more probable one.

As in most countries in the Diaspora a person is given both a secular name and a Hebrew name. The countries' official documents will, as to be expected, give the secular name. In this paper, the Polish and the Hebrew names are used interchangeably.

In Przedecz there were a relatively large number of people with the surname of Zielinski. Possibly they were members of the same extended family, but this paper is limited to my branch. Due to the fact that there are to be found identical first names of Zielinskis, (possibly they had been named after the same person), one cannot completely exclude the fact that there are instances where I mistakenly described the life of a member of the Zielinski family who was not a direct member of my family.

The City of Przedecz

Przedecz is today situated west of Central Poland midway between Chodecz and Klodawa. It is about 75 kilometres north-west of Lodz, 150 kilometres west of Warsaw and 130 kilometres east of Posen. Its co-ordinates on the map are: latitude – 52 degrees 20 minutes North; longitude – 18 degrees 54 minutes East. The south west side of Przedecz borders on Lake Przedecz.

In Yiddish the city was known as Pshaytsh.

The earliest mention of Przedecz is in the 12th century, and at that period it was in the possession of Archbishops. In the second half of the 14th century the king purchased Przedecz and the surrounding lands from the Archbishops. At about that period, it was a transit station for traders travelling from south to north and from east to west, and was a centre for trade for the surrounding farms.

Przedecz was granted the right to be known as a city before the end of the 14th century. Although in today's usage, Przedecz would be regarded as a "village," in this paper we shall use its official status and refer to it as a "city."

During the period when Przedecz was in the possession of the Archbishops, Jews were forbidden to live there and the beginning of Jewish settlement seems to have begun towards the end of the 14th century. The Jewish cemetery is about 600 years old.

In 1538, there was a big fire in Przedecz and most of the houses were destroyed. Ten years later, the king gave the right to produce and market liqueurs without paying taxes and to have a market day each week.

In the middle of the 17th century, during the war with the Swedes, the city was destroyed and only 40 houses remained. The financial situation of Przedecz flourished at the beginning of the 18th century when the king gave permission to have two market days each week and a fair six times a year.

In a census taken in 1793 the population consisted of 355 persons, 139 of whom were Jews. By 1827 it had grown to 1935 persons, 346 of whom were Jews. During the following 30 years the total population in Przedecz increased by only 20, whereas the Jewish population increased to 606. In other words, during these 30 years the percentage of Jews in this city radically increased. This occurred because Jews from the neighbouring villages moved to Przedecz. By 1921, the total population had increased to 3,040, of whom 840 were Jews.

Przedecz had only a few streets, but it had all the elements of a Jewish Community: Synagogue, Bet Hamedrash, Mikva, Jewish Schools, Yeshivah, Jewish Library, Jewish Cemetery, Eruv, welfare and cultural organisations. Przedecz had its own City Rabbi and it also had its own Shochet and Mohel. At first the Shechitah of animals took place in the courtyard of each butcher shop, and the Shechitah of fowl in the courtyard of the Shochet, However, before the Second World War, a large abattoir was built under the auspices of the Local Council. In this new abattoir, the sanitary conditions were better and there was also a regular veterinary inspection by the Polish authorities.

Many of the Jews were artisans - tailors, hatmakers, cobblers etc. They usually worked from their homes assisted by their children and other employees, and would then travel from city to city to sell their wares, in general, to the non-Jews. Some of the Jews were small traders.

Every place had its market day and for Przedecz it was Monday. On Mondays the non-Jews would come from the farms in the area and sell butter, eggs and chickens to the Jews and in turn these non-Jews would buy products such as salt, sugar and tobacco from the grocery shops, and clothes, shoes, hats etc. from the market. From morning to evening on Mondays, the market was crowded with people.

Apart from the main Synagogue of Przedecz, there was a "Chevrat Tehillim." This "Chevrat Tehillim" served as a Synagogue for the artisans of the city. Services were also held in the Bet Hamedrash. The Bet Hamedrash had its own library and on Fridays two boys aged 13-14 went around the houses collecting money to buy new books and to pay for the rebinding of the old ones.

The Mikvah was situated very near to the lake and quite near to the "Chevrat Tehillim." The city also had its own Eruv, which enabled the Jewish residents to carry in the streets on Shabbat. On occasions when this Eruv was broken, and this happened quite often, the children would carry the Siddurim and Tallitot to the Synagogue, and would also bring the Cholent to the houses from the bakery.

The religious affairs of the community were controlled by a Committee (Parnasai Ha'ir). Every year members of the Community would meet in the Bet Hamedrash and elect 8 members to this Committee. The function of this Committee was to fix the salary of the Rabbi and other religious officials, the price for Shechitah, the charge for the Mikvah, etc. A tax was levied on the families in order to pay for these services.

In Przedecz, there was a State Elementary School. There was no High School and thus pupils who wished to study in a High School had to go to neighbouring cities. The Elementary School was attended by both Jewish and non-Jewish children of the city. The usual secular subjects taught in schools were taught there. At first it was situated in the same building as the Town-Hall, the school being upstairs and the Town-Hall downstairs, but later a new large building was built for the school in Stoldona Street. For their religious instruction there was a "Bet Sefer Ivri," which would meet after regular school hours. Subjects such as Tanach (Bible) and Dinim (Jewish Law) were taught in this "Bet Sefer Ivri." In the religious education of the children, particularly of the boys, a love for Eretz-Israel was prominent. In addition, there was a "Bet Yaacov" school for the more religious girls, although in fact the overwhelming number of Jews in Przedecz were observant. In the courtyard of the Bet Hamedrash there was another more religiously orientated school. There was also a Yeshivah, whose Principal was Rabbi Yoseph Alexander Zemelman, the Rabbi of Przedecz. For those who wanted to learn a trade such as tailoring, hatmaking or cobblering, there were evening classes.

The city had a Jewish Library but it was more than just a library. It functioned as a cultural centre. People would meet there in the evenings and read books, dance, listen to lectures, have theatre performances, etc. The more religiously observant, instead of going to the Jewish Library would use the Agudah or the Mizrachi facilities instead.

There were also welfare organisations in Przedecz. A "Bikur Cholim" society would look after the poor sick. There was also a "Benevolent Fund" which would give loans without interest to needy Jews and this saved them from starvation.

In 1926, with the assistance of the "Joint" a Jewish Bank was set up in Przedecz. The main purpose of this Bank was the granting of loans. These loans were made according to usual banking procedures and required two guarantors who were acceptable to the Bank. This Bank closed in 1936 as a result of the difficult financial situation of the Jews at that period.

During the 20th century, various Zionist groups were established in Przedecz, including branches of the General Zionists, Poale Zion Yemin, Hashomer Hazair, the Mizrachi and the Revisionists. Money was collected in Przedecz for the J.N.F. There were also a few Bundists. In 1937 there were seventy people who had voting rights for delegates to the 20th Zionist Congress held in Zurich that year, of whom all but three utilised their rights. The establishment of these groups caused friction between those of the right and those of the left. As a result, those of the left stopped coming to the Jewish Library. For the younger people there was the Young Mizrachi and Betar. The programmes of these youth groups included activities on Shabbat afternoons.

Agudat Yisrael also had a branch in Przedecz, most of its members being Gerrer Hassidim. One of the people active in this branch was the Rabbi of Przedecz, Rabbi Zemelman. Until 1925 the Gerrer Chassidim had a shul which was located in a rented house in the courtyard of Yeshayahu Zielinski's house. I tried to track down further information on this shul and on 18 December 1997 I spoke to Avraham Moshe Segal who had an archive and was an expert on the Gerrer Chassidim in Poland. He didn't remember such a shul nor did he have any archives on it. In addition, he did not know anyone from Przedecz.

There was even "Hachsharah" (preparing people for Aliyah to Eretz-Israel) in Przedecz. This group had some fields in which young people planted and grew vegetables which they then sold in Przedecz.

The houses in Przedecz were mostly just one story high. Some were owned by the Jewish residents and others were rented from non-Jews. There was no running water in the houses. In the centre of Przedecz was a pump. Electricity was only installed in 1928 - until then people used gas lights. There were very few telephones in Przedecz and radio was a luxury found in very few houses. The Polish Telephone Directory of 1932/33 listed just eight telephones in Przedecz and some of these were for public institutions.

In September 1939, Germany entered Poland and the Second World War began. A few weeks later on the night of the Festival of Shemini Atzeret, 4 October 1939, the Germans set fire to the Przedecz Synagogue. On the day after the Festival, the Germans summoned the Rabbi of the City together with some of the leaders of the Community and they were forced to sign a statement that the Jews themselves had burnt down the Synagogue, and in addition they had to pay a fine for so doing!

The Germans changed the name of the city to Moosburg.

In 1940 there were 769 Jews in Przedecz and nearly half of them were sent to forced labour camps. The majority of them died there from hunger and disease. The Germans set up a ghetto in Przedecz which was situated in the Old Market. In early 1942, the Germans packed the remaining Jews into the local church, where they were left with no food or water for three days. Many of them died from lack of air. On 24 April 1942 - 7 Iyar 5702, the remaining Jews were sent to the Chelmno extermination camp and the Jewish community of Przedecz was thus finally liquidated. The 7 Iyar has become the Memorial Day for this Community.

The Rabbi of Przedecz managed to escape to Warsaw, where he took an active part in the Warsaw Ghetto uprising.

In the mid-1960s, some former residents of Przedecz went to revisit the place. Where the Synagogue had formerly stood, the Poles were building houses. All that remained in what had been the Jewish cemetery was a solitary tree. All the tombstones had disappeared. The Bet Hamedrash and the adjoining house of the Rabbi had been demolished.

In March 1998, my eldest daughter Ayelet went on a "Holocaust Study Trip" to Poland. On 30 March she made a brief trip to Przedecz, where she visited the site of the Jewish cemetery and photographed it. It had been destroyed by the Nazis. A memorial plaque had been erected there by the Local Council. At a later date the Buks family, who originated from Przedecz erected a memorial stone in the cemetery, whose inscription reads, "We honor the blessed memory of our Jewish ancestors from the town of Przedecz lovingly remembered by the Buks family - 1993." She lit a candle by this memorial stone. The Polish authorities have planted a forest over the site of the cemetery, presumably to preserve and beautify the area.

The Association of Jewish Genealogical Societies (AJGS) has established a "Cemetery Project" in which they give a report of the state of Jewish cemeteries in Europe. One of them is for this cemetery in Przedecz, and it was compiled together with Arline Sacks, and it appears on the Internet.

In this extract from their report, they write:

The Jewish cemetery was used by Orthodox Jews, and the date of the last known Jewish burial was 1939.

The cemetery is located in a suburban area on flat land; it is isolated and there is no sign or marker. It is surrounded by no wall or fence (although there was a wooden fence before the war) and has no gate. It can be reached by turning directly off a public road, and access is open to all.

The size of the cemetery before the Second World War was around 0.5 hectares; it is the same size now. There are no tombstones visible. Some of the tombstones removed from the cemetery are in a museum/conservation laboratory (5 pieces), and some are in the garden by the Municipality Office (3 pieces). Tombstones are datable from the 20th Century, and are inscribed in Hebrew. They are made of sandstone and are finely smoothed and inscribed stones. Some tombstones have traces of painting on their surfaces.

The cemetery is currently owned by the municipality, and is used for recreational purposes - a forest was planted from 1960-1965. The properties adjacent to it are residential - there is a house at the synagogues site (the pre-burial house?). The cemetery is occasionally visited by private Jewish visitors and local residents.

The cemetery was vandalized during the Second World War. There is now no maintenance done There are slight security, weather erosion, pollution, vegetation and vandalism threats facing this cemetery. There is also a slight threat from an incompatible nearby development.

I subsequently sent several of my daughter's photographs to the AJGS and also pointed out a small error in their report. They inserted this correction into their report and gave me the credit. They also included a photograph that I had sent them.

In addition to photographing the cemetery, my daughter photographed the houses which had been built over the site of the former Synagogue. Lack of time prevented her from viewing the tombstones which it was reported had been put in the museum/

conservation laboratory and in the garden by the Municipality Office. I now understand that these tombstones have disappeared.

Today there are no Jews in Przedecz, nor even signs of a former Jewish community. However, a number of Przedecz survivors from the Holocaust rebuilt their lives in Eretz Israel, where today they and their descendants live.

My stages in the research

[The information given below is not necessarily in chronological order]

My first "research" on the Zielinski family was in the form of several discussions with my maternal grandmother (who died when I was 14 years old) and whose husband was born in Przedecz. I remember she said that her husband's family came from a place which at the time sounded to me like "Shtaich," and she also gave me the names of all her husband's brothers and sisters. However, I remembered just a few of these names.

Decades passed during which I did nothing further to investigate the genealogy of the Zielinski family, almost all of whom had perished in the Holocaust. It was only towards the end of 1996, that my daughter Rachel, then aged 17 went on a "Holocaust Study Trip" to Poland and the Czech Republic, that I felt that this would be a good opportunity to investigate this branch of my family.

I learned that the name of the city in Yiddish was Psceich and that the Polish name was Przedecz. Thus armed with this name, I went to "Yad Vashem" - the Holocaust Martyrs' and Heroes' Remembrance Authority in Jerusalem. The librarian there referred to their computer and gave me the reference of the "Yizkor Book" for Przedecz.

At that time, I had no idea whatsoever where the geographic location of Przedecz was. I therefore opened a number of atlases on Poland which were in the Yad Vashem library and searched for and found its location.

The latter part of this Yizkor Book has brief biographies in Yiddish of the people of Przedecz who perished in the Holocaust.

These included a large number of people whose surname was Zielinski and I made a photocopy of these pages. I recollect that the photocopier in Yad Vashem was an old model and each time one wanted a photocopy one had to insert four coins of 10 agorot each. Since people do not normally carry around large quantities of such coins, one could exchange money there for packets of 10 agorot coins!

There were four editors of the Przedecz "Yizkor Book," which had been published over 20 years earlier in 1974. I tracked them down but learned that two of them had since died. The remaining two, were Moshe Mokotov and Reuven Yamnik. I spoke to both of them by telephone. Moshe Mokotov sent me a copy of this "Yizkor Book" and refused any payment for it. Reuven Yamnik informed me that all of the Zielinskis mentioned in this book were from the same family - cousins etc.

This Yizkor book includes reconstructed drawings from memory by Reuven Yamnik, who then lived in Przedecz, of the synagogue and of the roads in Przedecz.

This book also gave the names of former residents of Przedecz both in Israel and in the Diaspora. Although there were no Zielinskis living in Israel, there were three Zielinskis living in the Diaspora - two in U.S.A. (New York and Nebraska) and one in France (Paris). It was in October 1996 that I wrote to all of them. After introducing myself and explaining my precise connection with the Zielinski family, I requested the answer to several questions: "Are you from the same Zielinski family and if so, how are you related to me? What further information can you give me about the Zielinski's? I notice from this 'Sefer Yizkor' a large number of people with the name Zielinski from Pscheich who perished in the Holocaust. Are all these from the same family?" For the Zielinski living in Paris, I had my letter translated into French.

I never received replies from any of these three Zielinskis. In two cases - the Nebraska and Paris addressees - the letters were returned by the Post Office. This was not too surprising since the addresses were well over twenty years old, and also by my calculations these people would have been very elderly and possibly no longer alive.

This Yizkor book also gave the names and addresses of many former members of Przedecz living in Israel, but none of them were Zielinskis. From a program on my computer which enabled me to obtain any telephone number in Israel, I was able to draw up a list of telephone numbers of people who were still alive. Between December 1997 and February 1998, I contacted these people by telephone in order to see if they could give me information regarding the Zielinski family.

I kept a diary record of these conversations. It began in December 1997 and went on until February 1998. Here are some extracts.

16 December: Reuven Yamnik: Many Jews in Przedecz owned property including members of the Zielinski family. Alya Zielinski owned a house. [At a later date he amended this to a rented house.]

17 December: Reuven Yamnik: Alya lived in the New Market. There were no numbers on the houses as far as he remembers. Yeshayahu the brother of Alya lived in Warshavska Street, maybe no.1. Yeshayahu's wife was called Sarah. He suggests I speak to Levi Schweitzer.

17 December: Levi Schweitzer: He confirms Alya and Yeshayahu were brothers. Alya lived in the New Market. Yeshayahu lived in Warshavska Street.

18 December: Yehoshua Davidovitz: He remembers very little: He lived in the Old Market. There were tailors in the Old Market. He suggests I contact Bela Yachimovitz. He doesn't remember the Gerrer shul in Przedecz.

18 December: Bela Yachimovitz: She lived in the same house as Alya. The house did not belong to him but to someone called Woltersdorf. She thinks this house was demolished. The house was in a square. She does not remember where Yeshayahu lived. *[Whilst I was on the telephone, her son who was listening asked why I am asking her all these questions. She is not well. This ended the telephone call.]*

18 December: Mela Brand: She does not remember the Zielinski family.

18 December: Galilit Panini: She doesn't remember details of the Zielinski family, although she remembers the name Zielinski - a big family.

18 December: Moshe Mokotov: Alya lived in the New Market on a corner house. Possibly Bela Yachimovitz lived in the same building. Does not remember where Yeshayahu lived nor does he remember the Gerrer shul.

20 December: Esther Berg: (sister of Galilit Panini) She left Przedecz when she was young and so she does not remember details of the Zielinski family. She does remember that there was a widower in the family.

20 December: Fishel Goldman: Does not remember. Thinks there were numbers on the houses.

20 December: Reuven Yamnik: Alya lived in a rented house together with father of Bela Yachimovitz. Afterwards Bela went to live in 9 Kilinskiago Street. Alya also moved somewhere else – it seems to a rented house. Yeshayahu lived at 1 Warshavska Street. He owned the house.

29 December: Reuven Yamnik: Mendel Niemczowko lived on 2nd floor of a house and Itzik Zingerman on 1st floor. [I had meanwhile received a document from my Uncle Monty Zielin (described later) showing that they were the brothers-in-law of Alya and Yeshayahu Zielinski.] The house was owned by Zingerman and was situated in the Old Market. Itzik Zingerman was a blecher (*a person who smelts metals*).

3 January: Husband of Golda Grabinsky: He informed me that his wife had died just 5 weeks earlier. She was related to both the Zielinski and Zychlinsky families. Yeshayahu was her grandfather and Fishel Topolski his wife's uncle. [*Had I managed to speak to Golda, I am sure that I would have gained valuable additional information about the Zielinski family.*]

7 January: Sarah Mandlinger: Did not remember details but remembered that there were a lot of Zielinskis. She thought that they were more than one family – not related.

27 January: Moshe Mokotov: Did not remember if all the names in the Yizkor book are people who perished in the Holocaust or if it includes people who died in the years beforehand.

29 January: Fishel Goldman: Did not remember the name of Alya's wife. He will ask his sister Bela. He mentioned something about Alya's son Shmuel being ill – but was hesitant when pressed on this question.

1 February: Levi Schweitzer: Did not remember the name of Alya's wife. He confirmed that Alya lived in the New Market and Yeshayahu next to him at 1 Warshavska Street. Before being sent to Chelmno, the Jews were put in the Catholic Church.

11 February: Yehoshua Davidovitz. He thinks that Alya's son Reuven died before the war. There is a relative of Morgenstern (the father-in-law of Reuven Zielinski) alive in America today (Saul Morgenstern). He could not remember Alya's wife's name and could not confirm whether Eliahu Zielinski (appearing in the Yizkor Book) is the same person as Alya Zielinski.

16 February: Fishel Goldman: He had checked with Bela. Wife of Alya was called Rachel.

28 February: Levi Schweitzer and also *Reuven Yamnik*: They each gave me the names of the various educational establishments in Przedecz.

During the course of the above telephone conversations, I realised that I needed to have a much longer discussion with Reuven Yamnik and a face-to-face meeting would be best. He agreed to such a meeting and on 20 January 1998 I travelled to his house in Bnei Brak, armed with a cassette recorder and plenty of paper and spoke with him for two hours. [*Some of the questions I subsequently asked the former residents of Przedecz arose from this conversation.*]

[I should mention that during my subsequent research. I discovered that some of the details he had given me may not have been accurate, which is quite understandable after such a large period of time.]

From this meeting I learned several new facts regarding the Zielinski family. These included: Nachman Zielinski was a cousin. The daughter of Itzik Zingerman married a Goldman girl. The second son of Alya was Chaim Alta. He did not remember the names Rachael or Sarah Leah (two sisters of Alya). He also did not remember the Zielinski parents Azriel and Lieba. The Eliyahu Zielinski mentioned in the Yizkor Book is Alya. Alya and Yeshayahu generally davened in the "Chevrat Tehillim" shul.

Alya lived in the same house as Yoseph Goldman, the father of Bela Yachimovitz, with Bela living on the opposite side of the street. The house where Alya lived was owned by a Christian named Francis (Frankus) – it was a two-family house, on one side lived Yoseph Goldman, who had a bakery. Alya lived on the other side. Francis knocked down this house and built a larger house of 3-4 stories in the 1930s. Alya then moved to the opposite side of the street and rented a house and courtyard. Yoseph moved to 9 Kilinskiago Street and took his bakery there.

Reuven married Zipporah and went to live in Lodz. He was handsome and tall. He occupied himself with local cultural activities and the library. Maybe he also gave lectures. Alya's wife was a housewife. He didn't remember what the children did.

Yeshayahu was a member of the Committee for Visiting the Sick. He helped ill people who had no-one to help them. His son Chaim-Hersh was on the management Committee of the Jewish Library whose functions included buying books and giving lectures. Another son Woolf was active in the Hachshara for Aliyah. The daughter Sheina helped the needy. The trade of the son-in-law Fishel Topolski was preparing leather for shoes.

Itzik Zingerman (Sheva's husband) was gabbai of the Shul. Hersh was the son of Sheva. They also had a daughter Rachael Leah. There was another son called Alta who lived in Lodz.

Pesse (Alya's sister) was ill – she had blotches all over her face – and he thought she died before the war. [*I recollect my grandmother telling me that she died in about 1933.*] Mendel's (husband of Pesse) occupation was a travelling salesman. He was a member of one of the city's committees who would fix prices for Shechitah, the Mikvah and salaries of the Rav and the Shochet. He was also a comedian.

During this interview he also gave me additional information regarding Przedecz. These included facts on the activities which took place at the Jewish library, the physical living conditions (water from the well, when electricity was installed), market day, schools and curricula, political groups, and local Jewish elections. *(Details are given in section 1 of this paper.)*

I also asked him from where they got the information for the Yizkor Book. He answered that on every Erev Shabbat they would go round the houses and collect money for books. From the list of donors, they were able to prepare lists for the Yizkor book of Przedecz and that the names in this book were arranged according to the streets of Przedecz. I then asked where these lists of donors were and he answered that they no longer exist.

However, researchers who want the names of at least many members of the Jewish Community of Przedecz, can find them in the annual lists of the "Przedecz Jewish Community Membership Fee" which for at least many years are still extant and are located at the "Jewish Historical Institute of Poland." However, from the answer I received from Reuben Yamnik, it would seem that these are not the books referred by him which give the list of donors to the book fund.

I shall now return to describing the Holocaust Study Trip which took place at the end of 1996, in which my daughter Rachel was about to participate. The organisers had said that would try to incorporate into their itinerary visits to places where ancestors of the participants came from, provided they did not involve a real deviation from their planned route. I studied the planned itinerary which my daughter had received and saw that on the second day they would be travelling from Lodz to Chelmno. By a slight detour, they would be able to go via Przedecz. I spoke to Ezra Hartman, the organiser of this trip and he promised to consider going via Przedecz.

My daughter and I made a list of all the Zielinskis listed in this "Yizkor Book" - there were 61 of them. Since a married woman takes the surname of her husband, there were obviously an even higher number of Zielinskis from Przedecz who perished in the Holocaust. She also took some Yahrzeit candles to light in what had been the Jewish Cemetery of Przedecz. From this "Yizkor Book" we learned that all the tombstones had been uprooted. Before I learned that the cemetery had been destroyed, I suggested that she try and find any tombstones bearing the name Zielinski, copy out their inscriptions and also photograph these tombstones.

My daughter went on this trip and a few days later, the father of one of the other participants heard from his own daughter that some sort of detour had been made during the journey. From this, I assumed that they had managed to visit Przedecz. However, when Rachel returned, she told me that although the organisers had considered going through Przedecz, they found that the road leading to this place which was marked on the map, no longer existed. An alternative route would have involved a much larger detour, and since their schedule was very tight, a visit was not possible. Rachel did however recite the names of the Zielinski family who perished in the Holocaust, in a memorial service which they held at Auschwitz.

There was a further piece of information of the Zielinski family which I obtained from my mother's brother Monty Zielin. He had a list of the names of the brothers and sisters of his father. I wrote to him asking the source of such a list and he replied that during the Second World War, whilst serving in the British army, he was told to supply a list "giving the family names and addresses" in occupied Europe, in order not to be sent to those areas. I asked him for a photocopy of this list which he duly sent me. *(My subsequent research showed that there were some inaccuracies in this list of names, but since this was not first-hand information of his, this is understandable.)* The list was typed in

March 1942, and since in those days not many people had typewriters, he wrote to me: "It was probably typed by your father." In addition, my aunt had a document which gave the maiden name of my grandfather's mother and the date and place of her marriage.

When one does any research, it is essential to know where to find the source material, and this of course includes research into one's genealogy. I must admit that when I began this research, I was basically a novice on genealogy and had to begin from square one. Fortunately, this was already the era of the Internet and one could obtain the general information one required from this source. I downloaded a large amount of material, although I must admit that in the end, I used very little of it.

Amongst this general material that I downloaded were articles on "How to Trace your Family Tree – Suggestions for the Beginning Genealogist," "Genealogy Resources on the Internet," "Compiling an Oral Family History" and "Cyndi's List of Genealogy Sites on the Internet."

A journal on Jewish Genealogy which is published four times a year in the U.S.A. is "Avotaynu." On the Internet is an "Index to the First Twelve Volumes of Avotaynu." I downloaded this index and then went through it (most especially the section on Poland) marking the articles which I thought might help with my research. I then ordered the appropriate journals at the Jewish National Library and photocopied the articles I had marked off. These included articles such as the "Jewish Historical Institute in Poland," "Jewish Genealogical Research in Poland" and "Directory of Polish State Archives."

I also downloaded general genealogical material on Polish Archives. Much of this was put on the Internet by the "Polish Genealogical Society of America." Amongst this material was a list of the names, addresses and telephone numbers of the various "Archives in Poland."

One of the major difficulties (if one does not know Polish) is the language difficulty. Even if you write to an archive in English, they will reply in Polish! To assist the researcher, this "Polish Genealogical Society of America" has brought out a "Polish Letter

Writing Guide." They recommend writing to local civil records office in Polish. A long list of common phrases used in such letters is given in both English with the Polish equivalent. Apart from the difficulties in language, many of the letters in Polish have various symbols on them. Generally, one's computer will not have these fonts and one will have to add them by hand.

Another Internet site gives where one can find the various "Vital records in Poland" – namely, births, marriages and deaths. As I shall show later, this isn't as simple as it may seem. I have been told that records are not always where one expects them to be, or maybe they are no longer extant.

I would also search through various journals and magazine for any leads I might find on my family. From an article which I had photocopied from "Avotaynu" I learned of the existence of lists with the names of over 200,000 Jews of the Lodz Ghetto. I immediately realised that they could be relevant to my research, since several members of the Zielinski family had moved to Lodz from Przedecz.

I first searched for these lists in the Jewish National Library in Jerusalem but they were not there. Therefore, I then went to the Yad Vashem Library and found a set of four volumes listing all the members of the Lodz ghetto, which had been arranged in alphabetical order using a computer. I looked under the letter "Z" but could not find Zielinski. However, there was a "volume 5" which was a supplement containing names which had been omitted and there I found under Zielinski, Reuven's wife and two children – but not Reuven.

I then went to the archives room of Yad Vashem and found microfilms of the two original lists, which had been prepared on the basis of addresses in the Lodz ghetto. One had been prepared in 1940 and the other about 1942. In order to use these microfilms, one first looks in the computerised alphabetical lists to determine the address of a specific person in the Lodz ghetto and then one is able to find his name by looking up the street and house number in the microfilms. The latter list also gives the dates of birth, and sometimes the former addresses of the inhabitants and the dates that they were sent to the concentration camps. I ordered photocopies of the relevant frames in the microfilms.

As I mentioned, the name of Reuven was absent. Why? In Tel Aviv there is "The Organization of Former Residents of Lodz" (OFRLI). They have in their records about a third of the 180,000 Jews buried in the Lodz Jewish cemetery. It was in February 1998 that I telephoned them and asked them if the name Reuven Zielinski appears on their lists. They checked but it was not there. Since only a third of the names appear, it is by no means conclusive. A few weeks later I again contacted them and they said in addition to the very likely possibility that he had died before the Lodz ghetto list of 1940 was prepared, there is also the possibility that he fled to Russia, as many others had done, in the hope that later they would be able to bring out their families.

It was about a month later in March 1998, that my eldest daughter Ayelet was one of the leaders in a Holocaust Study Trip and I asked if she would be able to find information about my mother's cousin Reuven Zielinski who lived in Lodz. The itinerary included Lodz which included a visit to the Lodz Jewish cemetery, and I asked if she could see if Reuven was buried there. She went to the cemetery office and there they had found the burial certificate for Reuven who had died aged 28 in December 1937 and they made a photocopy for her. She then went into the cemetery and found the grave. The stone was in perfect condition. She photographed it and was one of the only ones in that area of the cemetery. My initial reaction was that the Nazis had removed most of the tombstones. However, on reflection I concluded that there could be another explanation. It was only just before the beginning of the Second World War and maybe not many burials had taken place in that part of the cemetery or stones had not yet been erected over the fresh graves. This subject needs further research.

From the lists of those in Lodz, we knew where he had lived and I suggested she try and photograph the building that Reuven Zielinski had lived in and also another building where it was possible that another relative had lived. She managed to find the location where Reuven had lived. However, that particular building had been demolished to build some sort of boutique. The house of the other relative was still standing.

On their subsequent route from Lodz to Chelmno, it seemed from their programme that they would pass by the junction with Przedecz. I asked if she could manage to incorporate a visit there. If so, she should photograph amongst other things, the site of the Jewish cemetery, the site of the former Shul, and the houses where the family had lived.

The group even managed to make a detour and pay a brief visit to the cemetery in Przedecz. Another leader of the group was studying the life of the Rabbi of Przedecz, Rav Yoseph Zemelman, who later escaped and took part in the Warsaw Ghetto uprising. This leader was thus able to support her in making the detour to Przedecz. To their credit, the Polish authorities had not built over the graves, but had planted trees and had put up a memorial stone. However, over the site of the Shul destroyed by the Nazis, they had in the 1960s built apartments. In one of her photographs, one can see the occupant closing the window. Maybe they were frightened we had come to claim the site.

A similar incident occurred when someone went to photograph the house (which incidentally a few years earlier had been rebuilt) where a relative of mine had owned and lived. Half of the city came out of their houses. Possibly they were worried that the Jews would claim this house! In fact this was not so theoretical!

It was in December 1997 that a long article appeared in the "Jerusalem Post" headed "Every house has a story" and subtitled "Now is the time for Polish Jews and their descendants to reclaim family property in Poland. Real estate prices are rising and unclaimed property will eventually be expropriated." Apparently, much had already been expropriated. My immediate reaction was, why allow any Government, let alone the Polish Government which had such a record of anti-Semitism, expropriate Jewish property. I therefore decided to investigate whether the Zielinski family-owned property in Przedecz?

The "Jerusalem Post" article had a sub-article, "How to stake a claim for property in Poland" and gave the names of three law firms in Israel who were dealing with property reclamation. I telephoned one of them who informed me that one could not proceed without the exact address of the property in Poland. The only way to obtain such an address, (short of travelling to Poland, and researching land registry records - assuming the Poles would allow it) was by contacting former residents of Przedecz now living in Israel, and asking them if they remembered addresses of 60 years ago!

I also contacted the other two law firms mentioned in the "Jerusalem Post" article. They both told me that the initial stage would be to find out in whose name the house was registered, whether it was still standing and whether it had already been expropriated. Just for these initial investigations they would charge $650 plus VAT! One of the lawyers also added that unless the property was a large one in a big city, it was not worth the outlay and trouble, both for the lawyer and for the client.

Although I later discovered that one of the members of the Zielinski family in fact owned a house, following the advice of the lawyers, I did not continue with this line.

In Przedecz there was a source of income for the Jewish community, namely, there was a "Przedecz Jewish Community Membership Fee." There are extant lists between the years 1924 and 1935, which gives the name of the member and the amount he paid in zlotys. At least a large majority of those on this list perished in the Holocaust.

Apart from this "Membership Fee List" and the "Przedecz Yizkor Book," one might ask whether the names of the Jews of Przedecz who perished in the Holocaust have been documented? The answer is that it was in the 1950s that Yad Vashem decided to try and document the names of the six million Jews murdered in the Holocaust. They then sent round officials to the houses of Jews in Israel asking them if they could complete forms entitled "Pages of Testimony" with this information. This documentation afterwards continued and until today (end of 2021) I understand there are about five million names have already been recorded.

By 1999, I had assembled information on many members of the Zielinski family and in May of that year, I went to Yad Vashem to fill in forms with such information. I went armed with the book I had written. There I requested a whole pile of forms and went into their library in order to complete them. The questions asked on these forms included: family name of victim, first name, age at death, date of birth, gender, place of birth, victim's parents' and spouse's name, place of work, date of death, place of death and circumstances of death. This was followed by details of the informant.

I spent hours filling in forms for about 36 members of the Zielinski family. In many cases I did not know the answer to many of the questions and therefore had to leave blanks. In the margin of each form, I added the source of my information. I personally feel that it would be useful for this to be incorporated as one of the questions. I also feel it would be good for those filling up these "Pages of Testimony" to add their Identity Card number.

A few years later all the information on these forms was transferred to a computer and at the beginning of 2005 it was put onto the Internet. I read that within a short period this site had been viewed three million times.

A side advantage of this website was that people discovered other relatives of theirs. This would occur when two different people would register the same victim. This indeed happened in my case.

As soon as this site became available, I entered it to see if the names I had registered had already been entered and saw that about 25 of them had. I also saw that for a number of them, a Sinai Aharonovitz of Tel-Aviv had also filled up forms describing himself as "cousin" to relatives of mine. Incidentally he had also mistakenly registered Reuven Zielinski as a Holocaust victim. At a later date, I recollect that someone else had also registered his name as a Holocaust victim, I pointed out this error to Yad Vashem, inclosing photocopies of Reuben's burial certificate and a photograph of his grave in Lodz Jewish Cemetery.

I decided to try and track down this "new found relative." Maybe he could also supply me with details I did not know about the family. His name did not appear in the Bezek telephone book. The Ministry of Interior told me that he was no longer alive – not too surprising since he would have been over a century old!

I asked someone who was experienced in genealogical research how to go about tracking down the family who had lived in a certain apartment in the 1950s. He suggested that I go to this apartment in Tel-Aviv and knock on the doors of the neighbours and ask. However, Tel-Aviv is not just "round the corner" and I found a quicker method. I entered the Bezek site 144 on the Internet, typed in the name of the street and the city Tel-Aviv and developed a reasonably quick way to find out the names and telephone numbers of people living in that and the adjacent buildings.

With this information, and following a few telephone calls, I was able to locate close relatives of Sinai Aharonovitz. They were pleased to hear from me and asked me for a copy of my research which I sent them. However, from our conversations we saw that when Sinai had written "cousins" it also meant a more distant relationship. We never worked out exactly how we were related to each other.

All countries keep (or should keep!) records of births, marriages and deaths, but it sometimes be difficult to track down where they are kept. I found this especially so with the Polish records.

At the end of December 1997, I sent to the "Polish Genealogical Society of America," a completed "Ancestor Index File Submission Form" together with a letter asking whether they could fill in gaps in my information. One of their volunteers replied saying that I would have to get documents from Poland adding that "we advise our members to give up because the price is ridicules.... The way I see it – poor people paid their dues when they were recorded. Now again they have to pay if you want information. Does the government own it? Such a steep price?"

The volunteer wrote to the Polish archives at Warsaw to ask what records that had of Przedecz. They replied they had none but they would look if they were anywhere else. I had also written to these archives in Warsaw at the beginning of January 1998.

Following a prompt acknowledgment of my letter, I received in June of that year a reply in Polish from the archives in Torun. They wrote that the records of Jewish births of Przedecz were destroyed probably during the Second World War. There were some records in the books of the population register of permanent residents of Przedecz between 1885 and 1931. These could be found in the archives in Torun.

However, from other sources, different information was received! In 1993, the Office Director of the Museum of Konin wrote to an inquirer, "Books of registrations birth and death are held in Town Hall of Przedecz (birth 1902-1916, 1916-1934, death 1903-1916). Another volume and all registrations of marriage has been burned during the War. Registrations from years before 1902 are, probably in the State Archives in Poznan (till 1985) and Bydgoszcz (1975-1902)."

On the Givat Ram campus of the Hebrew University are situated the "Central Archives for the History of the Jewish People." I thought that maybe I will find something there on the Zielinski family of Przedecz. I went there, looked at their catalogue and found they had a few fragmentary records from Przedecz from the mid-19th century. I ordered the file and found a few documents on the Zielinski family, written of course in Polish and in the Napoleonic format, as decreed by Napoleon at the beginning of the 19th century. I had these documents photographed.

From a certain Howard Kushel I received an e-mail in January 2004, "Unfortunately for Jewish records there are only the death records for 1875-1887 and these are found in the Poznan Archives…"

Yet a further "version" I received in a telephone call with Gary Mokatoff of "Avotaynu" in December 1998. He told me that these vital records (births etc.) do exist. For the last 100 years they are to be found in Przedecz. He added that he knows this fact because Moshe Mokotov got a birth certificate from there of his sister who died in the Holocaust. Those more than 100 years old are to be found in the archives in Warsaw.

The bottom line of all this is that as yet I have very few original vital records of my branch of the Zielinski family.

However, on the positive side, as a result of periodically putting my updated research on my website, I received in April 2004 a very nice letter from a non-Jew called Zbigniew Cmielewski. He wrote to me in English (and his English is very good): "I have just read your history of the Zielinski family of Przedecz. It is very interesting. I was born in Przedecz in 1956 and I was living there by 1971. I'm interested in history of Przedecz especially in its former residents .... I can give you some more details about Przedecz and eventually about its former citizens and I can send you some photos from Przedecz...."

A few weeks later he sent me a page from the Polish Business Directory of 1929. The entry for Przedecz contained the name Zielinski Ch. and Zielinski A. In the accompanying letter he wrote that the Ch "is Chaim because there aren't Polish names which start with 'Ch'."

After a further few weeks, I received a beautifully coloured brochure on glossy paper on Przedecz and the immediate vicinity – in Polish. Needless to say, I immediately acknowledged with thanks all these things he sent me.

A few months later, he sent me by e-mail a current colour photograph from Przedecz. In his opinion it was the house owned by Francis and in which Alya lived. Zbigniew told me that his mother had told him that this house owner's name was Francus and he was a German. A few days later I received an old photograph which included this Francus. The next photographs I received were of buildings where the Cheder and the school had been situated.

Soon after this, he saw online the Przedecz Yizkor Book. He wrote, "I'm very happy but I have got a hugh problem – I can't read it. It's a pity that this book is not in English." In order for him to be able to read this book, he wrote that he would have to learn the language and he had already started to teach himself the Hebrew alphabet. He concluded by asking, "Could you translate inscriptions into English on the street map of Przedecz?"

I made a big photocopy of this street map and next to all the Hebrew words wrote an English translation. When thanking me he added: "I recognised some of the houses and places. Most of the streets are the same names but many buildings vanished without a trace, For example: synagogue, psalms club, ritual bath, abattoir and 'Young Mizrachi' building. The others changed their destiny: library, post office, rabbi's house, house of study, bank and Betar building. They are dwelling houses now." He concluded by saying that this Yizkor Book should be translated into Polish and that many people should read it.

In the Przedecz Town Hall there are a number of Jewish birth and death records from the early part of the 20th century. These are to be found in three small thin books. I wrote to Zbigniew asking him if he could arrange to me to have photocopies of these books. He inquired but was told that records for the last 100 years were closed but they would let me have records appertaining to my family. I replied by giving him all the surnames of my various relatives. One of the workers at these archives began and he himself continued extracting the material from these records (which are in Cyrillic) and at the beginning of 2006, he sent the information to me by e-mail two lists in a tabulated form. The information included for the births: child's name, year of birth, father's name, mother's name including maiden name; for the deaths it included: name, year and often the actual date and/or age at death, and occasionally father's and/or mother's name. It seems from studying these records that some of the entries are from my direct family, whilst others are probably more distant relatives.

Zbigniew offered to send me photocopies of the original documents, moreover at his own expense, adding "Many of your relatives - who were on the list – perished in the Holocaust. Today is "March of the Living" in Auschwitz-Birkenau. This is my small step in it." Unfortunately for some reason I did not take this up with him at the time. It was many years later, towards the end of 2014, when I returned to my project on genealogy, that I sent him an e-mail reminding him of his kind offer. I then carefully went through the two lists he had sent me and found 10 birth records who were my immediate family and requested that he scan or photocopy these documents and send them to me, adding that I was prepared to pay for the expenses involved. However, I received no reply (despite sending him a further e-mail), probably indicating that he had changed his e-mail.

I made a further attempt to get photocopies of these 10 birth records via Noach Hall who lived in Telshstone near Jerusalem, and whose family came from Przedecz (although it would seem that he was not from my family). I had been in periodic contact with him for a number of years. Noach was in contact with Halina Ziecik, a Polish historian, who had made a film on the Jews of Przedecz in Przedecz and she had assisted Noach in his research, including sending him photocopies of documents connected with his family. I therefore I asked Noach in March 2017, whether Halina could photocopy these 10 documents for me, for payment, but he replied that Halina was at the time occupied with writing a book on Przedecz. Therefore, I still do not have these photocopies!

Prior to this, Noach had gone on a Holocaust Study trip and he informed me that he intended to take a day to visit Przedecz. I asked that if he had time could he photograph some sites connected with the Zielinski family and if he should see any archival documents mentioning this name photocopy them. After he returned, I met with him and then showed me the photographs he had taken. Amongst them was one where the house of Yeshayahu had been. I said "had been" since he was told that a few years earlier it had been rebuilt. He also related that when he came to photograph it, half the city came out of their houses. Possibly they were worried that the Jews would claim it! He had also photocopied from the archives in Przedecz a number of documents which mentioned the name Zielinski, although not necessarily my branch. Soon after, he faxed me copies of these documents.

To return to the period of about the year 2005. It was then that I received e-mails from two people who had seen my book on the "Zielinski Family of Przedecz" on the Internet. One of them was from Ken Rapoport an accountant from Illinois in the United States; the other, was from Gary Nelson a lawyer from London. Ken was related to the Zychlinsky's who were distant relatives of mine, and Gary to the Zielinskis. We worked out that my great great grandfather was Gary's great great great great grandfather.

171

Ken gave me a brief summary of his ancestry in Przedecz and suggested we share information, which of course I readily agreed to. Very soon after, he informed me that he was going to Poland to search out his roots. In reply I told him that he would likely find relevant material in the Przedecz Town Hall and at the Jewish Historical Society of Poland which is located in Warsaw. Those were all the sources I knew of at the time. I also told him: "I have learned from my personal experience that what you don't photocopy today, you might never have another opportunity to do so and it is thus worth laying out more money to do a greater number of photocopies."

He went to Poland in September 2005. Afterwards he wrote to me: "My trip to Poland was wonderful. I found a lot a lot of information and it was spiritually moving." At the Jewish Historical Society, he found quite a bit of material which included the annual Rolls of Przedecz Jewish Community Membership Fee Payers for the years 1924-1935, and several Rolls of Candidates for Members of the Board of the Przedecz Jewish Community. Since they were in Polish, he paid quite a lot of money there to have them translated into English. There was also the Polish Telephone Directory of 1932/33 and he had a photocopy made of the page which included Przedecz. There were just 8 telephones there at that period and some of these were for public institutions. He sent me photocopies of this material and it included entries on the Zielinski family. I could see from these records that only a fraction of the Jews in Przedecz paid these Jewish communal dues. However, these lists did give me the names of many of the Jewish families in Przedecz during the 1920s and 1930s.

In Przedecz, Ken had found great difficulty in gaining access to the records in the Town Hall and they would not even let him read through them. However, after much effort he was able to receive photocopies of the records appertaining to his family. He was very upset about their attitude and wrote to me: "It [these record books] is such a meaningless thing to them, but SO valuable to me and you and people with relatives in Przedecz." (I should mention that in contrast, Noach Hall had found them very helpful indeed. It obviously depends with which clerk one is dealing with!)

Also, towards the end of 2005, using mainly the Internet, I made a search of the sources of Jewish genealogical information appertaining to Przedecz. In addition to the sources stated above, I also found that there were some death records of the 1870s and 1880s at the Poznan archives and records of permanent residents of Przedecz (both Jews and non-Jews) from 1885 to 1930 at a branch of the Torun Archives situated at Wloclawek. At first, I wrote a general letter in English to the Torun Archives to which I eventually received a reply in Polish. I then wrote with the help of a friend of mine who lives in Kiryat Arba and was born in Poland, Mordechai Reback, a more specific letter in Polish. In their reply, they wrote that one cannot order photocopies of masses of material but one must state exactly which pages one wants to photocopy. However, as I shall now explain there will very soon hopefully be a simpler and more effective method to obtain the information one requires.

One of the people Ken was in contact with was Stanley Diamond who is the Executive Director of "Jewish Records Indexing – Poland." This organisation had already indexed a large number of the Jewish records in Polish archives. From my e-mails with him and with Ken, I learned that at that period (about 2005) there was a project then being commenced to index the Jewish entries in the "Lists of Permanent Residents" from the latter part of the 19th century and early part of the 20th century for the various towns in Poland. This was eventually done for Przedecz, and Ken sent me the relevant pages for the Zielinski family. These pages gave the names of Azriel and Libe Zielinski, *(my great grandparents)*, their dates of birth (possibly on the Julian calendar), the names of their parents, their occupations. It also gave all these details for their seven children (three boys and four girls), and in some cases for the next generation.

At first, I had understood that the Polish authorities had allowed this organization to microfilm these local residents' records from Przedecz and that this indexing would be done in America. I therefore wrote to Ken, who passed my message on to

Stanley, volunteering my services to help but to do this I would naturally have to receive photocopies of the records. But Stanley informed me that this was not the case. They could not make the microfilms. They were therefore employing Polish staff (which was much cheaper than sending over American research workers) to do the work.

With regards to the Poznan records, I searched on the Internet for the names of the members of the Zielinski family which appeared on them - a total of 7 death records - and passed the information on to Gary, who then ordered photocopies.

About that period, I informed Ken of a further source to reconstruct the genealogy in Przedecz. This was the Yad Vashem lists of those who had perished in the Holocaust. There, there were several hundred names connected with Przedecz. Ken however felt that although it was a "valuable resource" it was limited since "so many of the Jews in this district were murdered without leaving any survivors at all."

Incidentally, another person who on reading my book contacted me was Graham Calvert, whose family came from Przedecz, although he was not from my family. Coincidentally Graham had purchased my mother's house in Edgware (near London) when she came on Aliyah.

Azriel's brother Shiar had moved to England and that was where he finally died. The relevance of this point to my research is that as is customary, his tombstone gives the name of his father, namely Azriel's father. (Since this account is of the Zielinski family of Przedecz, the history of Shiar's family after arriving in England is not relevant.)

Gary Nelson, after much effort, succeeded in the summer of 2006 in locating, Shiar's tombstone in Edmonton Federation cemetery which is in London, which he then photographed. This confirmed the information that I had already found from the Polish records that the name of his father was Avraham Yehudah. I furthermore learned from this tombstone inscription that the way he spelled Yehudah was that the last letter was an "aleph" rather than a "hey."

From all the above research, I was able to write an account of the history of the Zielinski family of Przedecz. I freely admit that there are still gaps to fill, and should further records be discovered or released in Poland, hopefully some of these gaps could be filled.

Results of my research

The book "Jewish Family Names and Their Origins" states that the name Zielinski comes from Zelin which is the Yiddish name of Zolnica (East Galicia).

When did the Zielinski family first arrive in Przedecz? In the "Central Archives for the History of the Jewish People" are some fragmentary civil records of births and marriages which took place in Przedecz in the mid-19th century. These records are written in Polish, in the Napoleonic format, as decreed by Napoleon at the beginning of the 19th century. Some of these records include the names of members of the Zielinski family, although the precise link with my branch of the family has as yet not been traced. One of these documents dated 1847, states how Nachman Zielinski, a tailor, who had lived in Przedecz for 22 years, and was the husband of Ryfki Zielinski aged 18, appeared in the Registry Office together with witnesses. to notify them of the birth of a girl. The girl had been named Marys in a Jewish religious ceremony. Another document dated 1854, states that Rabbi Auerbach notified the Registry Office of the marriage of Zalman Zielinski, aged 20, who lived in Przedecz, to Gitel Rubinska, a spinster aged 20, and daughter of Rechil and the late Michal Rubinstein. It certifies that three notices were given to the Registry Office before the marriage. The document is signed by Rabbi Auerbach and the Mayor of Przedecz. Zielinskis were therefore already in Przedecz in at least the early 19th century.

We also know from the "Acts" of the "Administration of Internal and Spiritual Affairs" of Przedecz from the year 1852 that a discussion or decision of the Jewish residents to raise the salary of the Rabbi was signed by Mordche Zielinski and Hersz Zielinski.

175

In a book-keeping book from Przedecz from the years 1833-1834, the name Abram Zielinski appears in the column listing income coming in from old order merchants of commodities.

My great great grandfather was called Abram Zielinski. Whether or not it is the same Abram Zielinski mentioned above is not known. On the basis of the date that his son Azriel was born, the time period is about right. He married my great great grandmother Ryfka (or according to another record Chaya Ruchla) Zolna. Their dates of birth and marriage are unknown.

Azriel and Libe Zielinski

Azriel Zielinski, (*my great grandfather*), was born 22 June 1845 and he was the son of Avram and Ryfha. He died about the beginning in 1932, and his Yahrzeit is 22 Tevet, which would make the date of his death 1st January 1932. He married Libe Nejhaus, (*my great grandmother*) who was born in 1844, the day and month are unknown. She died probably in the 1920s, her Yahrzeit is 3 Shevat. They were married in Przedecz on 6 January 1867.

Libe Nejhaus' parents were Naftal Wolek Nejhaus, (*my great great grandfather*), and Chana Przedecka, (*my great great grandmother*). The dates of their birth and marriage are unknown.

Azriel and Libe had seven children: Rachel, Szawe (Sheva), Szai (Yeshayahu), Alie (Alya, Eliahu), Chaim my grandfather, Sure Laje (Sarah Leah) and Pessa.

My grandfather kept up a regular correspondence with his family in Przedecz and would send them parcels of clothes. After he died in 1934, the contact with the family in Przedecz became very tenuous and only one or two of them kept in contact. Clothes parcels were still sent until the start of the Second World War, although I understand their financial situation was not such as to make this clothing a great necessity.

The war began with the German invasion of Poland and there was no further contact with Przedecz. In addition, right at the beginning of the war all the children of Chaim Zielinski moved from Stamford Hill (North London) to Edgware Middlesex

(North West of London). Since the family in Przedecz did not know the address in Edgware, it is possible that even if they did write, letters were not forwarded to Edgware. To the best of the recollection of Betty Zielin, who used to send these parcels, she addressed them to Alya Zielinski, Zuma Kaliski (or Kaliska), POW Wlolclavek, Przedecz. Wlolclavek is the regional centre for Przedecz.

It is very likely that "Zuma Kaliski" is "in fact "Kilinskiago Street". We know that after Alya's rented house on the corner of Warshavska Street was demolished, he moved to the opposite side of the New Market. That is where Kilinskiago Street is situated.

Rachel

The eldest child of Azriel and Libe was called Rachel an she was born on 21 April 1866. Unfortunately, we do not know her married name, and so one cannot give further information about her. It is possible that one of the married Rachels appearing in the "Yizkor Book" refers to her. It is also possible that she married someone from outside Przedecz and moved away.

Sheva

The next child was a girl called Szawe (Sheva), born 3 August 1870. She married Itzik Zingerman. They lived on the first floor of a house which they owned and is situated in the Old Market.

Itzik (Sheva's husband) was a "blecher" - a person who smelted metals. He was religious and for many years he was gabbai in the Synagogue which he tended with great devotion.

Itzik's brother was called Shalom and he came from Konin and was a teacher at the "Bet Sefer Ivri" in Przedecz.

For a number of years, Itzik would pay the Przedecz Jewish Community Membership Fee. His payment in zlotys (the Polish currency) was: 1924, 8; 1925, 5; 1926, 5; 1927, 4; 1928, 5; 1929, 5; 1930, 6; 1931, 3; 1932, 5.

Sheva and Itzik had six children: Abram, Rachel Leah, Hersh (Hersz), Moszek, Mariam Hadja, and Channah. Five of the children were married and they all lived outside Przedecz. There were many grandchildren but not even one of them survived the Holocaust.

The eldest child was called *Abram (Avraham)*. The list of Jewish inhabitants of the Lodz ghetto, lists an Abram Zingerman who was born on 15 June 1897 and lived at Flat 3, 56 Marysinnska Street. *[After the occupation, the Germans renamed Marysinska Street, Siegfriedstrasse.]* His wife was called Temer and she was born on 25 April 1900. No previous address or date of deportation is given for them in this Lodz ghetto list. It is very probable that this entry refers to our Avraham Zingerman. Further confirmation is indicated by his date of birth which seems about right. My daughter Ayelet found that this house is still standing. Avraham, together with his brother-in-law visited Eretz-Israel in 1935. They wanted to settle there but to their great sorrow were not able to do so and they returned to Poland where they became victims of the Holocaust.

A daughter *Rachel-Leah,* date of birth unknown, was married to Chaim Roach, who was their eldest son-in-law. They lived in the same house as Itzik Zingerman at the side of the courtyard. Chaim traded in chickens and sold them in Lodz. He loved to tell stories and jokes. He was religious and prayed regularly in the Synagogue.

A son *Hersh (Hersz)* was born in 1912 and was a member of the "Young Mizrachi," In summer 1941, he was in the German Labour Camp at Inowroclaw, which was situated about 70 kilometres north west of Przedecz.

A list from the Przedecz Town Hall records gives as one of their children *Moszek* who was born in 1903. Other children were *Mariem Chaja* also born in 1903, and *Channah,* date of birth unknown. However, the Yizkor Book gives the names of only two of the boys (Avraham and Hersz) but for some unknown reason omits the name of Moszek.

Yeshayahu

The son Szai (Yeshayahu), the second oldest of the brothers was born 2 March 1873. He lived at 1 Warshavska Street in a house which he owned. Until 1925, the Gerrer Hassidim had a Synagogue was located in a rented house in the courtyard of his house, but in that year it closed for financial reasons.

He was married to Sura Gitel (Sarah) Plocka who was born on 21 October 1874, the date of their marriage is not known. She was the daughter of Abram Plocka and Frymet Rybinska, the dates of their birth and marriage are unknown.

Yeshayahu was religious and attended Synagogue services regularly. He was involved in communal affairs and gave money to charity. He helped ill people who had no-one to help them. His wife Sarah also assisted people in need.

He was a tailor and had a workshop in which his children worked until they got married. His finished clothing was sold in the market.

For a number of years, he would pay the Przedecz Jewish Community Membership Fee. His payment in zlotys (the Polish currency) was:1924, 8; 1925, 6; 1926, 5; 1927, 5; 1928, 8; (the relevant page seems to be missing for a number of years); 1933, 5; 1934, 5; 1935, 5.

They had six children. They were called Szajna (Sheina) Ruchla, Channah Ryfka, Naftal Wolek (Woolf), Chaim Hersz, Genendal and Laja (Leah). All the children were members of the Jewish Library.

The daughter *Sheina* was born on 25 November 1897. She gave a lot of support to the Jewish welfare organisations in Przedecz and her house was always open to poor people. Szajna was married to Yoseph Zychlinsky, who managed a work-shop for making hats. He had an apprentice in his work-shop and his products were sold in the market. He was religious. People would often see him sitting on the top of the stairs in front of his house reading a newspaper.

They had four children and they were given a Jewish, nationalistic education. The three sons were called Ya'acov, Yehudah and Chaim, all of whom perished in the Holocaust. The daughter Golda (Zehava) survived the Nazi camps and after the war attempted to go to Eretz Israel "illegally." As with many other "illegal" immigrants, she was interned by the British in Cyprus. It was there that she met her future husband Tzvi Grabinsky. In Israel, they lived in Haifa and Golda died towards the end of 1997.

A daughter was called *Chana Rivka (Ryfka)* and was born on 21 August 1899. She lived in Wlolclavek, which is about 35 kilometres north east of Przedecz.

A son called *Woolf (Naftal Wolek)* was born 22 October 1901. His was married and had a family, and they lived in Chodecz, which is about 9 kilometres north of Przedecz.

A son called *Chaim-Hersz (Hersh)* was born on 1 February 1904. He was on the management committee of the Jewish Library. The duties of the Committee included the buying of books and the giving of lectures. Chaim-Hersh was also one of the founders of the drama group which was attached to this Library. In the 1920s when the Hachshara group was established in Przedecz, he became one of the most active workers. In 1932, he opened his own independent tailor work-shop.

The daughter *Genendal* was born on 7 November 1907. She was a member of the Jewish Library. She was married to Fishel Topolski, date of his birth and marriage unknown, who was the son of Moshe Topolski. They lived in a very narrow lane in Przedecz. Fishel's job was preparing the leather for making shoes. He was both the founder and chairman of the "Poale Zion Yemin" Zionist movement. They had four children, one of whom was called Luba. Their whole family was murdered in the Chelmno extermination camp.

The youngest child of Shai and Sura was daughter called *Laja (Leah)* who was born on 30 November 1909.

Alya

Alya (Alie, Eliahu) was born on 8 September 1875. He was the only one of the family to visit England, and he did so in 1913. His brother Chaim *(my grandfather)* who had already been living in England for many years and had already married there and had several children wanted him to stay. According to my mother Sally Simons (nee Zielinski), he said that he would not be able to bring up his children in the irreligious atmosphere of London. My uncle Monty Zielin has a different version and says that he wanted to bring his family, but because the First World War started, this idea had to be abandoned and he returned to Poland.

Alya was a tailor and he would travel with his new merchandise to the markets. He lived in Rynek Street (the New Market) in a square at the corner of Warshavska Street, right next to his brother Yeshayahu who lived at 1 Warshavska Street. The house in which he lived was rented from a non-Jew called Francis. This was a two-family house, the other family living in this house was the family of Yoseph Goldman. Alya did his tailoring work from the house. Yoseph Goldman was a baker and his bakery was also in this house. At a later date, the owner Francis knocked down this house and built a 3 or 4 story house in its place. Alya then rented a house and a courtyard on the opposite side of the same street.

In the 1920s he went to Brazil in order to try and improve his financial position, but was not successful and so he returned to Przedecz and reopened his tailoring workshop.

He was religious and would pray in the "Chevrat Tehillim" and was one of those who helped to renovate this "Chevrat Tehillim." He was also active in the Jewish Library and in the Drama Group.

For a number of years, he would pay the Przedecz Jewish Community Membership Fee. His payment in zlotys (the Polish currency) was:1924, 10; 1925, 6; 1926, 8; 1927, 6; 1928, 10; (the relevant page seems to be missing for a number of years); 1933, 5; 1934, 5; 1935, printing of the amount is not clear.

Alya married Ruchla (Rechil) Aronowicz who was born on 12 July 1875 in Ozorkow, date of marriage not known. She was the daughter of Szmul Aronowicz and Ruchla Baujan, dates of their birth and marriage are not known. We can get an idea when Alya died from the inscription of his son Reuven's tombstone. From this inscription on this tombstone, we can see that Reuven's father Alya was alive when Reuven died in December 1937, or even when they erected the tombstone, which is often done amongst European Jewry about a year after the death. Thus we see that

Alya was still alive at the end of 1937 or even in 1938. One might also investigate why they wrote his name as Eli and not Eliyahu on the tombstone

They had three children, Abram Lajbus, Frajda and Rywin (Reuven). In addition, a still born son was born to them in 1907.

(The Przedecz Yizkor Book states that Alya also had a son called Shmuel and there is a photograph in this Yizkor book which includes a Shmuel Zielinski, but it is possible that it this Shmuel was not the son of Alya. This Shmuel was a member of the "Young Mizrachi" of Przedecz.)

Abram Lajbus was born on 14 December 1900 in Ozorkow.

Frajda was born on 14 November 1907.

Alie's son *Rywin (Reuven)*, who was born on 1 December 1909, was married to Zipporah Morgenstein, who was born on 5 May 1912. She was the daughter of Isser and Rachael Morgenstern, dates of birth and marriage not known. They had two children. One was a son called Isser (very likely named after Reuven's father-in-law), who was born on 18 September 1933 and a daughter called Channah who was born on 28 June 1937.

Like his father, Reuven was a tailor. He took part in the cultural life of the city and was a member of the Workers' Movement.

A few years before the Second World War, Reuven and his family moved to Lodz where they lived at 28 Rybna Street. This street was in the poorest quarter of the city and was next to the Old Jewish Cemetery of Lodz. When the Germans occupied Lodz, they changed all the street names to German ones and thus Rybna Street became Fischstrasse. We know that in 1937, Reuven was living in Lodz with his family. When in early 1940, the Germans set up a Jewish ghetto in a small area of Lodz into which they packed all the Jews, the address of Reuven's family is given as Flat 10, 28 Fischstrasse. This may mean, that as a result of the entry of a large number of Jews into the street where they already lived, Reuven's family were forced to occupy a smaller area in their building.

Reuven died on 16 December 1937 aged 28 and was buried the next day in the Lodz Jewish New Cemetery. (Location of grave: 8/12 8 grave no.102)

A list of residents who lived in the Lodz Ghetto, which was compiled in 1940, includes Zipporah and her two children. Their surname appears as Zielinska (the surnames of females ended with "ska" instead of the "ski" for males) and their first names as Cypra, Icek and Chana. The clerk who prepared the list erred and wrote Icek in place of Isser.

About 1942, a new list of residents of the Lodz ghetto was prepared. With regards to the Zielinski family, at least, this list is more accurate and the surname is listed as Zielinski and the first names as Cypra, Hana and Isser. This list also states that the family was deported on 25 March 1942. We know that those deported from Lodz at that period were sent to Chelmno concentration camp and exterminated there, usually on the day of their arrival. The names of the members of the Zielinski family (together with the names of many other families) has a line through it, indicating they had already been transported from the Lodz ghetto.

A point to note is that the name "Alya Zielinski" does not appear in the biographies in the "Yizkor Book." However, the name "Eliyahu Zielinski" does appear. "Alie" is a nickname for Eliyahu, and Reuven Yamnik assured me that the "Eliyahu" in this book was Alie. Although Alya died just before the war, the "Yizkor Book" does include some people who died at this period. Confirmation comes from Bela Yachimovitz, (a former resident of Pezedecz whose father lived in the same building as Alya) who stated that Alya's wife's name was Rachel - the "Yizkor Book" lists Rechil (the Yiddish form of Rachel) as Alya's wife. We also know from my family that Alya was a tailor and Eliyahu Zielinski is listed in the "Yizkor Book" as being a tailor.

Chaim (My grandfather)

He was born 10 April 1878. He served in the Russian army (since at that period Poland was a province of Russia). After finishing his military service in 1905-06, he came over to London with the intention of using it as a staging post before continuing on to America. However, he was introduced to my grandmother Hinda

183

Reichert (Richardson) and they were married in 1907. My Grandmother had arrived in London in 1898 from a place in Poland called Golina (Gliniany), which was situated only about 50 kms. south west of Przedecz. My grandfather died on 23 January 1934 - 8 Shevat 5694. However, after leaving Poland, his history is not part of the history of my family in Przedecz.

Sure Laje (Sarah Leah)

She was born in 1881 (day and month unknown). As stated above in the case of Rachel, we do not know her married name, and so one cannot give further information about her. It is possible that one of the married Sarahs appearing in the "Yizkor Book" refers to her. It is also possible that she married someone from outside Przedecz and moved away.

Pessa

She was the youngest child and was born on 6 March 1883. Pessa's husband was called Mendel Niemczowko, date of his birth and marriage are not known. They lived on the second floor of Itzik Zingerman's house.

She was in poor health and suffered a lot. There were blotches all over her face. Despite all this she invested much effort, within her limited ability, in assisting the poor people of Przedecz. She died about 1933.

Her husband Mendel was a travelling salesman. He used to travel to various places with produce such as chickens, wood etc. in order to sell them. He enjoyed involving himself in the affairs of the community and once he was elected to the Committee of the Jewish Community (Parnasai Ha'ir). He was a member of one of the city's committees who would fix prices for shechita, the mikveh, and salaries of the rabbi and the shochet. He was also a candidate of the trades-people to the Jewish Council of Przedecz. He was a very clever man with a great sense of humour and used to amuse people with his stories. He was religious and was a member of the "Chevrat Tehillim."

The "Yizkor Book" does not record that they had any children.

Conclusion

To the best of my knowledge, with the exception of Alya, Reuven and Pessa who died before the Second World War, and Golda who survived the concentration camps, all (or almost all) the children of Azriel and Libe Zielinski and their descendants, who at the time lived in Poland, were murdered in the Holocaust.

In this chapter, I have written down the information which I have at present on the Zielinski family of Przedecz. I have no doubt that more information could be obtained from the "vital records" in the possession of the Polish authorities. However, as I have stated above, even if one can cut through all the bureaucracy to get access to these records, it is extremely expensive to have them searched and photocopied!

Section Three

The Feasts of Lights and Lots

THE CHANUKAH MIRACLE OF THE CRUSE OF OIL
IS IT TO BE INTERPRETED LITERALLY OR IS IT JUST AN ALLEGORY?

Rabbi Dr. Chaim Simons

(Hebrew text was written in 2020
Translation into English was made in 2021)

Readers may put in a request to my e-mail chaimsimons@ gmail.com for original photocopied source materials quoted in this paper to be sent to their e-mails without charge.

Talmud Bavli

It is written in Masechet Shabbat: "What is Chanukah? Our Rabbis taught that on the twenty-fifth day of Kislev begins Chanukah which lasts for eight days during which it is forbidden to give eulogies or to fast. When the Greeks entered the Temple, they defiled all the oil which was there, and when the Hasmonean dynasty prevailed and defeated them, they searched and found only one cruse of oil with the seal of the High Priest. This oil was sufficient to burn for only one day, but a miracle occurred and it burned for eight days. On the following year they established these days as a festival with the recitation of Hallel and for thanksgiving."[1]

A question that can be asked is whether in fact this oil lasted for eight days, or was in fact an allegory for other things which occurred at that period?

A very small amount of oil which suffices to burn for eight days is indeed a miracle. During the course of past generations, the Jews witnessed miracles and wonderous events, for example the parting of the Red Sea, Yonah who was swallowed by a big fish, Hananiah and his friends in the fiery furnace, and Daniel in the lions' den.[2] Therefore, like the other miracles, the incident with the cruse of oil was, according to the plain reading of the text, also a miracle, and therefore before lighting the Chanukah candles one recites the berachah "who performed miracles for our fathers."

The miracle of the cruse of oil is not mentioned in the Mishnah, but it does appear in the Gemara of the Talmud Bavli, which was written at the period of the Amoraim [Rabbinical sages of the years 200-500, whose views are recorded in the Gemara.] Furthermore, there is no Masechet in the Shas called "Chanukah,"[3] and Chanukah is only mentioned a few times in the Mishnah. Of these mentions only one is in the context of Chanukah candles, and even there, the mention is in connection with fire damage being caused by the Chanukah lights.[4]

Megilat Ta'anit

The miracle of the cruse of oil is also mentioned in a book called "Megilat Ta'anit"[5] and the question to be asked is whether the source of the miracle of the cruse of oil that is presented in this Megilah was historically before or after the event was mentioned in the Gemara.

It is written in the Gemara that Hananiah the son of Hezekiah of the Garon family together with a number of others compiled the book "Megilat Ta'anit." In the Gemara "Megilat Ta'anit" is mentioned several times, and in addition it is also mentioned once in the Mishnah,[6] thus proving that this book was written during the period of the Tannaim [Rabbinical sages of the years 10-200, whose views are recorded in the Mishnah], or even at an earlier date.

Megilat Ta'anit was written in Aramaic. The date of its composition was probably just before the destruction of the Second Temple. Its contents include a list of thirty-five days on which happy events occurred for the Jews, during the years spanning the period from the days of Ezra until shortly before the destruction of the Second Temple.[7]

One of the events mentioned in Megilat Ta'anit occurred on the twenty-fifth day of the month of Kislev, namely Chanukah. In this Megilah it is written in Aramaic: "On the 25th day is the start of Chanukah, which lasts for eight days during which one may not eulogise."[8] However, the megilah then continues in Hebrew dealing with the miracle of the cruse of oil, using the identical words found in the Gemara.[9] Therefore one could come to the conclusion that the Gemara copied this passage from Megilat Ta'anit.

However, this is not the correct conclusion! In the original Megilat Ta'anit, after each date, appear a few words in Aramaic about what happened that day. The original Megilat Ta'anit itself does not mention the miracle of the cruse of oil. What appears today in Megilat Ta'anit after each event is a commentary (Scholion) on the Aramaic text written in Hebrew. This commentary was written after the period of the completion of the Talmud.[10]

Therefore, the passage found today in Megilat Ta'anit about the miracle of the cruse of oil is not copied in the Gemara, but on the contrary, Megilat Ta'anit was copied from the Gemara.[11]

Megilat Antiochus

The miracle of the cruse of oil is also mentioned in "Megilat Antiochus."[12] This Megilah was written in Aramaic, and at a later date was translated into Hebrew.[13] Rav Saadia Gaon (who lived between the years of about 892 to 942) prepared (or edited) the Arabic version of Megilat Antiochus.[14]

The style of Megilat Antiochus is similar to the style of the Book of Esther. This Megilah details the history of the Hasmoneans and includes the miracle of the cruse of oil:

"After this, the Hasmoneans came to the Temple, and rebuilt the gates which had been smashed, and repaired the breaches in the walls, and purified the courtyard from the corpses and from the impurity. They asked for pure olive oil with which to light the Menorah, but they found only one cruse which was sealed with the seal of the High Priest, and they knew that it was pure, but it was only sufficient for one day. And the Almighty who caused his name to dwell there, gave it his blessing and it lasted for eight days. Thus the children of the Hasmoneans together with the children of Israel made these eight days, days of feasting and rejoicing, in the same way as the Festivals written in the Torah, and also ordained lighting candles to publicise the victory which the Almighty did for them. Therefore it is forbidden to eulogise on these days nor to decree a fast on them, unless one of these days had been previously been accepted as a fast and a day to pray before the Almighty. However, the Hasmoneans and their children and brethren did not forbid working. From that time onwards there was no remnant of the Greek kingdom. The kingdom of the Hasmoneans and their sons from this time unto the destruction of the Temple lasted two hundred and six years. Therefore, the children of Israel wherever they are in the world observe these days. They call them days of feasting and rejoicing beginning on the twenty-fifth day of Kislev for eight days. From that time and for ever more will not depart from them what was established in the Temple by the Priests, the Levites and their Sages, and what they accepted upon themselves and their descendants will never be removed."[15]

The question arises as to what the earliest source of the miracle of the cruse of oil is? In order to answer this, it is necessary to understand when Megilat Antiochus was written - before or after the Gemara? On the subject of the date of composition there are many opinions and much discussion.

Rav Saadia Gaon's book "Sefer Hagalui" says of the Book of Antiochus: "It was founded ["yasdu" in Hebrew - "at-bito" in the original Arabic] by the Bnei Hachashmonai (Sons of the Hasmoneans)"[16] and there are discussions about what Rav Saadia meant by these words.

It is possible that the main opposition to the opinion that this Megilah was written by the Bnei Hachashmonai is that the conclusion of this Megilah refers to the destruction of the Second

Temple, which occurred hundreds of years after the Bnei Hachashmonaim! Although most of the manuscripts of the Megilah include these verses, there are two manuscripts from Yemen that do not include them,[17] and therefore, according to these two Yemenite manuscripts, the above verses are only a later addition.[18] However, in Rav Saadia's book these verses are found in this Megilah.[19] The intention of Rav Saadia was that the Hasmoneans founded [yasdu] Megilat Antiochus, which was transmitted orally, and it was later generations that made additions until the current version was finally reached.[20] Proof of this comes from a study of the writings in the Arabic language of Rav Saadia. There he did not write that the Bnei Hachashmoni "wrote" the scroll, but "founded" it.[21] One can also explain that Rav Saadia did not intend that his use of the words "Bnei Hachashmonai" should be taken literally, the reason being that in his time there were groups of Jews like the Karaites who did not accept the Oral Torah, including Chanukah, and therefore it was necessary to emphasise that Chanukah has a sacred source like the other Festivals, and hence he wrote that the Megilah was written by the "Bnei Hachashmonai."[22]

Before Rav Saadia was born, the book "Halachot Gedolot" was written, and there are various opinions on the question of the identity of its author, and there it is written that Megilat Antiochus was written by the "Elders of Beit Hillel and Beit Shammai,"[23] who lived at a later period than that of the Hasmoneans. However, there is another version of the Halachot Gedolot, and there in place of the words "Megilat Bnei Hachashmonai" [which is another name for Megilat Antiochus] it states "Megilat Ta'anit."[24]

There are several scholars who suggest other dates for the composition of Megilat Antiochus. They are of later dates, and include the first century, the Talmudic period, before the period of the Geonim, the eighth century, the ninth century and the eleventh century.[25] However, the suggestion of the eleventh century seems problematic because before that date Rav Saadia had already translated the scroll!

In addition to the above, there are two manuscripts which have a different version of "Megilat Antiochus." These manuscripts do not mention the miracle of the cruse of oil, and their title for Megilat Antiochus is "Tosefet Targum l'Roni v'Simchi." "Roni v'Simchi"[26] is an interpolated Targum [Aramaic translation] to the Haftarah of Shabbat Chanukah, and this version appears before the Targum of this Haftarah. The scholar Israel Abrahams believed that this addition was written in the Middle Ages.[27]

In conclusion, we see that "Megilat Antiochus" was written at least a few hundred years after the Hasmonean period, but it is not clear whether it was before or after the Gemara period. Because this scroll is not mentioned at all in the Gemara, nor in Midrashim,[28] it may be assumed that this is proof that it was compiled after the period of the Gemara.

Talmud Yerushalmi

The miracle of the cruse of oil is to be found in in the Talmud Bavli together with several pages that deal mainly with the laws of lighting Chanukah candles. However, the Talmud Yerushalmi does not even hint at the miracle of the cruse of oil.[29] Since the miracle happened in the Eretz Yisrael, it is amazing that the miracle of the oil is not mentioned in the Talmud Yerushami. In addition, almost no details are even mentioned regarding the mitzvah of Chanukah candles. In places where Chanukah is mentioned, it is limited to brief mentions. These include twice in connection with the mitzvot that depend on the Land of Eretz Yisrael, namely terumah (portion of produce given to the Kohen)[30] and orlah (fruit of trees during the first three years after planting),[31] once in connection with the laws of Shabbat Chanukah,[32] once in connection with the damage caused by Chanukah candles,[33] and once regarding the berachah which is recited when lighting these candles.[34]

Rabbi Yaakov Chaim Sofer (grandson of the author of the "Kaf Hachaim") wrote an article on why the Talmud Yerushalmi does not bring the halachot regarding the lighting of the Chanukah candles.[35] He quotes the son of the Vilna Gaon who wrote: "I heard from the father of the Vilna Gaon that the seven small Tractates are all that we have, but there are others ... Masechet

Chanukah ... but he did not explain to me who brought them and also how they were lost."[36] After these words, Rabbi Sofer quotes from the Ramban's sermon: "And we will see that this Masechet [Chanukah] is not to be found with the other Masechtot, but is a Jerusalemite [Masechet] and was not to be found in Babylon and in the two yeshivot."[37]

From all this, Rabbi Sofer concludes "by way of hypothesis," and he emphasizes that it is only a hypothesis, that this masechet - "the Jerusalemite" - is in place of the laws of Chanukah in the Talmud Yerushalmi.[38] It is clear that even if this hypothesis is correct, it does not prove that the missing Jerusalemite "Masechet Chanukah" mentions the miracle of the cruse of oil.

Summary of sources where the miracle of the cruse of oil is mentioned and sources that it is not mentioned

We see that the exposition of the miracle of the cruse of oil is limited to the Megilat Ta'anit, Talmud Bavli, and Megilat Antiochus, all of which were written hundreds of years after the dedication of the Temple during the period of the Hasmoneans.

On the other hand, we will see later, that there are a number of writings from the Hasmonean period or a relatively short time later, which do not mention this miracle even in allusion. And these are: the liturgical prayer "al Hanisim," the Apocryphal books I Maccabees, II Maccabees, and Yosephus.

The Liturgical Prayer "Al Hanisim"

It is written in the Shulchan Aruch: "All eight days of Chanukah, one says "al hanisim" in the second berachah of Birchat Hamazon (Grace after Meals), and in the berachah of Modim of the Amidah."[39] Its content is that at the time of the Hasmoneans, during the period of the second Temple (about 250 years before its destruction), the Greeks wanted the Jews to forget their Torah and cease to observe its Mitzvot. The Almighty caused the Jews to be victorious over the Greeks and made a great deliverance and redemption on that day. After that his children came into the inner sanctuary [the Heichal] of the Temple, cleansed the Temple,

195

purified the holy place, kindled lights in his holy courtyard, and appointed these eight days of Chanukah in order to give thanks and praise to his great name.[40] We immediately see that the miracle of the cruse of oil is not mentioned at all.

The author of the book "Zera Ya'akov" considered the words "and kindled lights in your holy courtyard" to be problematic, and wrote: "The correct location for the Menorah was in the Heichal and if they had not already said that they had already cleaned out the Heichal, one could say that the words 'in the courtyard' included the Heichal, but since they had already said that they had cleaned out the Heichal one should say that it was there that they kindled the lights."[41]

The "Chatam Sofer" brought the words of the "Zera Ya'akov" and then wrote "a great and immense innovation,"[42] namely, that "the lighting was permitted outside even if the Menorah were to be standing outside." He went on to say that the reason they lit the Menorah outside was because "then the Heichal was still full of idols.[43] Therefore, until they cleared the Heichal and purified the Temple, they did not kindle lights inside but in the courtyard." However, it is possible to question this from the wording of "al hanisim" where it states that the cleansing and purification appear before the kindling of the lights. If the lighting was in the courtyard and it was there that the miracle of the cruse of oil occurred, why is this not mentioned in the prayer "al hanisim"? Also, in the Book of Maccabees (see below) it is explicitly written that the Menorah was lit inside, namely inside the Heichal of the Temple.

When was "al hanisim" written? If it was written hundreds of years after the Hasmoneans, this omission could be understood. But that is not what happened. There are some Rishonim (great Rabbis who lived approximately between the 11th and 15th centuries) who identify the author. They are:

"Sefer haRocheach Hagadol" whose author was Rabbi Elazar of Germiza, (the gematria of "Rokeach" is "Elazar"), who wrote on the subject that the number of words in al hanisim is 125, the same gematria as the word "Kohanim," and because of the great modesty of Yochanan Kohen Gadol, he added one letter more than the gematria of Yochanan which is 124.[44]

The "Rokeach" also wrote a commentary on the Siddur[45] which included a commentary on Psalm 90. The words of this Psalm "Almighty, you have been our dwelling place" until "and the path for their children" numbers 125 which correspond to the 125 words which the Hasmoneans wrote in the al hanisim prayer which is recited on Chanukah, a prayer which Moshe recited when he set up the Mishkan [Tabernacle]. The words of the Psalmist "And the path for their children" were followed by the Hasmoneans, and being Kohanim they instituted the saying these 125 words the gematria of "Kohanim."[46]

Likewise, in the "Siddur Rabbeinu Shlomo" it is written: "Al hanisim: the number of words in this is the gematria of Yochanan when including the words 'kesham sheasita'." In the commentary of the Rokeach, it states that Yochanan the High Priest initiated this prayer. There are those who say that the number of words in this prayer is the gematria of "Kohanim" and they state that the Hasmoneans and their sons initiated it.[47] The author of this siddur is Rabbi Shlomo son of Rabbi Shimshon of Germiza who lived between the years 1030 and 1096. One can see that he brings the opinion of the Rokeach who lived between 1160 to 1240. However, how it is possible to quote someone who was not yet born?! Furthermore, the expression "Peirush of Rabbi Eliezer [the Rokeach]" appears many times throughout this siddur![48]

In addition, there are other Rishonim who also wrote that Yochanan was the author of al hanisim. They are:

Kol Bo: The name of the author is not known but apparently, he lived in the 15th century. He wrote: "We make mention of Chanukah in the berachah of hoda'a, and there are 124 words in al hanisim which correspond to the gematria of Yochanan who initiated it."[49]

Orchot Chaim: The author is Rav Aharon HaKohen of Lonil who lived at the end of the 13th century. He wrote on the subject: "Al Hanisim - there are 124 words which is the gematria of Yochanan who initiated it ... but we do not say in it 'and the Chashmonei and his sons,' since Yochanan was the Chashmonei, as is stated in the book of Yosifun."[50]

The book "Pri Tzedek" discusses the question as to whether the author "Yochanan" was the father of Matityahu, or was his son who was also called Yochanan.[51] However, in connection with this article there is no difference since they both lived at about the same period.

There is another version of "al hanisim" in Masechet Sofrim[52] and in this version also there is no mention of the miracle of the cruse of oil. In the commentary "Nachlat Ya'akov" written at the end of the 18th century by Rabbi Yaakov Noimberg who lived in Germany, he writes "The Hasmonean miracle on Chanukah" and not "the cruse of the oil miracle."[53]

Also, after the blessings for lighting Chanukah candles one recites "haneirot halalu" whose source is Masechet Sofrim[54] and even there, there is no mention of the miracle of the cruse of oil.

The Books of the Maccabees

In addition to the books of the Tanach, there is a collection of books known as the Apocrypha. Among the books in the Apocrypha are I Maccabees and II Maccabees, and their content is the history of the Hasmonean period.

The Septuagint contains the books of the Maccabees, but they are written in the Greek language. A question which arises is "was it translated from the Hebrew?" Two Christians who lived about fifteen hundred years ago wrote about this, and according to their research, the original I Maccabees. was written in Hebrew. One of the writers was Jerome who lived between the fourth and fifth centuries and his specialty was the Bible. In the year 391 Jerome wrote under the title "Prologus Galeatus," a preface to the books of Samuel and Kings. In it he wrote that the book I Maccabees was written in Hebrew, but that the book of II Maccabees was originally written in Greek as can be proved from its style of language.[55]

The other writer was Origen, who lived between the second and third centuries and he was high in the hierarchy of the church.

In the history of the church written by Eusebius, it states that Origen wrote that there are 22 books in the Hebrew Canon (roughly referring to what the Jews call the Tanach), and besides this, there are the Maccabees which are entitled Sarbeth Sabanaiel.[56]

Historians translate these words into Hebrew as "Sefer Beit Sar Bnei El," and therefore Origen believed that the original book of I Maccabees was written in the Hebrew language[57]

The original book of I Maccabees was written in Hebrew by a Jew, whose identity is unknown. However, it is no longer extant, and only the Septuagint translation into Greek remains. This book was written during the Hasmonean period.[58] II Maccabees was written in Greek.[59] At a much later date these two books were translated into Hebrew.[60]

In connection with Chanukah, it is written in I Maccabees: "They also rebuilt the Temple and the Heichal, and they sanctified it. They made new holy vessels, and placed the Menorah in the Heichal, and set up in the Temple the "Mizbach haketoret" [altar of incense], and the table, and the parochet [curtain] on the Ark. Then they burned incense on the altar and lighted the Menorah, which gave light in the Temple. They placed the "Lechem Hapanim" [shew-bread] on the table and hung up the curtains. Thus they finished all the work they had undertaken. Early in the morning on the twenty-fifth day of the ninth month, which is the month of Kislev, in the one hundred and forty-eighth year, they rose and offered sacrifice, in accordance with the halachah, on the new "Mizbeach" [altar of burnt offering] which they had built. At the very season and on the very day that the heathens had profaned it, it was rededicated with songs and harps and lutes and cymbals. All the people fell on their faces and worshiped and blessed Heaven, who had prospered them. So they celebrated the dedication of the altar for eight days, and offered burnt offerings with gladness; they offered a sacrifice of deliverance and praise. They decorated the front of the Temple with golden crowns and small shields; they restored the gates and the chambers for the Kohanim, and furnished them with doors. There was very great gladness among the people, and the reproach of the heathens was removed. Then Yehudah and his brothers and all the assembly of Israel determined that every year at that season the days of Chanukat Hamizbeach [dedication of the altar] should be observed with joy and gladness to the Almighty for eight days, beginning with the twenty-fifth day of the month of Kislev."[61]

A number of things can be understood from this passage. Not mentioned, and not even hinted at, was the miracle of the cruse of oil. More than that, it is written that the reason for the Chanukah celebration was the "Chanukat Hamizbeach." Rabbi Moshe Isserles (the Rema, who lived during the 16th century) states in the Shulchan Aruch that "there is somewhat of a mitzvah in adding meals because during those days there was the Chanukat Hamizbeach."[62]

It can also be seen that they placed and lit the Menorah in the Heichal and not in the courtyard.[63]

Chanukah is also mentioned in II Maccabees. but not the miracle of the cruse of oil! There it is written: "It happened that on the same day on which the Temple had been profaned by the gentiles, the purification of the sanctuary took place, that is, on the twenty-fifth day of the same month, which was Kislev. And they celebrated it for eight days with rejoicing, in the manner of the feast of Sukkot, remembering how not long before, during the festival of Sukkot, they had been wandering in the mountains and caves like wild animals. Therefore bearing "aravot" [willows] and "lulavim" [palm branches], they offered songs of thanksgiving to the Almighty who had given them the strength and deliverance to purify the Temple. They publicly decreed in all the cities of Yehudah that the Jews should celebrate these days every year.[64]

From this one can see, that in that year due to the war they could not celebrate the Festival of Sukkot and to compensate for this they began to celebrate it on the 25th of Kislev, and for eight days took the "arba'at haminim" (the four species taken during the Festival of Sukkot), but it seems not for only seven days as stated in the Halacha!

I Maccabees and II Maccabees are among the books of the Apocrypha that the Rabbis did not include in the books of the Tanach.

The question can thus be asked as to whether the Rabbis indeed quoted from these books?[65]

The answer is indeed yes. Rabbi Yom Tov Lipmann Heller, author of the "Tosafot Yom-Tov" on Masechet Megillah writes: "And I found in the book of Maccabees that when the Hasmoneans conquered the Greeks they found the altar in an abominable state, and they therefore rebuilt and beautified it and consecrated it on the twenty-fifth day of Kislev."[66]

This is not an isolated case of a mention of the Apocrypha in the Rabbinical literature. The Gemara brings a number of quotes from the book of Ben-Sira (Ecclesiasticus),[67] and a part of the liturgical poem "k'ohel hanimtach" recited during the mussaf service on Yom Kippur is based on the book of Ben-Sira.[68] This book is also mentioned in a Midrash[69] and in the Tosephta.[70] The Ramban's commentary on the Torah mentions "Megilat Shushan" and its intention is the Apocryphal book of Yehudit.[71] Due to an event found in the book of Yehudit, it is customary to eat cheese on Chanukah.[72] There is also a book called "Chayei Enoch" that is not included in the Apocrypha," but is mentioned in the Zohar.[73]

Yoseph son of Matityahu - Yosephus Flavius

He was born in the year 38 in Jerusalem and died about the year 100. He was a Jewish historian and author of several books,[74] one of them being the "War of the Jews - the Antiquities of the Jews." This book includes twenty volumes, the first ten being about the period of the Tanach, and the remainder from the Persian period in Israel up to the great revolt against the Romans.[75] This book is an important source for the history of the Jewish people, especially during the Hasmonean period.

In Volume 12 Yosephus writes that after the victory of the Jews against the army of Antiochus, Yehudah assembled the people together and told them that they should go up to Jerusalem, and purify the Temple and offer the appointed sacrifices. But as soon as Yehudah, along with all the multitudes of people, came to Jerusalem, they found the Temple desolate, its gates burnt down, and plants growing in the Temple itself. After they carefully cleansed the Temple, they brought new vessels, namely the Menorah, the Table [for the shew-bread] and the Mizbach haketoret [altar of incense], and they built a new altar of stones for the burnt offerings. On the twenty-fifth day of the month of Kislev, they lit the Menorah, offered incense on the altar, and put the "lechem hapanim" [shew-bread] on the table, and offered burnt offerings on the new altar.[76]

Yehudah celebrated the festival for the restoration of the sacrifices of the Temple for eight days. The people were very glad at the revival of their customs. They greatly rejoiced at the restoration of the daily schedule in the Temple after such a great interval. The people were very happy about the revival of their customs after a long time of intermission, that they made it a law for posterity that the Jews should keep a festival for eight days on account of their eight-day Temple worship. And from that time, we celebrate this holiday, and call it "Lights" (Chanukah). Yosephus concludes that this name was given and wrote that he held that the reason was because this freedom was beyond all their hopes, and thence the name given to the holiday was Lights.[77]

From the words of Yosephus, who does not mention the miracle of the cruse of oil at all, it appears that the reason for celebrating Chanukah was the victory and re-dedication of the Temple.

A Discussion of this Subject

According to the plain language from the Gemara there was a miracle concerning the cruse of oil and there is no doubt that there are miracles in every generation. However, the question arises as to why this miracle is not mentioned in the writings from the Hasmonean period, namely in the prayer "al hanisim" and in the books of the Maccabees. The first time the miracle of the cruse of oil is mentioned is in the Talmud Bavli written at least four hundred years after the Hasmonean period.

Therefore, it is possible that the language of the Gemara is to be taken not literally, but only allegorically. On this, there are a number of questions to be asked.

Why does the Gemara state that Chanukah was established because of the miracle of the cruse of oil and not because of the victory of the Hasmoneans? Several reasons have been suggested. One was written by Rabbi Yehudah Loew, the Maharal of Prague, (who lived in the 16th century) who writes that the main reason for establishing Chanukah was the defeat of the Greeks. However, because of the fear that the people would attribute the victory to their own prowess and not to the Almighty, it was stated that Chanukah was to celebrate the miracle of the cruse of oil, so that everyone would know that the war in which the Jews defeated the Greeks was due to a miracle from the Almighty.[78] Thus the Maharal by giving this answer removed the apprehension that the people would say that the success was due to "my power and might of my hand"[79] and not from the Almighty.[80]

Another reason was written in the "Ozar Midrashim" by Rabbi Yehuda Eisenstein: The Rabbis in the period of the Greeks and Romans did not want to arouse the anger of the rulers resulting from the Jews celebrating the defeat over them, and therefore the Rabbis gave the reason for the celebration as the Chanukah miracle of the cruse of oil which had been found in the Temple after the Hasmoneans had cleansed it. Thus the Rabbis concealed the defeat of the enemy caused by the strength and might of the Maccabees, and they only wrote it as a hint in the prayer "al hanisim."[81]

This phenomenon can also be seen in other cases. For example, the Rabbis did not want to write the reason for the fast on the ninth day of Tevet.[82] The reason seems to be because two of the reasons given for this fast were related to Christianity.[83] Another example is that the "Anshei Hamamad" [Jews who were on duty in their local Synagogues as their contribution to the sacrifices being offered up in the Temple in Jerusalem] fasted on most of the days of the week but they did not fast on Sundays because of the "Notzrim" [possibly it means Christians].[84] Rabbeinu Gershom (who lived in 10th-11th centuries) explains that this was because Sunday was their festival (Sabbath) and the Jews fasting would anger them.[85]

Can a connection be found between the details of the miracle of the cruse of oil and the events that happened during the period of the Hasmoneans?

After Antiochus conquered Israel, he wanted the Jews, as stated in "al hanisim": "To forget their Torah and to force them to transgress the commandments contained in it." We see from the "Book of Maccabees" that there were Jews who followed the Greek religion: "In those days lawless men came forth from Israel, and misled many, saying, Let us go and make a covenant with the Gentiles round about us. ... Many even from Israel gladly adopted the Greek religion; they sacrificed to idols and profaned the Sabbath."[86] Also at that time in the gymnasiums of the Greeks the athletes went naked, so everyone saw that the Greeks were not circumcised. This caused embarrassment for the circumcised Jews who took part in the activities in the gymnasiums and they therefore performed surgeries on themselves to hide the results of the circumcision: "and removed the marks of circumcision, and abandoned the holy covenant."[87] However, after the victory of the Hasmoneans, the Jews returned to mitzvah observance.[88]

On Purim, just the day after the victory, feasting and rejoicing was established. On the other hand, of Chanukah it is written "on a later year."[89] The question arises: Why wait a year? The reason was that Purim commemorated a physical rescue and thus the results seen immediately. On Chanukah, however, there was spiritual rescue and thus only after a year could it be seen whether the Jews, after many years of Greek influence, had really returned to keeping Torah and mitzvot.[90]

The Gerer Rebbe explained that unlike on Purim where there is drinking and feasting, on Chanukah spiritual things such as the recital of Hallel take place.[91]

In every generation there are Jews who stop keeping Torah and mitzvot, and sometimes the reason is that they were never taught Torah and mitzvot and they are called "tinok shenishba" [a captive baby.] However, there is almost always something small that these Jews observe - for example, going to synagogue once a year for a few hours on Yom Kippur. This can be compared to the "one cruse of oil" found in the Temple.(92) The people who are engaged in drawing Jews back to observance of mitzvot, build on this tiny amount and make efforts to persuade people to keep mitzvah after mitzvah. It is similar to the Chanukah candles that increase one by one every night until on the eighth night the Chanukah menorah is completely full of light,(93) that is, it will be full of light, and shines forth like the "great light" of keeping all the mitzvot. The word "Chanukah" includes the word "Chinuch" [education] and reminds one of the obligation to educate every Jew to observe more and more mitzvot.(94)

It can be said that the miracle of Chanukah during the Hasmonean period, was that Jews who accepted the influence of the Greeks and stopped observing the Torah, returned to observance after the victory of the Hasmoneans to have.

Here we must ask whether it is permissible to say that an explicit ruling of Chazal is not to be taken literally?

Regarding this, Rav Saadia Gaon who lived in the 9th-10th centuries wrote in his book "Haemunot Vehadayot [The Book of Doctrines and Beliefs]: Everything in the books of the prophets is to be taken literally when it can be seen from its meaning and that it is obvious from its wording. However, he then adds that there are four cases where one does not follow the literal meaning. They are: when it goes against one's sense, or against one's intellect, or contradicts something else, or rebuts what earlier people have received.(95)

There are for instance a number of commentators who say that the first chapters of Genesis are not to be taken literally, whilst others say the opposite. These deal with the creation of the world, and the serpent in the Garden of Eden.

Literally, in the first chapter of Genesis, every day of the week of the creation of the world was 24 hours, and some commentators consider this to be the case.(96) However, in his book "Moreh Nevuchim, [The Guide to the Perplexed]," Rabbi Moshe ben Maimon (the Rambam) writes: "The account given in the Torah of the creation is not as is generally believed, intended to be in all its parts literal."(97)

In his book "L'nevochei Hador" written by Rabbi Avraham Yitzchak Hakohen Kook, (probably in the first years of the 20th century, but published only in 2014), he writes: "There is nothing in the account of the creation of the world to be taken literally, since there is the depth of a parable in it, as the Rambam has already written. In any case, this is not the gist of the Torah."[98] Rabbi Kook continues:" And even if we interpret according to a parable, the creation of man, his placement in the Garden of Eden, his naming of the animals, the creation of his wife from his rib, there is nothing which opposes the foundations of the Torah."[99]

With regard to the incident with the "snake" in the Garden of Eden, according to Rabbi Ovadia Sforno, who lived in the 15th-16th centuries the "Satan is the evil inclination,"[100] and according to Rabbi Levi ben Gershom the "Ralbag," who lived in the 13th-14th centuries it is an allegorical figure that represents "the imaginary power" of man.[101] However according to Rabbi Yitzchak Abarbanel, (who lived in the 15th-16th centuries), it was literally the serpent, although Abarbanel was also amazed at the fact that the serpent that was not a human and could not speak, was able to incite and entice.[102]

What was the opinion of Rabbi Avraham Ibn Ezra, who lived in the 11th-12th centuries? Was the period of the creation of the world to be taken as literally or allegorically? From his commentary on the Torah it is not clear. He himself writes "And the serpent: some say that the woman [Eve] would understand and know the language of the beasts ... and others said it was a devil."[103] However, the Abarbanel writes critically about Ibn Ezra: "There are among the commentators, those who interpret this chapter in accordance with the plain meaning of the verses ... Rabbi Ibn Ezra claims that he favours this approach ... However, in reality, he does not imagine things to be so, nor does he think so in his heart."[104]

In summary we can see that even for certain things which are written in the Torah there are commentators who argue that they do not have to be taken literally. Thus how much more so, should things like the miracle of the cruse of oil not be taken literally.

Conclusion

On the one hand, some accept literally what is written in Masechet Shabbat in the Talmud Bavli about the miracle of the cruse of oil, just as in the case of other miracles that appear in the Holy Books.

On the other hand, the issue of the cruse of oil was mentioned for the first time only a few hundred years after the Hasmonean period, and furthermore, writings during the Hasmonean period do not even mention nor even hint at the miracle of the cruse of oil, but they do mention celebrating Hanukkah to commemorate the victory of the Jews, the re-inauguration of the Temple, and the return of Jews to observing the Torah. It is therefore possible that what appears in the Gemara in Masechet Shabbat was only intended to be allegorical, and it is possible to say this in the same way as the Rabbis who believe that things that are explicitly written at the beginning of Genesis are only allegories.[105]

References

(1) Talmud Bavli Shabbat 21a

(2) These miracles and others are found in the liturgical poem "mi sheasah" which is recited towards the end of the selichot.

(3) The grandson of the Chatam Sofer in the name of his grandfather states that the reason that there is no Masechet Chanukah, and that there is hardly any mention of the Hasmoneans in the Gemara, was because they took over the kingship even though they were of the tribe of Levi, and the kingship must be from the tribe of Yehudah (Rabbi Avraham Yitzchak Sperling, *Ta'amei Haminhagim Umekorei Hadinim*, (Eshkol: Jerusalem), par.847, (p.365); "Why is there no Masechet Chanukah?" (Atar Yeshivah, Ask the Rabbi, Why is there no Masechet Chanukah: Rabbi Yitzchak ben Yosef, 13 Kislev 5779, (Internet)

(4) Mishnah Bava Kama chap.6 mishnah 6

(5) Talmud Bavli Shabbat 13b

(6) Mishnah Ta'anit chap.2 mishnah 8

(7) Megilat Ta'anit, (Warsaw, 5634)

(8) Megilat Ta'anit, op. cit., chap.9, Kislev, (p.14)

(9) Ibid.

(10) *Encyclopedia Yehudit*, Megilat Ta'anit (Daat); *Encyclopedia Judaica*, (Keter Publishing House: Jerusalem, 1972), vol.11, col.1230, Megilat Ta'anit

(11) Written apparently in error, in the siddur *Seder Avodat Yisrael*, (Rabbi Yitzchak ben Aryeh Yosef Dov (Zeligman Baer), (Shukan publishers,

5697) "An account of the miracle is also related in Masechet Shabbat 21b in accordance with Megilat Ta'anit chap.9 p.444 footnote 1, stating that it was the Gemara which was copied from Megilat Ta'anit. The same error appears in Louis Ginzberg, *Jewish Encyclopedia*, Funk and Wagnalls Company: New York, 1901, vol 1, p.637

(12) Also known as Megilat Yevonit, Megilat Benai Hachashmonei, Megilat Chanukah

(13) Megilat Antiochus in Aramaic with translations into Hebrew and English, (Tzvi Pilipavski: London, 1851)

(14) S. Atlas and M. Perlmann, "Saadia on the Scroll of the Hasmonaeans," *Proceedings of the American Academy for Jewish Research*, vol.14, (1944) p.1; Aryeh Kasher "The Historical Background of Megillath Antiochus", *Proceedings of the American Academy for Jewish Research*, vol.48. (1981), pp.214, 216

(15) Megilat Antiochus, op. cit., verses 66-74, translation of the text from Aramaic to Hebrew

(16) Rabbi Yehudah Zibled, "Chelko shel Rav Saadia Gaon b'arichat megilat Antiochus..." *Kovetz Chatzi Giborim*, vol.10, Nisan 5777, (Lakewood, New Jersey), p.754

(17) Adolf Neubauer, "Two Monographs by Dr. M. Gaster" *The Jewish Quarterly Review*, vol.6, no.3, April 1894, (University of Pennsylvania Press), p.574

(18) Zibled, op. cit., p.5755

(19) Ibid.; Kasher, op. cit., p.215

(20) Zibled op. cit., p.5755

(21) Ibid.

(22) Atlas, op. cit., p.22; Kasher, op. cit., p.216 also fn.29. p.218

(23) *Halachot Gedolot* (Bahag), (Venice, 5308), Hilchot Sofrim, p.141

(24) *Halachot Gedolot*, Ezriel Hildesheimer, (Chevrat Makitzei Nirdamim: Berlin, 5648), Sefer Bet Hashmonai, p.615; Kasher, op. cit., p.213

(25) *Transactions of The Ninth International Congress of Orientalists*, vol.1, London, 1893, p.xxxvii; Israel Levi, "La Meguillat Antiochos" *Revue des Etudes Juives*, vol.45, Paris, 1902, pp.172-75; *Jewish Encyclopedia*, op. cit., pp.637-38; Adolph Neubauer, op. cit., pp.571-77; Kasher, op. cit., p.229; Tzvi Kadari, "In which Aramaic was Megilat Antiochus written?" *Leshoneinu*, manuscript to research the Hebrew language and areas which are similar to it, vol.23 no.3, Nisan 5719 (Academy for the Hebrew language), p.130

(26) Biblical book, Zecharia chap.2 verse14 – chap.4, verse 7

(27) Israel Abrahams, "An Aramaic Text of the Scroll of Antiochus," *The Jewish Quarterly Review*, vol.11 no.2, January 1899, (University of Pennsylvania Press), p.295

(28) Neubauer, op. cit., p.572

(29) Kasher, op. cit., p.220

(30) Talmud Yerushalmi Terumot chap.11 halachah 6

(31) Talmud Yerushalmi Orlah chap.1 halachah 1

(32) Talmud Yerushalmi Shabbat chap.2 halachah 1

(33) Talmud Yerushalmi Bava Kama chap.6 halachah 8

(34) Talmud Yerushalmi Succah chap.3 halachah 4

(35) Rabbi Yaakov Chaim Sofer "Why the Talmud Yerushalmi does not include the laws of lighting the Chanukah candles, Forum Otzar Hachochmah, 9 December 2015, (Internet)

(36) Rabbi Avraham son of Vilna Gaon, *Rav Pealim*, (Warsaw, 5654), Introduction, p.8 (15)

(37) Derashot of the Ramban for Rosh Hashanah, Lecturer: Rabbi Nechemia Tayler, Tishri 5778

(38) Rabbi Yaakov Sofer, op. cit.

(39) Shulchan Aruch, Orach Chaim [henceforth: SA OC], chap. 682 par.1

(40) "Al Hanisim" can be found in every siddur

(41) Rabbi Yaakov ben Yitzchak David Ginsberg, *Zera Ya'akov*, (Prague, 5574), Masechet Shabbat chap.2 first word: umadai, (p.13)

(42) Chanukah, (Zera Berach Institute, Maarechet shiurei Torah l'tzfiya), Chanukah 5776, (Beinenu), (Internet)

(43) Rabbi Moshe Sofer, *Chatam Sofer - Derashot*, vol 1, Tishri-Nisan, (Sarata Bokavina, 5689), for Chanukah 5592

(44) *Sefer Rokeach Hagadol*, (Warsaw, 5640), Hilchot Chanukah, chap.225

(45) Until less than 30 years ago, this commentary (or extracts from it) could only be found in a number of manuscripts in the Bodleian Library in Oxford. Rabbi Moshe Hershler and his son Rabbi Yehudah went over it, and prepared a printed commentary

(46) Commentary on the siddur by the Rokeach, part 1, (Machon Harav Hershler: Jerusalem, 5752), p.96

(47) *Siddur Rabbeinu Shelomo*, (published by Rabbi Moshe Hershler, Jerusalem, 5732), chap.84 - al hanisim – Chanukah, p.197

(48) Ibid. e.g. pp. 86, 101, 200

(49) *Kol Bo*, (Piorda (Furth), 5542), chap.44, Hilchot Chanukah v'Din haTefillah, p.34, chap.122 din gematriot v'notrikon, p.3b

(50) Rabbi Aharon Hakohen m'Lonil, *Orchot Chaim*, (Pirinazi (Firenze), 5510), hilchot Chanukah, chap.22

(51) Rabbi Tzadok Hakohen m'Lublin, *Pri Tzadik*, part 1, (Lublin, 5661), l'zot Chanukah, p.182

(52) Masechet Sofrim, chap.20 halachah 8

(53) Rabbi Yaakov (Jacob) ben David Noimberg, *Nachalat Yaakov*, (Piorda (Furth), 5653), Masechet Sofrim, chap.20 halachah 8

(54) Masechet Sofrim chap.20 halachah 6

(55) Jerome on the Canon, *Praefatio Hieronymi in Libros Samuel EtMalachim*, "Macchabeorum primum librum hebraicum repperi ..."

(56) *Eusebius Caesariensis- Historia ecclesiastica - The Church History of Eusebius*, Book 1, chap.xxv par.2

(57) Guy Darshan, "The Original Language of 1 Maccabees: A Reexamination", *Biblische Notizen*, Biblical Notes, Nr. 182 (2019), (Herder Freiburg: Basel, Wien), p.92; *Encyclopedia Biblische Judaica*, (Keter Publishing House: Jerusalem, 1972), vol.11 Maccabees I, col.656

(58) Darshan, op. cit., p.91; *Encyclopedia Judaica*, op. cit., vol. 11: cols.656-658

(59) *Encyclopedia Judaica*, op. cit. vol.11, Maccabees II, cols.658-660

(60) e.g: I Maccabees, translation by Avraham Kahana in the year 1931 in Eretz -Yisrael, and II Maccabees, translation by Yitzchak Sekel Frankel in the year 1888 in Warsaw

(61) I Maccabees chap.4, verses 47-57, translated to Hebrew by Avraham Kahana

(62) Rema SA OC chap.670 par.2 haga

(63) 1 Maccabees chap.4 verse 48

(64) II Maccabees chap.10 verses 8-11, translated into Hebrew by Yitzchak Sekel Frankel

(65) In a book giving translation to Hebrew of I Maccabees translated by Avraham Kahana, there are approbations from five Great Rabbis

(66) Rabbi Yom Tov Lipmann Heller, *Tosafot Yom-Tov*, Megilah chap.3 par.6 first word: banesiim

(67) e.g. Talmud Bavli: Chagiga 13a, Yevamot 63b, Bava Kama 92b, Nidah 16b; Talmud Yerushalmi, Berachot chap.7 halachah 2

(68) Ben-Sira, chap 50

(69) Bereshit Rabba, parashah 8, first words: page 2 Rabi Chama, (Vilna); Bereshit Rabba, parashah 91, first words: page 3 Vayavou benei; Midrash Tanchuma, parashat Vayishlach chap.8, (Warsaw); Midrash Tanchuma, parashat Chukat, chap.1 (Mantova)

(70) Tosefta, Yadayim chap.2 par.5

(71) Rabbi Moshe ben Nachman (Ramban), *Commentery of the Ramban*, (Warsaw, 5641), Sefer Devarim, chap.21 verse 14, first words: lo titamer ba

(72) Rema SA OC chap.670 par.2 haga

(73) Zohar, parashat Noach, p.72b (par.295)

(74) Encyclopedia Judaica, op. cit., vol.10, Josephus Flavius: col.251

(75) Flavius Josephus, *The Antiquities of the Jews,* translated by William Whiston

(76) Josephus, op. cit., vol.12, chap.7 par.6

(77) Ibid., par.7

(78) Rabbi Yehudah Loew (Maharal from Prague), *Ner Mitzvah,* (first printing was in Prague 5360), Ner Chanukah, p.22

(79) Sefer Devarim chap.8 verse 17

(80) Rabbi David Silverstein, The Miracle of Chanukah, (Orayta)

(81) *Ozar Midrashim*, part 1 aleph-lamed, editor: Rabbi Yehudah David Eisenstein, (Eisenstein: New York, 5675), Chanukah, p.185

(82) SA OC chap.580 par. 2

(83) Chaim Simons, *Reasons for the fast of ninth of Tevet,* (Nehemia Institute: Kiryat Arba, 5753), pp11-17

(84) Talmud Bavli, Ta'anit 27b

(85) Rabbeinu Gershom on Ta'anit 27b

(86) Maccabees I, chap.1 verses 11, 43

(87) Ibid., verse 15
(88) Maccabees I, chap.2
(89) Talmud Bavli, Shabbat 21b
(90) "Chanukah Quiz" *Haderech* no.2, Chanukah 5713, (Keren haTorah Committee Educational Department: London), p.18, (compliled by Rabbi C. Wilchanski)
(91) Ibid., in the name of the Gerer Rebbe
(92) Talmud Bavli, Shabbat 21b
(93) SA OC chap.671 par.2
(94) Chanukah - Chinuch l'hadlaka or l'hanacha? Rabbi Ezra Cohen, Kislev 5778, (Atar Hayeshiva Beit Hamidrash), (Internet)
(95) Rabbeinu Saadia Gaon, *Haemunot Vehadayot*, (The Book of Doctrines and_Beliefs), (David Slotski: Leipsig 5624), seventh paper, Techiyat Hameitim, p.109
(96) e.g. Rabbi Moshe ben Nachman (Ramban), Bereshit chap.1 par.3, and in our generation Rabbi Menachem M. Schneersohn, (Lubavitcher Rebbe), *Challenge*, ed: Aryeh Carmell and Cyril Domb, (Association of Orthodox Jewish Scientists. London, 5736 -1976), pp.142-149
(97) Rabbi Moshe ben Maimon (Rambam), *Moreh Nevuchim* (The Guide for the Perplexed), part 2, (Vienna, 5588), chap.29, (p.40)
(98) Rabbi Avraham Yitzchak Hakohen Kook, *Lanvuchai Hador,* (Yediot Aharonot and Sifrei Hemed: Tel-Aviv, 5774), chap.5, p.38
(99) Ibid. p.40
(100) Rabbi Ovadiah Sforno, Bereshit chap.3 par.1
(101) Rabbi Levi ben Gershom (Ralbag), (Venice, 5307), Bereshit p.14b
(102) Rabbi Don Yitzchak Abarbanel, *Peirush al haTorah,* (Jerusalem, 5724), question 25, (p.82)
(103) Rabbi Avraham ibn Ezra, Bereshit chap.3 par.1
(104) Rabbi Abarbanel, ibid., question 42, (p.85)
(105) This incident is similar to what occurred at a later date. Many people connect the Maharal of Prague with the Golem. However, at the period of the Maharal there was no mention of the Golem, neither in the Maharal's writings nor of those of his family, nor of anyone else. The first mention of the Golem was only two hundred years after the death of the Maharal! (see paper: The Adventure of the Maharal of Prague in London: R. Yudl Rosenberg and the Golem of Prague, by Shnayer Z Leiman, which appeared in the journal *Tradition*, (Rabbinical Council of America), vol.36 no.1, Spring 2002, pp. 26-58)

LIGHTING CHANUKAH CANDLES WITH PIG FAT

Rabbi Dr. Chaim Simons

(Hebrew text was written in 2021

Translation into English was made in 2021)

Readers may put in a request to my e-mail chaimsimons@ gmail.com for original photocopied source materials quoted in this paper to be sent to their e-mails without charge.

Introduction

The norm for a Torah observant Jew, is for him not to use pig fat (lard) for the lighting of Chanukah candles. In the past, however, there have been rare cases that required the use of fat from non-kosher animals. This situation occurred in Auschwitz, during the Second World War, when before Chanukah, the Jews feared that they would not find oil for lighting Chanukah candles. On the eve of Chanukah, one of the kapos told the Jews that they would receive a double serving of margarine, but the margarine would be smeared on the floor and to use it they would therefore have to scrape it off the floor. Among the Jews was an elderly rabbi who collected the margarine and said it was a "miracle from heaven." Using this margarine, the Jews lit the Chanukah candles.[(1)] (In the past, margarine was made from oils from unclean animals, including pigs.)

Part One
General Principles

[Throughout this paper the expression "clean animal" refers to a "kosher species of animal" and the expression "unclean animal" refers to a non-kosher species of animal]

Oils for Chanukah candles

It is written in the Shulchan Aruch: "All oils and wicks may be used for the lighting of Chanukah candles."[2] From this language it seems that one may use, without exception, all sorts of oils and wicks, namely from both kosher and non-kosher sources, to light Chanukah candles.

However, the Gemara writes elsewhere: "For a Heavenly work only the skin of a clean animal was declared fit,"[3] namely, for the observance of a mitzvah only parts of clean animals may be used. It should be emphasised that it is the species which is the determinant, and therefore it is permitted to use "nevailot" (animals that died or were not killed by shechitah) or "treifot" (animals with a physical blemish) from a clean species of animal.[4]

The opinion of the "Magen Avraham"

The "Magen Avraham" (Rabbi Avraham Aveli Halevi Gombiner, 17th century) writes: "The whole Torah is compared to tefillin."[5] His source is the Torah statement on the subject of Tefillin: "The Torah of the Almighty should be in your mouth,"[6] namely, that in order that a particular item may be used for fulfilling a mitzvah, it must be permitted to put the item into one's mouth.[7] From the wording of the Magen Avraham, this is not limited to tefillin but also relates to other mitzvot

Also, according to the Magen Avraham, not only is it forbidden to use parts of an unclean animal to fulfil a mitzvah, but it is even forbidden to use for this purpose, a material that is non-edible, such as a raw material which is not food.[8] As an example, if one needs to stick together two pieces of parchment in tefillin, one can only use something that has originated from a clean animal, and not a different material, for example, a synthetic

213

material.[9] A further example concerns gold, but here there are two opinions. One is that gold is not fit to be eaten, and therefore according to the opinion of the Magen Avraham, one would not be permitted to use gold in the fulfillment of a mitzvah. The second opinion is of the "Noda b'Yehudah" (Rabbi Yechezkel Landau, 18th century) who holds that edibility is not relevant in the case of gold, and therefore it is permitted to use gold.[10] An example of the use of gold would be if the outside of a shofar was covered with a layer of gold, the shofar would remain fit for use (on condition that the gold does not cause a change in the sound of the shofar).[11] One needs to make a further study as to whether according to the Magen Avraham such gold would make the shofar unfit for use.

According to the Magen Avraham, the principle of what is "permitted to put in one's mouth" applies to all mitzvot. However, two hundred years before the Magen Avraham, the Ran (Rabbi Nissim ben Reuven Gerona, 14th century) held an opinion which did not accord with that of the Magen Avraham's, and he permitted in the performance of mitzvot, the use of materials which were forbidden to be put in one's mouth. However, he made one exception to this, namely with the shofar. He compared the shofar to tefillin since the shofar is blown as a "zicaron" (remembrance) and this term is also used in connection with tefillin.[12]

In addition, other Rabbinical authorities disagree with the opinion of the Magen Avraham, and they believe that with all mitzvot, including the shofar, but with the exception of tefillin, it is permitted to use items that are forbidden to be put in one's mouth.[13] However, they did not agree with the opinion of the Ran that the prohibition also applies to the shofar. It follows that there are many instances, where in the observance of mitzvot, items are indeed used that are not permitted to be put in one's mouth.

In summary, there are three opinions on the subject:

1. The opinion of the Magen Avraham that the rule "from what it is permissible to put in one's mouth" applies to every mitzvah.

2. The opinion of the Ran that the rule applies only to tefillin and shofar.

3. Opinion of other Rabbinical authorities that the rule applies only to tefillin.

In this article we will look at this topic as it applies to various mitzvot, and we will then try to reach a conclusion regarding oil for the lighting of the Chanukah candles.

Holy Artifacts and Mitzvah Artifacts

Artifacts for mitzvot can be divided into two groups. The first group is holy artifacts, and they include Torah scrolls, tefillin and mezuzahs. It is written in the Gemara, "Holy artifacts are put into a genizah [store house for holy materials]," [14] namely, that after they are no longer in use, they must not be thrown away, but must be put in a genizah or buried.

The second group is materials which were used in performing a mitzvah and they include shofar, tzitzit, sukkah, and the arba'at haminim. According to the halachah, after their use the Gemara states "Artifacts of religious observances may be thrown away," [15] but in practice this is disgraceful [16] and they should be used for another mitzvah. For example, the aravot (willows) from Hoshana Rabba are burned with the chametz on erev Pesach, [17] a tzitzit is used as a bookmark. [18] It is written about the "Chatam Sofer" (Rabbi Moshe Sofer (Schreiber), 18th–19th centuries) that he did not allow a potential student to study in his yeshiva because he saw through the window that this student stepped on the schach (roof covering of sukkah) that was on the ground after being removed from the sukkah after Sukkot. [19]

There are those who make a distinction between these two types of materials, namely that only in the case of holy artifacts, the principle that it has to be "from what is permitted to put in one's mouth" is applicable. [20] Furthermore, one can see from the Gemara that it is permitted to use a "tied-up elephant" for the wall of the sukkah, [21] although an elephant is an unclean animal.

There are mitzvot whose observance is not related to things which are eaten, such as trees or stones, so the principle "from what is permitted to put in one's mouth" cannot apply to them, [22] an example being the walls of a sukkah, which can be not only an unclean animal but made of any durable material, such as iron.[23]

However. even though according to the Gemara one can use a tied-up elephant for the walls of the sukkah, it seems that the "Sdei Hemed" holds that this is not in accordance with the opinion of the Magen Avraham. He writes: "In any case, according to Magen Avraham who compares the entire Torah to Tefillin, an elephant would be forbidden for the wall of a sukkah,"[24] but he concludes that further study is required on this subject.

A further question on this subject is related to the supports ("ma'amidim") of the schach for the sukkah. A question to be asked is whether it is permitted to use the bones of an unclean animal for the supports for the schach? One of the things that disqualifies the schach is whether it can receive ritual impurity.[25] Does the same restriction apply to the supports for the schach? On this, the Mishnah Berurah writes: "At the outset one must be careful not to place the schach on something which can receive ritual impurity. However, if this has already been done, or if one has no alternative, then it is permitted to stand the schach on something which can receive ritual impurity."[26] Therefore, the use of the bones of an unclean animal for the supports for the schach would not disqualify the sukkah.

A further example: At the beginning and the end of the parchments in the Torah scroll there are the "atzei chaim" (wooden Torah rollers (poles) which are attached to the two ends of the parchment).[27] In practice, they are made of wood, but there is a debate as to whether the bones of unclean animals can be used for the "atzei chaim." Rabbi Bezalel ben Yisrael Moshe Hakohen, (19th century, Vilna) author of the book of responsa entitled "Reshit Bikkurim" wrote: "I have a doubt on the question of whether one can make the 'atzei chaim' from something which is not permitted to put in one's mouth, such as bones from unclean animals ... nevertheless, if they are to be made from bones, one should use the bones only from clean animals."[28]

Mitzvot d'Rabbanan

Mitzvot may be divided into two categories, namely Mitzvot from Torah and Mitzvot from the Rabbis. The first category includes tefillin, shofar, sukkah, and eating matzah on the first night of Pesach. The second category includes washing the hands before eating bread, recitation of Hallel, Shabbat candles and Chanukah candles.

The "Sdei Hemed" is a set of encyclopedia-type books that includes ten volumes written in the nineteenth and twentieth centuries by Rabbi Chaim Hezekiah Medini. There he writes concerning the mitzvot from the Rabbis: "One does not need to utilise the principle regarding 'everything that is permitted to be put in one's mouth',", and then adds regarding it: "And even the Magen Avraham who holds that 'the entire Torah is compared to Tefillin,' only applies this dictum with regard to mitzvot from the Torah which are compared to Tefillin ... which is not the case with mitzvot from the Rabbis."[29]

However, one should mention that there is an exceptional case, related to the laws of the shofar, which is a mitzvah from the Torah. There is an opinion that allows a shofar from an unclean animal to be used on Rosh Hashanah.[30] However, one can immediately see that there is a contradiction to this opinion because it is written in the Mishnah: "All animals that have horns have cloven hooves (a sign of a clean animal)."[31] The "Be'er Hagolah" (Rabbi Moshe Rivkas (Rabkash), 17th century, Poland and Lithuania) resolves this contradiction as according to him one is speaking of a shofar from a clean animal born from an unclean animal.[32] However, Rabbi Shimon Yair Bachrach (17th century, Magnesia Greece) writes in his book "Chavat Yair" that this explanation is "very forced."[33] According to the opinion of the "Be'er Hagolah" it appears that there is an inconsistency in the principle "what is permitted to put in one's mouth," and the Sha'ar haTzion [which gives the sources for the Mishnah Berura] resolves the inconsistency by stating: "this [what is permitted to put in one's mouth] is not relevant to the shofar which is only a mitzvah artifact."[34] Regarding the use of the horn of an unclean animal, there is a ruling that "one can be lenient when there is no other shofar available."[35]

Destined to be consumed by fire

In the event that the artifact is to be consumed by fire, such as Shabbat candles and Chanukah candles, the rule "from what is permitted to be put in one's mouth" does not apply to such an artifact.[36]

Tiny amount in the mixture

Does the principle "from what is allowed to be put in one's mouth" apply to the presence of just a tiny amount of material, for example, whose function is only for colouring? It seems from the language of the "She'arit Yosef" (Rabbi Yosef ben Shem Tov ben Yeshua, 16th century) that a tiny amount of material like a gold coating on tefillin, is not enough to disqualify the artifact for the reason of what is forbidden to be put in one's mouth.[37]

The composition of tefillin leather boxes is skins, material for blackening the boxes, straps, sinews to sew up the boxes, and hairs. These items must be from a clean animal. What is the law regarding the blackening material used to blacken the straps? Making the straps a black colour is one of the ten things regarding tefillin that is "halachah l'Moshe miSinai" (laws Divinely communicated to Moshe at Mount Sinai).[38] Therefore, the blackening material must be "from what is permitted to put in one's mouth."

In addition to the actual blackening material for the straps, it is customary to mix this colouring material with the fat of an unclean fish, in order "to improve the appearance and soften the leather of the straps." The question to be asked is how is it possible to utilise material from an unclean fish? On this the "Noda b'Yehudah" rules that it does not disqualify the tefillin because this unclean material is only there for the sake of appearance and therefore has no significance.[39] Rabbi Yitzchak Dov Halevi Bamberger (19th century, Germany) brings the "Noda b'Yehudah" but adds "and in any case it is good to be particular and use kosher fat."[40]

At a later period, a question was asked about adding glycerin (a substance made from animal oils) to the colouring matter that blackens the straps. The function of the glycerin is to "stick the colour on the skin of the straps, since because without it, the black colour will not be absorbed." It was ruled that using glycerin is more prohibitive than using the fat of an unclean fish, and therefore could not be used. Even though the amount of glycerin was less than one sixtieth (which is generally regarded as a quantity insufficient to disqualify something), it is still forbidden because it is a "davar hamamid" [an indispensable ingredient].[41]

Materials from unclean creatures - silkworm and hilazon
There are two types of unclean creatures that are used extensively in an item for mitzvah observance. They are both especially used in the mitzvah of tzitzit, and they are silk (meshi) and colouring from a certain type of snail (hilazon).

Silk: It is possible to observe the mitzvah of tzitzit not only with wool and linen, but also with (among other materials) silk.[42] Silk originates from the silkworm (the domestic type called *Bombyx mori*, and the wild type called *Bombyx mandarina*), and this worm is an unclean species. The Rabbis are divided as to which area of this worm the silk is produced from. The "Pri Megadim" (Rabbi Yosef Teomim, 18th century, Germany) writes: "Apparently it originates from the body of a silkworm."[43] However, there are other opinions, namely that the origin of silk "is the silkworm saliva."[44] The principle is similar to bees' honey,[45] so the question arises: Why is bee honey kosher, even though it comes from an unclean insect? The method of production of bees' honey is as follows: Worker bees suck nectar from flowers with their proboscis (mouth). The nectar mixes with saliva and is swallowed into the honey sac where enzymes from the saliva break down the nectar into honey. It should be noted that the nectar is never digested but is just transformed into honey by the saliva.[46]

It is stated in the Shulchan Aruch that it is permissible to make the garments for tzitzit from silk fabric and that even the threads for the tzitzit may be made from silk.[47] Rabbi Yeshayahu Halevi Horovitz (16th-17th centuries) writes in his book "Shnei Luchot Habrit" that when putting on the tallit (the garment with the tzitzit), one should be particular that the side which is adjacent to the head should always be in this position, and therefore it is customary to make an attractive "atara" (neck-band) at the top of tallit for recognition purposes, and thus ensure that it is always at the top of the tallit, and not instead be at the bottom.[48] In addition, he added that it is preferable to make the garment for the tzitzit from wool. It would therefore appear that his intention is that the "atara" should be made of silk which is sewn on to the woolen garment. The book "Orach Neeman" (Rabbi Menachem Natan Neta Auerbach, 19th-20th centuries, Jerusalem) understands that this is the way to understand the words of the "Shnei Luchot Habrit."[49]

The reasoning behind the opinion that the mitzvah of tzitzit can be performed by wearing a garment made of silk is that the rule "from what is permitted to be put in one's mouth" does not apply to artifacts for mitzvot, and tzitzit is one of such artifact. Another halachah is that when the fabric of the garment is made of silk, the tzitzit threads must also be made from silk and not from other materials (with the exception of wool and linen).[50]

Tzitzit from silk is not the only case where there is a controversy regarding unclean animals. There are also controversies where the fabric of the garment and the strings of the tzitzit are made from the wool of camels and rabbits which are unclean animals.[51] According to the opinion that "from what is permitted to put in one's mouth" does not apply to most mitzvah artifacts, there will be no impediment to the making of threads for tzitzit from the wool of unclean animals such as wool from camels and rabbits, provided that the actual garment is made from the same source.[52] However, there are those who disagree, and in the book "Misgeret Zahav" Rabbi Moshe Izrael of Visaki Lithuania writes in the name of the "Malbim" (Rabbi Meir Leibush Wisser, 19th century, Eastern Europe): "One requires further study as to whether on making a tallit from wool of camels, one may put tzitzit from camel wool on it, since they did not permit Heavenly work except from something originating from a clean species."[53]

Furthermore, there are Rabbinical discussions as to whether it is permitted to use silk threads in a Torah scroll which is classed as a holy artifact. A Torah scroll consists of sheets of parchment sewn together. The "Tur" (Rabbi Yaakov ben Asher, 13th-14th centuries) writes: "One may only sew a Torah scroll with the "gidim" (tendons) of a clean animal."[54] The question arises as to whether it is permitted to do this sewing by using silk threads for the gidim. The Rema (Rabbi Moshe Isserles) in his commentary "Darkei Moshe" writes: "Sheets sewn together with silk thread are invalid, since one has to use gidim." However, he adds, that in an emergency, when one does not have gidim, and at the outset, if the sheets were already sewn with silk thread, the use of such a Sefer Torah it would be permitted under exceptional circumstances.[55] The "Sdei Hemed" writes that in order to reconcile the different opinions, it should be said that one is speaking of coloured threads, whose colour is permanent, and which have therefore undergone a change.[56] The same thing applies regarding the "atzei chaim" which are sewn at both the beginning and end of the Torah scrolls. It should be noted here the use of silk threads is being permitted, even though a Sefer Torah is a "tashmish kedushah" (a holy artifact)."

Rabbi Yonah Landsofer, (17th-18th centuries, Bohemia), discusses this subject in his book "Bnei Yonah" and writes that the reason for putting two rollers on a Sefer Torah is so that when rolling it, one does not have to touch the parchment itself. One of the rollers is put at the beginning and one at the end, and the ends of the parchment are wrapped around these rollers, and then sewn onto the parchment. The question is, whether in a case of need when it is impossible to sew the ends of the parchment using gidim, silk threads could be used? Rabbi Landsofer answers that according to halachah the rollers do not require sewing on to the parchment, thus if the rollers are not sewn at all, the Sefer Torah will not be unfit. Furthermore, even if there is an absence of sewing, maybe one may use this Sefer Torah, and how much more so if the rollers were sewn with silk thread, since there is no obligation to sew. Perhaps furthermore one can be lenient even if the rollers are completely absent, if there is no other Sefer Torah available. and hence, not doing so, would necessitate omitting the Reading of the Torah.[57] One can learn from this that in a time of need, one may use silk thread to sew the sheets of parchment together, especially to sew the ends of the parchment to the rollers.

The prohibition on the use of silk in the observance of mitzvot was given by Rabbi Bahya ben Asher ibn Halawa, (who was known as "Rabbeinu Behaye") in his commentary on the words "gold and silver and copper"[58] that appear in the Torah at the beginning of Parashat Teruma. He writes: "Three sorts of metal and three sorts of wool are mentioned, but one does not find silk in the things donated for the building of the Mishkan (Tabernacle), since this is something out of the body of a creeping thing that is a worm and one is only permitted to use pure things for Heavenly work."[59]

To reconcile the contradiction as to why Rabbeinu Behaye says that we did not give silk to the Mishkan, whilst on the other hand, we use silk, for example, for the mitzvah of tzitzit, it is suggested that there is a difference on one hand, between religious artifacts such as Torah scrolls, tefillin and mezuzahs, and on the other hand, between mitzvah artifacts such as tzitzit where the principle "which is permitted to be put in one's mouth" does not apply.[60]

Rabbi Avraham Halevi (17th-18th centuries, Egypt) in his book "Ginat Veradim" disagrees with Rabbeinu Behaye and explains that in his opinion the reason that it is permitted to sew with silk thread which originates from worms was because it was never forbidden to eat silk since it is was from the saliva of a worm (as is cobwebs), which is not forbidden to be eaten since it has no taste and thus is like the dust of the earth.[61]

The Chatam Sofer suggests a further reason to permit the use of silk, possibly, in "tashmishai kedushah." He writes that it seems to him that our custom to permit the use of silk in a Synagogue is because when weaved into a garment, the silk is completely changed and becomes something new. This is like anything originating from impurity which after it has been changed it can be used for something holy. However, this ruling is not in accordance with Rabbeinu Behaye.[62]

Another possible use of silk threads is for the wicks of Shabbat candles or Chanukah candles, and the question is whether this is allowed? It may be suggested that since these candles are a mitzvah artifact it would be permissible.

Snail (Hilazon): In the mitzvah of tzitzit, in addition to white threads, there are threads whose colour is "techelet," which is the colour of the sky.[63] The source of "techelet" is the blood of the hilazon,[64] and the hilazon is an unclean creature.

What is the identification of the hilazon? The problem is that a few hundred years after the destruction of the Second Temple the identification of the hilazon was lost.[65] Recently, however, there have been many attempts to identify this creature.

The first attempt was by Rabbi Gershon Henoch Leiner, the Admor of the Radzyn chasidim (19th century). He searched in Italy and identified the fish *Sepia officinalis* as the hilazon. His chasidim extracted from this species the techelet, and dyed their tzitzit with the resultant colour.[66] Until this day, his followers wear tzitzit with this techelet. He wrote three books on the subject of techelet.[67]

During the First World War, Rabbi Yitzchak Isaac Halevi Herzog researched the subject thoroughly and wrote a thesis on this subject for a doctorate at the University of London.[68] His conclusion was not that of Rabbi Leiner's. At first he agreed, with the opinion of Wilhelm Gesenius (a non-Jew, expert in the Hebrew language), that the *Janthina* is the source of techelet.[69]

After that, Dr. Israel Hakohen Zeiderman, scientific director of the "Techelet Foundation," researched the issue in an orderly fashion and concluded that the techelet color is extracted from the snail *Murex trunculus* (the banded dye-murex). In accordance with his research, techelet is today extracted.[70] In recent years more and more people are wearing tzitzit with techelet in accordance with the identification of Dr. Zeiderman.

In the book "Nechmad Lemareh" written by Rabbi Nissim Avraham ben Rafael Ashkenazi, (19th century), a dilenna is posed: "We have to know how it is possible that techelet which is "melechet shamayim" is the blood of an unclean fish, and such blood is forbidden to be eaten.[71]

In his book "Ptil Techelet," Rabbi Leiner realises the problem that the fish that he identifies as the hilazon is unclean, and is therefore not "permitted to put it in one's mouth." Hence how is it possible to be used in tzitzit? He discusses the subject and then suggests an answer to the problem: "The hilazon is a species of fish that is unclean, but by Torah law its blood is permitted, and the blood of all unclean fish is not forbidden by the Torah, since the prohibition of blood is limited to cattle, wild beasts and birds, but in contrast the blood of insects, fish and locusts is not forbidden."[72]

In his third book called "Ein Hatechelet", Rabbi Leiner puts forward a new suggestion to solve this problem. He argues at length that in addition to the Ran's opinion regarding the shofar, it is also possible to say with regard to techelet that it can be regarded as a "zicaron" (awakens remembrance), and thus the mitzvah of techelet is similar to the mitzvah of shofar.[73]

It is written in the Tosephta: "Techelet is not kosher except from the hilazon and that which is not from this very snail is unfit for the mitzvah."[74] Therefore, there can be no substitute even with another creature which follows the principle "what is permitted to be put in one's mouth."

The fact that the Torah allows and even requires, (but does not to compel), a person to wear techelet, since it is written in the Mishnah "Techelet does not impair the validness of the white, and white does not impair the validness of techelet."[75] From this, one can see that techelet in clothing proves, (on the assumption that the identification of the hilazon is right) that the Torah, at least on this subject, does not hold according to the principle: "what is permitted to be put in one's mouth."

Second part

As stated above there are situations that can permit the use of artifacts that are not "from what is permitted to be put in one's mouth." These include: things that are only mitzvah artifacts (as distinct from holy artifacts); mitzvot that are only Rabbinical;

things which are about to be burned. We will discuss how these rules apply to materials for the lighting of Chanukah candles.

It is written in the Shulchan Aruch: "All oils and wicks are permissible to use for the lighting of Chanukah candles."[76] From the plain words, one can interpret this as meaning that anything without exception is allowed to be used as the oil for lighting the Chanukah candles. But this is indeed not the case, and there are a number of things which are not permitted, or for which there are differences of opinion, with differing reasons, regarding their use.

Meat with milk: In the Torah it is written on three occasions "You shall not boil a kid in its mother's milk."[77] We learn from this that the Torah forbids cooking meat from a domesticated animal with milk from a domesticated animal, and then eating or deriving benefit from such a mixture.[78] The Rabbinic Sages discuss whether, for example, if one having cooked meat fat with butter, it is permissible to use the mixture for lighting of Chanukah candles. Such discussions include rules such as "mitzvot were not given for enjoyment" and "with something which has to be burned, its size is already to be regarded as if it was already burned."[79] Some people forbid using such a mixture for the lighting of Chanukah candles.[80] However, the Maharsham (Rabbi Shalom Mordechai Hakohen Schwadron, 19th-20th centuries, Galicia) permits it *post facto* (if it has already been done).[81] Rabbi Epraim ben Yaacov Hakohen, the "Shaar Efraim" (17th century, Vilna) goes further than the Maharsham and writes that *ab initio* (from the outset), it is permitted to light Chanukah candles from butter from which it is forbidden to get benefit,[82] (it had already been cooked with meat).

Orlah: According to the Torah, it is forbidden to eat and even enjoy the fruits of a tree in the first three years after its planting (such fruit is known as "orlah.")[83] Discussions about using oil from orlah fruit for Chanukah candles are similar to discussions on a mixture of meat and milk.[84]

In summary, as detailed above, it is forbidden to derive benefit from a mixture of meat with milk, and from orlah. However, some forbid, and others allow, the use of such oil for the lighting of Chanukah candles. The question arises, what is the halachah on this subject regarding pig fat?

We will begin by looking at what is written in the Rabbinical literature about pigs. A pig is a species of unclean animal which may not be eaten because it has only one of the signs of a clean animal, namely, it has a cloven hoof. However, it does not have the other sign, namely chewing the cud, and in fact it is the only animal which has a cloven hoof but does not chew the cud.[85]

According to the halachah, there are restrictions on raising unclean animals. However, with regard to the pig there are even more restrictions, as it is written: "A Jew may not raise pigs anywhere, even to use them to treat leather, it goes without saying that one may not raise them for purposes of commerce."[86] One of the reasons is "because of an incident which occurred in the days of Hyrcanus and Aristobulus."[87]

However, there are exceptional cases that allow pigs to be in a Jew's possession and to be traded. On this it is written "If one had inherited dogs and pigs, we would not require him to sell them together but may sell them little by little."[88] That is, pigs will remain in his possession for a certain period of time. In addition, there is also another case where if a Jew receives pigs in repayment of a debt, he is allowed to keep them until he is able to find someone who buy them at their proper value.[89] Rabbi Yaakov Chaim Sofer (19th-20th centuries, immigrated from Baghdad to Eretz Israel), wrote in his book "Kaf Hachaim" that if a non-Jew owes a Jew money, he may receive pigs from him as payment of the debt.[90]

The question arises as to what is written in Halachah about deriving benefit from pigs? "Trading [with pigs] is forbidden by the Torah just as one is forbidden by the Torah to trade in food which is forbidden to be eaten, even when it is permitted to derive benefit from it."[91] The "Kaf Hachaim" writes: "It is permitted to buy the fat of pigs to use for candles or soap."[92]

Sometimes however deriving benefit from pigs is allowed, and the question to be asked is whether this includes the use of pig fat for observance of mitzvot like the lighting of Chanukah candles?

We have seen above that it is forbidden to benefit from a mixture of meat and milk, and of orlah, but some allow these things for the lighting of Chanukah candles. Therefore, since there is no prohibition on gaining benefit from pig fat it seems to be permitted.

The Gemara gives a list of oils that may not be used for Shabbat candles and then adds: "Wicks and oils that the Sages said are not to be lit for Shabbat may be used on Chanukah."[93] One of them is the oil "shemen kik." The question which arises is what is "shemen kik"? The Gemara gives several possibilities. Some of them are types of plants, and one of them is a bird.[94] In masechet Chulin, the Gemara writes that the species of bird called "kik" is an unclean bird.[95] Therefore, according to this, it is possible to use "shemen kik" which is from an unclean creature for Chanukah candles.[96] According to this reasoning, it should also be permitted to use pig fat.

In addition, there are some responsa dealing with the question as to whether it is permissible to use this a mixture of pig fat and olive oil to light Chanukah candles?

One of these responsa was written by Rabbi Shlomo Dreimer (19th century, Galicia) in his book "Beit Shlomo." The author writes that he was asked "whether it is permissible in these times to light Chanukah candles with the fat of ostriches because it is common to mix it with pig milk." The questioner held that this was forbidden, because even with Rabbinical commandments one should be particular to use things which can be put into one's mouth. The "Beit Shlomo" does not agree with this opinion, because in the Talmud we do not find having to be particular about this principle except in the case of Tefillin.[97]

Another answer was written by Rabbi Shaul ben Tzvi Hirsch (18th century, Berlin) who authored the book "Besamim Rosh." He also objects to the prohibition of a mixture which includes pig oil and even writes that "pigs are more to be found than clean animals." He adds that the ban on using what is forbidden to put in one's mouth applies when "writing a Torah scroll on pigskin,"[98] and the "Sdei Hemed" understands from his words that his intention is that the prohibition is only relevant for a Sefer Torah, but "in the case of the mitzvah of Shabbat and Chanukah candles there is no argument."[99] Chanukah candles are only mitzvah artifacts and therefore, as written above, the halachah of "from what is permitted to put in one's mouth" does not apply to them.

Another reason for permitting pig fat for the lighting of Chanukah candles is given by Rabbi Shlomo Yaakov Yosef Kluger (18th–19th centuries, Galicia) who authored the book "Shenot Chaim," and this is also brought down in the book "Beit Yitzchak" written by Rabbi Yitzchak Yehuda Shmalkish (19th century, Lvov). His reasoning is that since the fat is about to be burned, one is not particular as to what is fit for Heavenly purposes and therefore the principle "what is permitted to put in one's mouth" does not apply.

On this subject, there is also a question involving "bitul" [nullifying a forbidden food]. The question is; What happens if in a mixture of olive oil with pig fat, there is sixty times as much olive oil as compared with the pig fat. In such a case, is the pig fat nullified? Rabbi Shneur Zalman Fradkin, (19th century, Lublin), the author of the book "Torat Chesed" discusses this question and concludes that if there are sixty times the permitted oil as against the pig fat, it is "completely permitted," and he adds that even if there are not sixty times the amount, there are still several reasons to allow it.[101]

Conclusion: Many Rabbis hold that pig fat or a mixture of oil with pig fat may be used for the mitzvah of Chanukah candles.[102]

Epilogue: Rabbi Chaim Ben Atar (18th century, Morocco) asks: "Why is the pig ("chazir") called a pig?" And he answers that one day it will return ("chazor") to be permitted to be eaten.[103] When we, *bezrat Hashem,* reach that day, there will be no question or doubt about the use of pig fat for the lighting of Chanukah candles!

References

Abbreviations
SA = Shulchan Aruch

OC = Orach Chaim
YD = Yoreh Deah
CM = Choshen Mishpat
MB = Mishnah Berurah

(1) Moshe Prager, *Nitzuzei Gevurah* (Sparks of Glory), (Netzach: Tel-Aviv), pp.95-101
(2) SA OC chap.673 par.1
(3) Talmud Bavli, Shabbat 28a
(4) SA OC chap.32 par.37
(5) Magen Avraham on SA OC chap.586 par.3
(6) Sefer Shemot, chap.13 verse 9
(7) Talmud Bavli, Shabbat 108a
(8) *Piskei Teshuvot* sorted and arranged by Rabbi Simcha Rabinowitz, (Jerusalem, 5767), chap.32 par.73, first words "aize 'devek'"
(9) Ibid.
(10) Rabbi Yechezkel Landau, *Noda b'Yehudah*, vol.1, (New York), responsum 1, first word "v'hinei gam"
(11) SA OC chap.586 par.16
(12) Chidushei haRan on Masechet Rosh Hashanah, (New York, 5706), chap.3, page 26b, first word "umayhu"
(13) Rabbi Chaim Hezekiah Medini, *Sdei Hemed*, collection of laws, section on chametz umatzah, section on Chol Hamoed and Chanukah, (Warsaw, 5656), chap.14, p.181, first words "hinai heiveiti"
(14) Talmud Bavli, Megillah 26b
(15) Ibid.
(16) SA OC chap.21 par.1, Rema
(17) MB chap.445 par.7
(18) MB chap.21 par.8
(19) Rabbi Yosef haKohen Schwartz, *Zichron l'Moshe*, (Oradea Romania, 5698), chap.18 par.2, (p.134)
(20) Rabbi Yechezkel Landau, *Noda b'Yehudah*, vol.2, (New York), responsum 3, first words "uvar min din"
(21) Talmud Bavli, Succah 23a
(22) *Sdei Hemed*, op. cit., p.180 first word "uvadaf," p.185 first word "ve'al"
(23) Biur Halachah, OC chap.630, first words "kol hadevarim"
(24) *Sdei Hemed*, op. cit., p.175, first word "veod"
(25) SA OC chap.629 par.1
(26) MB chap.529 par.22
(27) SA YD, chap.278 par.2
(28) Rabbi Bezalel ben Yisrael Moshe haKohen, *Reshit Bikkurim*, (Yerushalayim, 5729 – first printing was Vilna 5629), chap.10, first words "v'im toma lomar baze"
(29) *Sdei Hemed*, op. cit., p.178, first word "ulinyan dina"
(30) MB chap.586, par.8
(31) Mishnah, Masechet Nidah, chap 6 mishnah 9

(32) Rabbi Moshe Rivkas (Rabkash), *Be'er Hagolah*, OC chap.586 par.5; Dirshu on MB, (Dirshu, Kislev 5777), chap.586 par.10

(33) Rabbi Shimon Yair Chaim Bachrach, *Chavat Yair*, (Lemberg (Lvov), 5656), chap.20

(34) Sha'ar haTzion on MB, chap. 586 par.14

(35) Rabbi Eliyahu ben Binyamin Wolf Shapira (Spira), *Eliah Rabah*, (Sulzbach, 5517), OC chap.586 par.5

(36) Rabbi Yitzchak Yehudah Smelkish, *Beit Yitzchak*, (Faramisla (Przemsl), 5649), YD chap.145, first word "teshuvah"

(37) Rabbi Yosef ben Shem Tov ben Yeshua Chai, *She'arit Yosef*, (Warsaw, 5650), Masechet Megillah 24b

(38) SA OC chap.33 par.3

(39) *Noda b'Yehudah*, second volume, op. cit., responsum 3, first word "umayata"

(40) Rabbi Yitzchak Dov Halevi Bamberger, *Melechet Shamayim*, second edition, (Hannover, 5620), principle 20, hochmah, chap.2 par.5; Rabbi Shlomo Ganzfried, *Kesset Hasofer* brings similar wording in chap.23 par.2

(41) Rabbi Akiva Sofer, *Daat Sofer*, (Yerushalayim, 5725), YD chap.117

(42) SA OC chap.9 par.3

(43) Rabbi Yosef Teomim, *Pri Megadim*, (Warsaw, 5649), Mishbezot Zahav, chap.32 par.28

(44) *Piskei Teshuvot*, op. cit., chap.9 par.4

(45) Rabbi Chaim Hezekiah Medini, *Sdei Hemed*, vol 3, (Avraham Yitzchak Friedman: New York, 5722), maarechet ha-Lamed, principle 81, first words "ve'al mah shecatavti"

(46) "Do Bee don't Bee – A Halachik guide to Honey and Bee Derivatives," Rabbi Dovid Heber Star-K Kosher Certification, Maryland, Baltimore, Fall 2010, (Internet)

(47) SA OC chap.9 par.3

(48) Rabbi Yeshayahu Halevi Horowitz, *Shnei Luchot Habrit*, (Amsterdam, 5408), Shaar haOtiyot, p.112

(49) Rabbi Menachem Nathan Neta Auerbach, *Orach Neeman*, (Jerusalem, 5684), parts 1-2 on SA OC chap.9 par.3

(50) SA OC chap.9 par.3

(51) Sefer Vayikra, chap.11 verses 4, 6, Sefer Devarim, chap.14 verse 7

(52) *Pri Megadim*, op. cit., Mishbezot Zahav, OC chap.32 par.28; *Piskei Teshuvot*, op. cit., chap.9 par.4

(53) Rabbi Moshe Yizrael ben Yisrael Yosef of Visaki Lithuania, *Misgeret Zahav*, par.7 on *Kitzur Shulchan Aruch*, chap.9

(54) Tur YD chap.278

(55) *Darcei Moshe* (Rema), YD chap.278 par.1

(56) *Sdei Hemed*, op. cit., p.174, first words "ela d'kashe"

(57) Rabbi Yonah Landsofer, *Bnei Yonah*, (Prague, 5563), chap.278

(58) Sefer Shemot, chap.25 verse 3

(59) Rabbeinu Bahya ben Asher ibn Halawa, *Midrash Rabbeinu Behaye al Chamisha Chumshai Torah*, (Grosswardein (Oradea),5702), Parashat Terumah, chap.25, par.3

(60) Rabbi Gedaliah Moshe ben Tzvi Hirsch Halevi, *Hemed Moshe*, (Piorda (Fuerth), 5529), chap.586 par.3

(61) Rabbi Avrahami Halevi, *Ginat Veradim*, (Kustantina (Kushta, Constantinople), 5476), OC, rule 2, chap.16, first words "ach ma sheyire"

(62) Rabbi Moshe Sofer (Schreiber), *Chatam Sofer*, section OC, (Bratislava, 5601 – New York, 5718), responsum 39, first words "veod yitbaer"

(63) Talmud Bavli, Menachot 43b

(64) Techelet, (Encyclopedia Yehudit, Da'at, Michlelet Herzog), (Internet)

(65) Rabbi Mois Navon, Threads of Reason, Conclusion, (Internet)

(66) Techelet, Encyclopedia Yehudit, op. cit.

(67) S'funei T'munai Chol, (5647); Ptil Techelet, (5648); Ein haTechelet, (5651)

(68) Rabbi Dr. Isaac Herzog, *Semitic Porphyrology*, Doctoral Thesis, University of London, c.1913

(69) Ibid., pp.2, 99, 113, 126

(70) Techelet, *Encyclopedia Yehudit*, op. cit.

(71) Rabbi Nisim Avraham ben Rafael Ashkenaz1, *Nechmad Lemareh*, (Saloniki, 5592-5606); Talmud Yerushalmi, Kilayim chap.9 p.96b, first word "ulechora"

(72) Rabbi Gershon Henoch Leiner, *Ptil Techelet*, (New York 5712), chap 1, first words "hen emet" and first word "vehanire"

(73) Rabbi Gershon Henoch Leiner, *Ein Techelet*, (Warsaw, 5652), pp.73-74

(74) Tosephta, Masechet Menachot, chap.9 halachah 6

(75) Mishnah, Menachot, chap.4 mishnah 1

(76) SA OC chap.673 par.1

(77) Sefer Shemot, chap.23, verse 19, chap.34 verse 26, Sefer Devarim, chap.14 verse 21

(78) SA YD chap.87 par.1

(79) Dirshu, op. cit., chap.673 par.4

(80) *Shaarei Teshuvah*, chap.673 par.1; Rabbi Shlomo Zalman Braun, *Shearim Metsuyanim baHalachah* al Kitzur Shulchan Aruch, (Feldheim, Yerushalyim, 5731), chap.139 par.4; Rabbi Efraim ben Yaakov haKohen from Vilna, *Shaar Efraim*, (Lemberg (Lvov), 5647), OC responsum 38, first words

(81) Rabbi Shalom Mordechai haKohen Schwadron, *She'eilot U'teshuvot Maharsham*, (Yerushalayim, 5734), chap.122, first words "umah shenistapek"

(82) *Shaar Efraim*, op.cit., OC responsum 38, first word "omnam"; *Sdei Hemed*, op. cit., p.182, first words "ela shemidivrei"

(83) SA YD chap.294 par.1

(84) *Shearim Metsuyanim baHalachah*, op. cit., chap.139 par.4

(85) *Encyclopedia Talmudit*, vol 13, (Talmudit Encyclopedia Publishing: Yerushalayim 5730), chazir, cols.443-444

(86) SA CM, chap.409, par.2
(87) Talmud Bavli, Bava Kama 82b; Meirat Einayim, par.3 on SA CM 409
(88) Tur CM chap.409; SA CM chap.409 par.4
(89) MB chap.324 par.30
(90) Rabbi Yaacov Chaim ben Yitzchak Baruch Eliyahu Sofer, *Kaf haChaim*, YD chap.117 par 36, comment by Rabbi Ovadia Yosef
(91) Meirat Einayim, par.4 on SA CM chap.409
(92) *Kaf haChaim*, op. cit. YD chap.117 par.14, comment by Rabbi Ovadia Yosef
(93) Talmud Bavli, Shabbat 21b
(94) Talmud Bavli, Shabbat 21a
(95) Talmud Bavli, Chulin 63a and Mesoret haShass, par 5; *Sefer haAruch*, (Lublin, 5634), vol.1, letter ha"kof" "kk"
(96) Rabbi Tzvi Hirsch Chayot (Chajes), *Chidushei Maharatz Chayot* on Masechet Shabbat 21b; Rabbi Shneur Zalman Fradkin, *Torat Chesed*, (Warsaw, 5643), chap.60, first word "hasheailah"
(97) Rabbi Shlomo Drimer, *Beit Shlomo*, part 1, (Yerushalayim, 5747), responsum 108
(98) Rabbi Tzvi Hirsh Levin, *Besamim Rosh*, (Berlin, 5553), chap.320
(99) *Sdei Hemed*, op. cit., p.176, first words "v'chen mitbaer"
(100) Rabbi Shlomo Yaacov Yosef Kluger, *Shenot Chaim*, (Lemberg (Lvov), 5616), Kuntres Derech Hachaim; *Beit Yitzchak*, op. cit., YD chap.145; *Sdei Hemed*, op. cit., p.170, first word "neirot"
(101) *Torat Chesed*, op. cit., OC chap.60, first word "veyesh litmoah"
(102) Rabbi Shlomo Avraham ben Daniel Ze'ev Razachta, *Bikurei Shlomo*, (Pieterkov, 5654), suggested a different reason which is not connected to "what is permitted to put in one's mouth" to forbid the oil which is mixed with pig fat - it would be despicable. Omissions from volume OC chap.2
(103) Rabbi Chaim ben Attar, *Or haChaim* on Chamisha Chumshei Torah, (Zolkava, 5559), Sefer Vayikra, chap.11 par.3

THE DATE OF PURIM IN KIRYAT ARBA

Rabbi Dr. Chaim Simons

(Hebrew text was written in 2020
Translation into English was made in 2021)

Readers may put in a request to my e-mail chaimsimons@ gmail.com for original photocopied source materials quoted in this paper to be sent to their e-mails without charge.

Introduction

With the exception of Purim, there is a uniform date for all events in the Hebrew calendar. The question therefore arises: Why is Purim exceptional?[1]

The answer is found in the Book of Esther: In the days of Mordechai and Esther, when G-d performed a miracle for Israel, the Jews fought their enemies on the thirteenth of Adar, rested from war on the fourteenth of Adar and made it a festive and joyous day. However, in the city of Shushan, the war continued on the fourteenth of Adar and they thus rested on the fifteenth, and made the fifteenth a festive and joyous day. Since, for that generation, there were differences, depending on one's location, in the date to celebrate Purim, when Mordechai and Esther, with the agreement of the "Men of the Great Synagogue," established the festival of Purim for future generations, they made it for two days, the date to be observed being determined by location. They ruled that in every city that was then surrounded by a wall there would be a day of feasting and rejoicing and the megillah would be read on the fifteenth of Adar, as was done in the capital city Shushan,

233

but in other places they would observe Purim on the fourteenth of Adar. However, since at that period, Eretz-Israel was in ruins and therefore there were then no walled cities, for the honour of Eretz Israel they decreed that in cities that were walled in the days of Yehoshua bin Nun, Purim would be observed on the fifteenth of Adar, and in other places on the fourteenth of Adar.[2] This rule also included all the villages found to be "near and visible" to this walled city.

Because Yehoshua bin Nun lived about 3,300 years ago, there is a doubt as to which cities (with the exception of Jerusalem) had a wall in Yehoshua's time. Therefore, there are opinions that such doubtful cities should observe Purim, for two days, namely, on both the fourteenth and fifteenth of Adar.

There is a difference of opinion as to whether the original city of Hebron, namely Tel Rumeida, is one of these cities. The settlement of Kiryat Arba, established in 5731 (1971) is located, in ariel footage (or as sometimes stated by the expression "as the crow flies,") more than, two thousand amot, (which is about one kilometer), from Tel Rumeida.

In this paper, we will examine the date on which Purim should be celebrated in Kiryat Arba. To reach a conclusion, one must first discuss in general terms subjects relevant to the date of Purim in the wider world. These topics are:

- Is it permissible to observe Purim in a walled city on the fourteenth of Adar?
- What is the maximum distance between a walled city and the location of a "near and visible" place?
- Is the observance of Purim for two days, in a city where there exists a doubt whether or not it was surrounded by such a wall, a halachic [Jewish law] requirement or just an act of piety?
- Was the original Hebron (Tel Rumeida) a walled city?

It is important to emphasize that this article is only a study of the subject and not a Halachic ruling.

Part One

General Discussion

a) Purim in an undoubted walled city

According to the halacha, Purim is observed on the fifteenth of Adar in a city which was undoubtedly surrounded by a wall at the time of Yehoshua. However, what happens if the inhabitants of such a city observe Purim only on the fourteenth of Adar, as in unwalled cities?

The Talmud Bavli does not mention this subject, but this point is to be found in four places in the Talmud Yerushalmi: "Everyone fulfills the Mitzvah of Purim on the fourteenth."[3] On this Rabbi David ben Naftali Frankel, (18th century, Berlin), who composed the commentary "Korban ha-Edah" on the Talmud Yerushalmi writes: "Even if a walled city reads the megillah on the fourteenth, they do not have to read it again on the fifteenth."[4]

The question is whether or not we rule according to the Talmud Yerushalmi? The Shulchan Aruch and the Rambam do not mention this Yerushalmi. However, the "Kaf Hachaim" (Rabbi Yaakov Chaim Sofer, 19th-20th centuries, Baghdad and then Yerushalayim) writes that "b'dieved" (post facto) members of walled cities fulfil the mitzvah on the fourteenth as stated in the Talmud Yerushalmi.[5]

The Vilna Gaon, who is accustomed to brevity in his writings, notes on this subject only "since on the fourteenth he has fulfilled the mitzvah b'dieved."[6] The "Damesek Eliezer" (Rabbi Eliezer ben Shmuel Landau) who clarifies and elaborates on the words of the Vilna Gaon writes that the source of the comment of the Vilna Gaon is from the Talmud Yerushalmi.[7] There are also other Poskim (great Rabbinical authorities) who hold the same way.[8] Among them is Rabbi Ovadia Yosef who writes: "A resident of Jerusalem who read the megillah on the fourteenth of Adar, fulfils the mitzvah b'dieved."[9]

However, the "Chazon Ish" (Rabbi Avraham Yeshaya Karelitz, (20th century), who discusses the issue, holds that members of a walled city who read the megillah on the fourteenth

according to the Talmud Yerushalmi, would only fulfil the mitzvah
if they had erred by reading it on the fourteenth, but if they had
read the megillah deliberately on the fourteenth they would then
be obligated to read it again on the fifteenth. He added that if a
person were to tell someone to read it on the fourteenth and not
on the fifteenth he should not be listened to, because if one does
so, one has overridden the ruling of when a walled city should
read the megillah.[10]

b) Near and visible
What is the law in a village which is situated in proximity to a
walled city?

On this subject, it is stated in the Gemara: "A walled city and
any place near to it and which is visible from it is regarded as if it
is within the walled city. Up to what distance ... a mil (about a
kilometre)."[11] [One should not confuse the word "mil" with the
word "mile."] The question arises as to what exactly the Gemara
means by the words "near" and "visible" in connection with the
word "mil." There are a number of different opinions of the
"Rishonim" (Medieval Rabbis) and the "Acharonim" (post-
Medieval Rabbis) on how to interpret this Gemara.[12]

There are many "Poskim" [Great Rabbinical authorities] who
are of the opinion that the distance for both "near" and "visible"
is a mil. If so, what is the difference between the two? The answer
is "near" is walking by foot and thus this includes the hills and
vales in the course of the walk, and "visible" is measured in an
aerial footage."[13] Needless to say, in this way "visible" will be
farther away than "near."

There are some opinions that "near" is a distance of up to a
mil, which is about one kilometer, but "visible" is what can be
seen even if it is much more than a mil,[14] but they do not
explicitly write what the maximum distance of "visible" is. It is
thus possible that this distance will be tens of kilometres! In a
commentary by Rabbeinu Nissim (known as HaRan) of Gerona
(14th century), he writes that there is a limit to the distance for
"visible," namely less than a few parsaot (one parsa is 4 mils), but
he does not give a definite figure.[15]

In addition to all this, there is disagreement among the Poskim in a case when one sees only part of the village from the walled city. What then is the halacha? Some rule that due to the principle that "you should not separate into different groups" there cannot be a situation where one part of the village will read on one day, and the other part will read on another day. Thus, in such a case everyone should read on the fifteenth.[16] In contrast to this, there are those who hold that the principle of not separating into different groups is not relevant to the laws of Purim and the reading of the megillah. Thus, if half of a nearby village is visible or half is near, and half is neither near nor visible, it would seem that only that part that is near and visible joins the walled city, and the part that is neither near nor visible does not join in.[17]

Another question is whether one should be able to see from the ground of the walled city the ground of the village, or is it enough if one sees only the houses in the village? There are also differing opinions about this.[18] An interesting point emerges from the opinion that the ability to see the houses will determine the date of Purim, since by building a new tall building in the village it is possible to change the date of Purim in the village![19]

There is yet another opinion that "near" is within the "ibura" of the city, namely 70 amot (about 35 metres) from the outer limit of the city, and "visible" is a mil.[20]

As we shall now see, there are several ways to increase the distance of "near and visible."

Continuum of buildings
On this the "Chazon Ish" writes: "It seems that if houses were to be added outside the wall of the city, even if they extended beyond the "techum" [over a mil outside the city] and there were no houses either near or visible, the megillah should still be read on the fifteenth, since the city is regarded as if it is 4 amot (2 metres) large and its location is within the techum. This is provided that there is no plot of empty land between the buildings extending to 70 amot (or 141 amot) in accordance with the Sabbath laws of techum.[21] What is the difference between these two dimensions? Seventy amot is applicable when there is only

one house, but when there are three houses, the empty land is doubled to 141 amot.[22]

However, there are a number of other Poskim who write that a break of seventy amot is sufficient for the reading to be on the fourteenth, and they do not even mention 141 amot.[23] There is also an opinion which mentions a break of one mil.[24]

Municipality

According to Rabbi Shlomo Zalman Auerbach: "All the neighborhoods that are under the jurisdiction of the city [surrounded by a wall] for such matters, as for example, taxes and local rates, are regarded as part of the walled city. Purim there is observed on the fifteenth and not on the fourteenth.[25] The source for this is to be found in writings of the Rishonim. Rabbeinu Nissim writes that [the area (?)] is regarded as being within the city limits,[26] and Rabbi Yom Tov Asevilli (known as the Ritva, 13th-14th centuries, Spain) writes that it is so if the residents participate in the affairs of the city.[27] One of the Acharonim, the "Pri Megadim" (Rabbi Yosef Teomim 18th century), explains the words of the Ritva as meaning that perhaps they are liable for "taxes and local rates and other things."[28]

Within the Eruv

An eruv is a construction around a specific area, which permits carrying within that area on Shabbat.

According to Rabbi Shlomo Zalman Auerbach: "Every place within the Eruv of the walled city is to be regarded as part of the walled city.[29] (It is not clear whether the intention of his words "every place" is only when they are in the same municipality.) On the other hand, there are many Poskim who disagree with him and argue that the law of eruv is separate and the law of megillah is separate and the laws are not related to each other.[30] Rabbi Yitzchak Ratzabi also quotes these different opinions."[31]

There is also an opinion which reduces the distance of "near and visible." This is the opinion of Rabbi Yechiel Michel Tucazinski (19th-20th centuries, Jerusalem) in his book "Ir HaKodesh v'Hamikdash." In it there is a long chapter on the reading of the megillah in Jerusalem, and at the end he concludes that "all the neighborhoods that are more than one mil from the wall of the Old City, and are not visible within the border area of the Old City - I find no reason for them to be attached to the Old City of Jerusalem with regards to Purim." He gives a list of areas that are inside and those outside the above-mentioned mil. We learn from this that only a very small part of today's Jerusalem is within the above-mentioned mil.[32] Consequently, every year it is publicised that there will be a reading of the megillah with berachot on the night and the day of the fourteenth in the "Etz Chaim" neighbourhood opposite the bus station at the entrance to Jerusalem.[33] It was reported that two renowned Jerusalem Rabbis, namely Rabbi Shmuel Salant[34] and Rabbi Eliyahu David Rabinowitz-Teomim (known as the Aderet)[35] agree with Rabbi Tucazinski.

Another question is whether the law of "near and visible" also applies to a city where there is a doubt regarding the antiquity of its wall. On this there are differing opinions.

Rabbi Moshe Yisrael (17th-18th centuries), author of the book "Masat Moshe" was the first to rule on the question of the principle of "near and visible" in a doubtfully walled city. Even though, according to him, one reads the megillah on both days for a doubtful walled city, this does not extend to "near and visible" of such a city.[36] At a later date, other Poskim ruled likewise. They include the "Birkei Yosef,"[37] the "Kaf Hachaim,"[38] and the "Biur Halacha."[39]

However, the "Chazon Ish" disagrees with this and writes, that one cannot distinguish between a walled city and an area in its proximity without a source, and therefore they must be regarded as equal.[40]

c) Purim in a doubtfully walled city

It is written in the Talmud Bavli: "Rav Assi read the megillah in the city of Huzal on the fourteenth and on the fifteenth being in doubt whether or not it was walled at the time of Yehoshua bin Nun.[41] (The city of Tiberias is also mentioned, but for a different reason.) The conclusion is that in such cities, two days Purim should be observed, that is, on the fourteenth and on the fifteenth of the month of Adar.

However, there are discussions among the Rishonim as to whether this is halacha or only an act of piety. According to the Rambam, this is the halacha, and he writes: "In a city for which there is a doubt as to whether it was walled at the time of Yehoshua bin Nun, or was walled at a later date one reads the megillah on the two days which are the fourteenth and the fifteenth and on their nights."(42) On the other hand, Rabbeinu Nissim of Gerona (HaRan) is of the opinion that this is just an act of piety stating: "In Tiveria (Tiberias) and Huzal they would read the megillah on the fourteenth and on the fifteenth as an act of piety."(43) The Shulchan Aruch rules according to the Rambam stating: "A walled city where is a doubt whether or not it was walled at the time of Yehoshua reads the megillah on the fourteenth and fifteenth and their nights."(44) In contrast to this the Vilna Gaon writes that the Geonim [leading Rabbis of the period from about the year 600 to about the year 1000], held that one should only read the megillah on the fourteenth, since the ruling follows the majority of cities in the world, and furthermore when there is a doubt in a Rabbinical enactment one takes the lenient view. However one may not cancel completely the mitzvah of reading the megillah, and therefore it should be read just on the fourteenth, exempting a reading on the fifteenth.(45)

Another question related to a doubtful walled city is whether one recites the beracha (blessing) before reading the megillah, and if so when, namely on the fourteenth and / or the fifteenth. There are several possibilities for this:

1) To recite the beracha on both the fourteenth and the fifteenth. This was once the custom in the city of Tyre (today in southern Lebanon), and a question was submitted to the Rambam on this subject: "Are they or are they not transgressing by making an unnecessary beracha?" The Rambam answered that they were pronouncing the Divine name in vain, and that if they continued to do this and recite the beracha on the fifteenth, it would be proper for every

scholar and G-d fearing person to turn away and refrain from answering Amen on such a beracha, and anyone who were to answer Amen on an in vain beracha, or on a beracha for which there is a doubt, would have to give an accounting for this in the future.(46)

2) Not to say the beracha on the fourteenth or on the fifteenth. The source is the "Tur" (Rav Yaakov ben Asher, 13th-14th centuries), who writes that his brother held that they should read the megillah without a beracha on both days. He explains that they should not recite the beracha on the fifteenth because it may not have been a walled city, and not to recite the beracha on the fourteenth because it may have been a walled city hence the time for reading had not yet arrived and it would therefore be a beracha in vain.(47)

3) To recite the beracha on the fourteenth and not on the fifteenth. This is the opinion of the Rambam who writes: "One recites the beracha only on the fourteenth because this is the date for reading in the majority of the world."(48) The Chazon Ish explains that they fixed reciting the beracha on the fourteenth and not on the fifteenth since even if it were a walled city, one would have fulfilled the mitzvah by reading the megillah on the fourteenth, and thus in a doubtful walled city one would definitely be keeping the mitzvah. (49)

d) The city of Hebron

The Torah writes about six cities of refuge, three on the east side of the Jordan and three on the west side of the Jordan.(50) One of the cities of refuge on the western side was Hebron. Cities of refuge were unwalled, however, there are discussions among the Poskim as to whether there was a wall around Hebron in the days of Yehoshua bin Nun.

Rabbi David ben Shlomo ibn Zimra, (16th century), known as the "Radbaz" writes that the city of Hebron was not a walled city and the "goel hadam" (the blood avenger) would therefore not try to enter it in order to kill the murderer.(51) Walled cities were highly populated and it would thus be easy for a goel hadam to go undetected there. In contrast, a city of refuge which is not walled would not have a large population, hence the goel hadam would be easily detected if he tried to enter. Therefore, he does not try.

Furthermore, Rabbi Shaul Yisraeli writes that the observance of the mitzvah of reading the megillah and the other laws of Purim in Hebron applies only on the fourteenth of Adar. [52]

However, Rabbi Chaim Yosef David Azulai (the "Hida," 18th century), author of the book "Birkei Yosef" disagrees and states that although the Radbaz writes in a responsum that it is obvious that Hebron was not a walled city at the time of Yehoshua and one thus reads the megillah on the fourteenth, there is however an ancient custom to read the megillah on both the fourteenth and the fifteenth due to a doubt. [53] However, he gives no reason for the custom.

In contrast, Rabbi Yehosef Schwartz (19th century) in his book "Divrei Yosef" gives an explanation for the custom of two days of Purim in Hebron. He claims that during the conquest by Yehoshua bin Nun, Hebron was surrounded by a wall, and only when it became a city of refuge was it necessary to break through its walls. [54]

In accordance with the custom of two days of Purim in Hebron, each year in the "Luach (calendar) Tucazinski for Eretz Yisrael" Hebron appears, among other cities, as a city where two days of Purim are observed due to a doubt as to whether it was walled from the days of Yehoshua. [55]

However, Rabbi Ido Elba (21st century, Hebron) claims that as a result of archeological studies of Hebron, Purim in Hebron should be only on the fifteenth of Adar and on this he writes: "According to the strict halacha, in Hebron and the surrounding area one should read the megillah on the fifteenth." However, he adds that "one can also find support as to why it is customary to read the megillah on the fourteenth and on the fifteenth. [56]

Part Two

Purim in Kiryat Arba
The custom in the city of Hebron until the year 1929 was to observe Purim on the fourteenth and fifteenth of Adar. [57]

In 1968, a number of people established a group called the "Mitnachalei Hevron" (Hebron Settlers), and their living quarters were in the local Military Government Building. This building was located on the summit of a high hill before the entrance to the city of Hebron.[58] There is no doubt that it was not "near" to Tel Rumaida (the site of the original city of Hebron). Furthermore, according to the opinion that "visible" means that it is within an ariel footage of a kilometre, it was indeed not within this kilometre. According to the opinion that "visible" means that one is able physically to see the place irrespective of the distance, it seems that at that period no-one checked that fact. However, on their first Purim in Hebron which was in 1969, the Hebron settlers observed two days of Purim. In the evening services of both days, one of the settlers, Yitzchak Ganiram read the megillah. The men were seated in the dining hall of the settlement and the women in the adjacent kitchen. For the morning readings, some of the settlers went down to the Cave of Machpelah and there the megillah was read in the "Ulam Yitzchak" (the burial area for the Patriarch Yitzchak) by Rabbi Moshe Levinger. This was the first occasion after hundreds of years that the reading of the megillah took place in the Cave of Machpelah.[59]

The first Purim in Kiryat Arba, was in the year 1972 and at that stage all the residents lived in the area known today as the "Lev Hakirya." They continued to observe two days of Purim. Several years later in the year 1983, some of the residents began living in an area known as "Ramat Mamre" or "Givat Hacharsina" whose location was several kilometres from Lev Hakirya.[60] Two days of Purim were also observed there.

The question is whether according to the halacha there is a source for the observance of Purim for two days in Kiryat Arba? We will use the information given above to examine the issue regarding Kiryat Arba.

a) Purim in a city without any doubt surrounded by a wall

Even in a city that is without doubt surrounded by a wall (namely Jerusalem) if the megillah is read only on the fourteenth of Adar, the mitzvah is observed. How much more so, is this the case if the megillah is read only on the fourteenth of Adar in Kiryat Arba, which possibly could come under the principle of "near and visible" to a walled city.

b) Near and visible
Is Kiryat Arba "near and visible" to Tel Rumeida?

Near: The distance of "near" is up to one mil, (about one kilometre). The distance between Tel Rumeida and Lev Hakirya, and even more so to Ramat Mamre, is more than a kilometre. However, as explained above, there are cases that allow an increase in this distance, and this happens if there is a continuum of houses between two places, provided there is no empty space of (according to different opinions), just over seventy amot (about 35 metres), 141 amot (about 70 metres), or one mil (about one kilometre), between these two places. The question therefore is, whether there is actually a continuum of buildings between Kiryat Arba and Tel Rumeida? In fact, in this area there are places where there is no continuum of houses.[61] However, professional measurements are needed in order to establish whether the empty space is large enough to eliminate the "near." Also, there are opinions that even if there is a continuum of buildings, a distance beyond a mil (about one kilometre) is not called "near," and according to this opinion Lev Hakirya, and especially Ramat Mamre, are not considered "near" to Tel Rumeida.

Visible: What is the reality of "visible" in relation to seeing Kiryat Arba from Tel Rumeida? According to the opinion that "visible" is only up to a mil by aerial footage, since Kiryat Arba is more than a mil from Tel Rumeida it is outside the area of "visible." However, there is an opinion that "visible" is what can actually be seen even if the distance is more, or even much more, than a mil. The reality is that when there is good visibility from Tel Rumeida, one can see, with some difficulty, a few isolated buildings in Kiryat Arba.[62] What is the halacha in such a situation? There are opinions that if you can see a small part of the village, following the rule that "you should not separate into different groups," it is possible that Purim should be observed in the whole village on the fifteenth of Adar. Why did we write the word "possible"? The answer depends on the meaning of the words "small part." This is relevant here because we can see only the "tiniest part" of Lev Hakirya from Tel Rumeida, and the question is whether this is sufficient for Purim to be observed throughout Kiryat Arba on the fifteenth of Adar? In fact, the matter is even more complicated because there is an opinion that only in the area of the village which can be seen from the walled city does one read the megillah on both the fourteenth and the fifteenth, and in other areas only on the fourteenth. In addition to all this, there is another controversy. Is it enough to see only the buildings of Kiryat Arba from Tel Rumeida in order to read the megillah on the fifteenth as well, or is it necessary to see the ground? Another question that is difficult to answer is whether were the buildings not there, it would be possible to see the ground of Kiryat Arba from Tel Rumeida.

Municipality: Some Poskim say that the reason that in all of Jerusalem Purim is observed on the fifteenth, is that there is one municipality for the whole city, and all residents pay taxes and property taxes to the Jerusalem municipality. However, this is not the case in Kiryat Arba and Hebron.[63] There are two bodies, namely, the Kiryat Arba Local Council,[64] and a Committee for the Jewish Community of Hebron.[65] Even though in the paper work of the Kiryat Arba Local Council, they add the word "Hebron" after the word "Kiryat Arba," Hebron is not within their jurisdiction. The Jewish Hebron residents do not have the right to vote in the municipal elections of Kiryat Arba.

Eruv: There is an opinion that if there is an "eruv" (a construction around a specific area, which enables carrying within that area on Shabbat) around the city surrounded by a wall and its surroundings, the entire area inside the eruv is considered "near and visible." Today there is an eruv that includes the whole of Kiryat Arba, the road to Hebron, the Jewish area in Hebron, Tel Rumeida and the Cave of the Patriarchs.[66] Rabbi Dov Lior, who was formerly the Chief Rabbi of Kiryat Arba, wrote: "Kiryat Arba has a common eruv which includes Hebron, and they are considered as one city for this purpose [to hold Purim on the fourteenth and fifteenth]."[67] However, there are many who disagree with this opinion and claim that there is no connection between the eruv and the date of Purim.

If, according to the halacha, it is the eruv that determines the date of Purim, why are there all the arguments as to which day Purim is observed in different areas of Jerusalem such as Har Nof and Ramot?[68] Rabbi Yaakov Yisrael Kanievsky (the Steipler) and Rabbi Ovadia Yosef write that according to the opinion (with which neither agrees) that the eruv sets the date of Purim, in the case of an eruv being made around the whole of Eretz Israel, then all Eretz Israel would be like the walled city of Jerusalem and everyone would thus observe Purim only on the fifteenth of Adar![69]

In a doubtful walled city is there the rule of "near and visible"?
There are disagreements as to whether the law of "near and visible" applies to a city doubtfully surrounded by a wall. This is a further reason not to hold two days of Purim in Kiryat Arba.

c) Purim in a doubtfully walled city
The Gemara discusses when to observe Purim in a doubtful walled city. There are discussions on how to interpret the Gemara, on this subject, namely whether it is halacha or only an act of piety to observe Purim in a doubtful walled city on the fourteenth and fifteenth of Adar. The Vilna Gaon writes that according to the Geonim, [leading Rabbis of the period from about the year 600 to about the year 1000], Purim is celebrated on the fourteenth and not on the fifteenth. Therefore, according to an opinion, it is only an act of piety to observe two days of Purim, and perhaps there is no mitzvah at all to observe Purim on the fifteenth. Furthermore, this is all the more so in a place which is only "near and visible" to a doubtful walled city such as Kiryat Arba.

d) The city of Hebron
Even though it has been customary for centuries to observe two days of Purim in the city of Hebron itself, it should be remembered

that the Jewish Quarter ("Ghetto") in Hebron was, before 1929, in the area of the Avraham Avinu synagogue,[70] which is relatively close to Tel Rumeida. This is not so with the location of Kiryat Arba which is much further away from Tel Rumeida. At the time that Kiryat Arba was established in 1971, the residents continued the Hebron tradition of two days of Purim.

In the year 1976, Rabbi Dov Lior came to live in Kiryat Arba and according to his opinion Purim should be observed only on the fourteenth. However, because it had already become a custom to observe two days of Purim in Kiryat Arba he did not try to change the custom.[71] This was such an accepted custom in Kiryat Arba that in 1978 he published a page with "A few of the Halachot of Purim" which began "In Kiryat Arba and Ramat Mamre and in the city of Hebron it is customary to observe Purim for two days."[72] One should note his use of the word "customary"! In contrast to some of the other doubtful walled cities in Eretz Yisrael,[73] all the Synagogues in Kiryat Arba read the megillah on both days.

In contrast to the above, Rabbi Ido Elba came to the conclusion that "according to the strict halacha, it would seem that in Hebron and its environs one should read on the fifteenth." He explains its "environs" as "the Cave [of the Patriarchs] including Kiryat Arba and Ramat Mamre."[74]

However, Rabbi Elba does not indicate whether there is anyone who supports his opinion on this issue. We can see that the Rabbi of the city, Rabbi Dov Lior, does not agree with Rabbi Elba's conclusion, because in 2009, which was eight years after Rabbi Elba's paper, Rabbi Lior published a "Pinat Halacha" (a halacha sheet) and there he wrote: "We have the custom to observe two days of Purim but the main one is the first day."[75]

Furthermore, Rabbi Elba does not specify when one should recite the berachot (blessings) for the reading of the megillah. Does he believe that because in his opinion the date of Purim in Hebron and Kiryat Arba is on the fifteenth, one should recite the berachot only on the fifteenth, and read the megillah without a blessing on the fourteenth? In support of this, there is a letter from Rabbi Avraham Yitzchak Hakohen Kook. Rabbi Kook was asked in 1931 about the reading of the megillah in Bayit Vagan in Jerusalem.[76] His answer (with the agreement of the Rishon Lezion Rabbi Yaakov Meir) is: "One should read it on the fourteenth without a beracha and on the fifteenth with a beracha." However, in contrast, Rabbi Yehuda Zoldan writes: "In the writings of the Poskim... one does not find that one can read the megillah on the fourteenth without a beracha and on the fifteenth with a beracha, as was suggested by Rabbi Kook!"[77]

Concluding remarks: The Radbaz even praises those who read the megillah on the fourteenth and fifteenth days of Adar, even if there is no need for it: "One should not rebuke those who read the megillah on the fourteenth and fifteenth since by reading it without a beracha nothing is lost, and I wish that the wonderous deeds of the Almighty be remembered every day."[78]

Summary

Due to many doubts (even more than a "sfek sfaika" – a double doubt!), it seems to me that Purim occurs only on the fourteenth of Adar in Kiryat Arba. However, there is already a "tradition" of half a century in Kiryat Arba to celebrate the two days of Purim. In Kiryat Arba, on the fifteenth of Adar (Shushan Purim), the megillah is read without a beracha in all the synagogues, the residents distribute food packages ("misloach manot") and money to the needy ("matanot laevyonim").

References

Abbreviations
SA = Shulchan Aruch
OC = Orach Chaim
MB = Mishnah Berurah

(1) On the subject on the date of Purim one can say that to "the making books there is no end" (Kohelet chap.12, verse 12). Therefore, this paper is limited to a summary of the more relevant points on this subject. [A further difference in dates is that, two days of each Festival are observed in the Diaspora as distinct from one day in Eretz Yisrael.]

(2) Rabbi Moshe Harari (editor), *Mikraei Kodesh, Hilchot Purim,* (Yeshivat Mercaz Harav: Jerusalem, 5759), chap.5, laws of unwalled and walled cities, p.90

(3) Talmud Yerushalmi: Megillah: chap.1, halacha 1; chap.1 halacha 3; chap.2 halacha 3; Shekalim chap.1 halacha 1

(4) Rabbi David ben Naphtali Frankel, *Korban ha-Edah* on Talmud Yerushalmi, Megillah, chap.1 halacha 3, chap.2 halacha 3

(5) Rabbi Yaakov Chaim Sofer, *Kaf Hachaim,* OC chap.688 para.26

(6) Biurei HaGra (Vilna Gaon), OC chap.688 para.4

(7) Rabbi Eliezer ben Shmuel Landau, *Damesek Eliezer,* part 1, (Vilna, 5628), OC chap.688, para.8

(8) Rabbi Moshe Sternbuch, *Teshuvot veHanhagot Hashalem,* vol.2, (Jerusalem, 5754), OC chap 347 first word: v'achshav

(9) Rabbi Yitzchak Yosef ben Rabbi Ovadia Yosef, *Kitzur Shulchan Aruch, Yalkut Yosef,* (Machon Chazon Ovadia: Jerusalem, 5757), chap.688 para.1

(10) Rabbi Avraham Yeshaya Karelitz, *Sefer Chazon Ish, Orach Chaim, Moed,* (Bnei Brak: 5754) chap.153 para.2, first word: badin

(11) Talmud Bavli, Megillah, 2b

(12) See paper "samuch v'nireh l'krach", betmidrash.org.il, (internet)

(13) Rabbi Yechiel Michel Tucazinski, *Ir HaKodesh v'Hamikdash,* vol.3, (Jerusalem, 5729), chap.27 sub.chap.3 para.1, p.412

(14) MB chap.688 para.6 and Sha'ar Hatziun para.5

(15) Rabbeinu Nissim of Gerona (HaRan) on Megillah, chap.1, (p.2), first word: amar

(16) Rabbi Moshe Yehoshua Yehuda Leib Diskin, *Shut Maharil Diskin,* (Jerusalem, 5671), Kuntrus Acharon, para.103

(17) *Ir HaKodesh v'Hamikdash,* op. cit., chap.27, para.6, first word: k'tzuram, (p.405); chap.10, para.3, (p.415)

(18) Dirshu on MB vol.6, ("Dirshu" edition: Jerusalem, Kislev 5777), chap.688, para.7, first word: v'ir

(19) Dirshu, ibid.

(20) Bet Yosef on Tur, OC chap.688, first word: vechen

(21) *Chazon Ish,* op. cit., hilchot megillah, chap.151, first word: nireh

(22) Paper "Samuch venire – zeman kriat hamegillah b'shechunot hahadashot bi'Yerushalayim", Din, Bet Hahoraa Hamercazi l'Dayanut, 18 Adar I 5779, (Internet)

(23) Rabbi Sternbuch, op. cit., OC chap.347, first words: veikar ta'am

(24) Rabbi Yitzchak ben Rabbi Ovadia Yosef, *Yalkut Yosef, Moadim Hilchot Purim,* (Aish Pituchim: Jerusalem, 5773), chap.688, (p.228), first words: ulfi ze

(25) Rabbi Shlomo Zalman Auerbach, *Halichot Shlomo al Moadei Hashanah, Tishri – Adar,* (Jerusalem, 5764), dinei ir vkrach, para.8

(26) Rabbeinu Nissim (HaRan) on Megillah, op. cit.

(27) Rabbi Yom Tov ben Avraham Asevilli, *Chidushei Haritva al Masechet Megillah,* (Jerusalem, 5727), chap.1, first words: vead kama

(28) Rabbi Yosef ben Meir Teomim, *Pri Megadim,* vol.1, (Frankfurt der Oder, 5547), OC chap.688, Mishbetzot Zahav, first word: vehineh

(29) *Halichot Shlomo,* op. cit., dinei ir vkrach, para.9

(30) Rabbi Yitzchak Yaakov Weiss, Responsa *Minchat Yitzchak,* vol.8 (Minchat Yitzchak Publishers: Jerusalem, 5753), para.62, first word: nitorer; *Yalkut Yosef Hilchot Purim,* op. cit., p.329. first words: veain haeruv

(31) Rabbi Yitzchak Ratzabi, *Shaarei Yitzchak,* (Mosdot Yad Maharitz: Bnei Brak, Tevet-Adar, 5770), the seventh shiur – Parashat Terumah, "Suburbs which are a distance from old city of Jerusalem, for example, the suburb of Ramot, when do they observe Purim", pp.166-67

(32) *Ir HaKodesh v'Hamikdash,* op. cit., vol.3, chap 27, para.16, first word: hasicum, (pp.424-25)

(33) For example: Luach (Tucazinski) l'Eretz Yisrael for the year 5780, p.45

(34) Rabbi Yaakov ben Chaim Menachem Halevi Epstein, *Chevel Nachalato,* vol.20 chap.30; *Ir HaKodesh v'Hamikdash,* op. cit., vol.3, chap.27 para.1 (p.381)

(35) *Chevel Nachalato,* ibid; *Ir HaKodesh v'Hamikdash,* ibid.

(36) Rabbi Moshe Yisrael, *Masat Moshe,* (Kushtadina, (Kushta, Constantinople), 5502), OC chap.3

(37) Rabbi Chaim Yosef David Azulai (Hida), *Birkei Yosf,* (Livorno, 5534), chap.688 para.9

(38) *Kaf Hachaim,* op. cit., OC, chap.688 para.9

(39) *Biur Halacha on* Mishnah Berurah, OC chap.688, first word: oh

(40) *Chazon Ish,* op. cit., Hilchot Megillah, chap.153, para.3, first words: b'Mishnah Berurah

(41) Talmud Bavli, Megillah 5b

(42) Rambam (Maimonides), Mishneh Torah, Hilchot Megillah, chap.1, halacha 11

(43) Ran (Rabbeinu Nissim) on Masechet Megillah, chap.1 p.2, first word: ul'inyan

(44) SA OC chap.688, para.4

(45) Biurei HaGra (Vilna Gaon), OC chap.688 para.4

(46) Rambam (Maimonides), *Teshuvot HaRambam,* (published by Yehoshua Blau, Mekitzei Nirdamim: Jerusalem, 5718), vol.1, responsum 124

(47) Tur, OC chap.688

(48) Rambam (Maimonides), Mishneh Torah, Hilchot Megillah, chap.1, halacha 11

(49) *Chazon Ish,* op. cit., Hilchot Megillah, chap.153, para.2, first word: uvimkom

(50) Sefer Bamidbar chap.35 verses 13-14

(51) Rabbi David ben Shlomo ibn Zimra, Responsa of *Radbaz,* vol.2, (Jerusalem, 5747), responsum 681

(52) Rabbi Shaul Yisraeli, appendix to article "What is the date of Purim in the settlement in Bet-El and the military camp there" *Tehumin,* vol.1, (Zomet -Yad Shapira: Alon Shvut, Gush Etzion, winter 5740), p.123

(53) *Birkei Yosef,* op. cit., OC chap.688 para.4

(54) Rabbi Yehosef Schwartz, *Divrei Yosef,* (Jerusalem, 5622), responsa, question 2, p.12

(55) For example: Luach (Tucazinski) l'Eretz Yisrael for the year 5780, p.49

(56) Rabbi Ido Elba, paper "Reading the Megillah in Hebron and the Surrounding Area" *Melilot – Mehkarim Torani'im,* vol.2, (Machon l'Rabbonei Yishuvim: Kiryat Arba, 5761), p.295

(57) *Birkai Yosef,* op. cit.; Luach (Tucazinski) l'Eretz Yisrael, op. cit.; Recorded evidence on the custom in Hebron until the year 1929 by former residents of Hebron, Yosef Kastel (17.10.1982) and Yitzchak Toker (14.10.1985)

(58) Chaim Simons *Three Years in a Military Compound* (in Hebrew), (Kiryat Arba, 5778), p.11

(59) *Three Years in a Military Compound,* op. cit., pp.58-59. There is a photograph of Reading the Megillah, p.58; Chaim Simons, "Hayishuv Sheli – Kiryat Arba- Hevron, Purim", (Nehemiah Institute: Kiryat Arba, Adar I 5757), p.8

(60) Givat Haharsina (Ramat Mamre), Wikipedia, (Internet)

(61) Photograph of part of the break in the continuum between building 303 in Kiryat Arba and the Arab house on the other side of the fence.

(62) Photograph (by the Afarsamon family) taken at Tel Rumeida in the direction of Kiryat Arba

(63) Map of the areas under the jurisdiction of the Kiryat Arba Municipal Council. There are 24 separate areas under their jurisdiction.

(64) Logo of Kiryat Arba Municipal Council

(65) Logo of the Committee of the Jewish Community of Hebron

(66) Responsum of Rabbi Dov Lior on the Eruv in Kiryat Arba, (website "Yeshiva, Ask the Rabbi", 9 Sivan 5762), (Internet)

(67) Rabbi Dov Lior, *Dvar Hevron,* (Kiryat Arba-Hebron), OC section, chap 621, Purim in Kiryat Arba

(68) For example: Rabbi Yehuda Zoldan, article "Reading the Megillah in the suburbs of Jerusalem" (Yeshiva website, 21 Adar I 5768, Internet); Rabbi Shlomo Zalman Auerbach, *Minchat Shlomo,* (Machon Otzrot Shlomo: Jerusalem, 5759), chap.57

(69) Rabbi Yaakov Yisrael Kanievsky, (The Steipler), *Karyana D'Igarta,* vol.2, (Bnei Brak: 5750), part 4, letters on decisions and guidance in halachah and in Orach Chaim, chap.105, whether a general eruv can make an area into one city and thus it be regarded as a walled city; *Yalkut Yosef Hilchot Purim,* op. cit., p329, first words: v'ain haeruv

(70) Gershon Bar-Kochva, "The old Jewish quarter in Hebron at the beginning of the twentieth century", *Katedra,* (Yad Ben-Zvi: Jerusalem), vol.169, Tishri 5779, p.51, drawing

(71) Oral evidence by Moshe Kaufman and the Afarsamon family, Adar 5780

(72) The page written by Rabbi Dov Lior can be found in the booklet "Mitzvot Yemai Hapurim b'Ir Safek Mukefet Homa" written by Chaim Simons, (Nehemia Institute: Kiryat Arba, Shevat 5758), p.29

(73) Ibid., pp.6-8

(74) Rabbi Ido Elba, op. cit., p.295
(75) Pinat Hahalacha by Rabbi Dov Lior, Rabbi of Kiryat Arba, can be found
      in "Chemdat Avot," publication of the local Religious Council, 10 Adar
      5769
(76) Letter in the handwriting of Rabbi Avraham Yitzchak Hakohen Kook can
      be found in the monthly magazine, "Meged Yerachim" issue no,113, Adar
      5769 (an organisation whose aim is to publish the writings of Rabbi
      Kook). Due to a printing error the year is written as 5780 instead of 5791
(77) Rabbi Yehuda Zoldan, op. cit.
(78) *Radbaz*, op. cit., vol.1, responsum 252

I emphasize that the above article is just for the study of the subject and not a ruling of Halacha. These rulings are for the great Poskim.

PAPERS OF MINE IN HEBREW WHICH WERE PUBLISHED IN SCHOLARLY JOURNALS

On some occasions the editorial board of the journal did a small amount of editing on the paper. At a later date, I sometimes made some additions to my papers which were mainly unpublished.

The titles of the papers are here translated into English

Papers in the journal "Sinai" published by the Mosad Harav Kook in Jerusalem

- The blackening of the straps of Tefillin including the inner side *(volume 153, 2020, pp.200-216)*
- Does a boy who is an orphan begin to put on Tefillin at the age of 12? *(volume 151, 2018, pp.99-106)*
- The Date for the start of reciting the blessing for rain in the Diaspora *(volume 111, 1992, pp.73-92)*
- Differences in the Sabbath morning Torah readings between those living in the Land of Israel and those living in the Diaspora *(volume 106, 1990, pp.33-40)*
- The connection between the time of the average astronomical new moon and the time for reciting the prayer for the Creator of the moon *(volume 117, 1995, pp.77-90)*
- Reading the scrolls of the Song of Solomon, Ruth, Lamentations and Ecclesiastes *(volume 118, 1996, pp.26-42)*
- Visiting the graves of the righteous in the month of Iyar *(volume 108, 1991, pp.77-92)*
- Is the chapter "Days on which one fasts" the last chapter of the Scroll of the Fast Days? *(volume 107, 1990, pp.58-64)*

253

- Reasons for the fast of the ninth of the month of Tevet *(volume 106, 1990, pp.138-151)*
- The Chinese Citron *(volume 149, 2016, pp.106-123)*
- The Reading of the Torah on the Eighth Day of the Solemn Assembly (Simchat Torah) in the Land of Israel *(volume 103, 1989, pp.239-247)*
- Eating of cheese and pancakes on the Festival of Chanukah *(volume 115, 1994, pp.57-68)*
- The commandments to be performed on the Festival of Purim in a doubtfully walled city *(volume 118, 1996, pp.193-210)*
- Two headed Siamese Twins – Aspects in Jewish Law *(volume 144, 2012, pp.107-120)*

Paper in the journal "Elonei Mamrei" published by Yeshivat Kiryat Arba

- Heter Mechirah or Imported Vegetables – Which should one choose? *(volume 121, 2008, pp.24-38; volume 122, 2009, pp.196-201)*

Section Four

Selection of Autobiographical Jottings

THREE TIMES BIRCHAT HACHAMAH

The least frequent mitzvah in the Jewish calendar is that of Birchat Hachamah, the blessing of the Creator of the sun. This mitzvah is only performed once every 28 years and it is recited on a Wednesday during the month of Nissan. Since it depends on the sun and the civil calendar is based on the sun, (at present) it is recited every time on 8 April.

I have been privileged to take part in this ceremony three times. The first occasion was in England and the next two occasions in Eretz Israel.

In this paper, I record my reminiscences of each occasion.

I pray to the Almighty that I will again be able to take part in such a ceremony in 5797/2037.

Wednesday, 23 Nisan 5713 – 8 April 1953

My first Birchat Hachamah was when I was 10 years old and took place at the Edgware United Synagogue which is located just outside North-West London.

This Synagogue was first built in 1934 in Mowbray Road, Edgware. The land had been donated by a far-sighted land developer who realized that a Synagogue in the area would draw Jews to live in Edgware. He was right! At the time there were very few living there, but in the subsequent years a very large number of Jews moved there.

The Synagogue, then known as Edgware District Synagogue, was one of the United Synagogues. It was a one-story building and as with many Synagogues in England at the time, its Bimah was at the front. On weekdays the Baal Koreh faced the Ark when leining, but on Shabbat he faced the congregation.

In 1939, a two-story communal hall known as the "Rose Harris Hall" was built adjacent to the Synagogue. On the top floor was the communal hall, and on the lower floor were, as I recollect, four classrooms for the Hebrew Classes. At a later date, as the Hebrew classes grew in size movable partitions were erected in the communal hall to divide it into four additional classrooms. The stone commemorating its opening was dated 3 September 1939. However, this was the day that Britain entered the Second World War and the opening ceremony was cancelled at a few hours' notice.

By at least the late 1940s, there was not enough room for all the worshippers who attended on Rosh Hashanah and Yom Kippur in both the Synagogue and the "Rose Harris Hall" and a marquee was therefore erected in the grounds of the Synagogue as a venue for an additional service.

During the year 1953 there was the ceremony of Birchat Hachamah. This occurred that year on Isru Chag Pesach and I attended Synagogue that morning with my father. The Synagogue then held services every morning and evening, and on weekdays most of the worshippers were mourners saying Kaddish.

After the Shacharit service, the then Minister, Rev. Saul Amias, announced there would be the ceremony of Birchat Hachamah and as an encouragement to the worshippers to remain for it said there would be a mourners' kaddish at the end. The worshippers then went outside the Synagogue to the courtyard with their Siddurim. Rev. Amias had a list of the prayers to be recited at this ceremony and he announced them to the congregation. That day a bright sun could be seen in the sky and we were thus able to say the berachah "oseh ma'aseh beraishit." At the end of the ceremony, I recollect one of the elderly worshippers saying that in 28 years time, B'ezrat Hashem, he will be able to participate in this ceremony again.

Wednesday, 4 Nisan 5741 – 8 April 1981

I was 38 years old at my second Birchat Hachamah and it took place in Kiryat Arba – Hebron, City of the Patriarchs.

In the summer of 1978, I had returned from Liverpool in England, where I had been Director of Jewish Studies at the Jewish

High School there. In Liverpool I had made a special study of the use of audio-visual materials in teaching Jewish Law. At the beginning of 1981, I happened to mention to Yigal Kutai, a resident of Kiryat Arba of this study I had made. He replied that I had been sent to him by Heaven. He had just got the Kiryat Arba Local Council to purchase a whole variety of video equipment, but having no-one to operate it, he had thought he would have to return it. He said that I had spoken to him at the ideal moment and I was then immediately appointed by the Local Council to be the Director of the Audio-Visual Centre which was then set up.

A few weeks later was the ceremony of Birchat Hachamah and as we shall soon see, I filmed on video one of the local ceremonies.

Meanwhile in the period preceding this ceremony, a number of booklets and leaflets were published (or republished). These include a small book by Rabbi Yechiel Tuchachinsky and a booklet by Mercaz Agudat Yisrael. Also, as far as I remember, Rabbi Zalman Koren, who then lived in Kiryat Arba, and was an authority on matters connected with the Jewish calendar, gave a public shiur on Birchat Hachamah in Kiryat Arba.

Needless to say, that all the Synagogues in Kiryat Arba had the Birchat Hachamah ceremony. Amongst them was the Kiryat Arba Religious Primary School. Since it was on 4 Nisan, the school had not yet broken up for the Pesach vacation.

In 1981, there were only Primary Schools in Kiryat Arba. The Ulpana and the Yeshivah Tichonit were things of the future. By far, the largest school was this Religious Primary School and it was situated in the building which is today shared by the Talmud Torah and the Secular School. The Headmaster of the Religious Primary school was Rabbi Shalom Horowitz.

As stated above, the Local Council had just purchased the video equipment and I had started to film events in Kiryat Arba. The ceremony of Birchat Hachamah at the Religious Primary school was one of them.

As is customary when this ceremony takes place, one has a "vatikin minyan" for Shacharit which is followed by this ceremony. That morning I took the video equipment to the School, and davened Shacharit there. After the service, we went out to the courtyard outside the main door of the upper story of that building and I attached the camera to the tripod. As the ceremony progressed, I would film many the pupils participating in the ceremony. Unfortunately, the day was cloudy and it was not possible to then say the berachah "oseh ma'aseh beraishit." I say "then" since soon after I returned to my own apartment, someone called out from the street that the sun had appeared and people ran out of their apartments to say the berachah.

Wednesday, 14 Nisan 5769 – 8 April 2009

I was 66 years old at my third Birchat Hachamah and, as on the previous occasion, it took place in Kiryat Arba – Hebron, City of the Patriarchs.

The weather forecasts of the previous days had been pessimistic that the day would be cloudy and people were thus apprehensive that they would miss the opportunity to say the berachah. Being also erev Pesach, which is always a very busy day, we realised that the day would be even busier on account of this "once in 28-year Mitzvah".

The Local Religious Council of Kiryat Arba had duplicated pages with the Order of Service for the Mitzvah, and its Chairman gave me a pile of these sheets to distribute in the "Chasdei Avot" Synagogue, where I was the Honorary Rabbi, which I did.

It is customary in many places to have a "vatikin minyan" on such a day, so that one would be able to perform this mitzvah at the first available moment. The time of sunrise in Kiryat Arba on that day was 6.18½, and thus to have a "vatikin minyan" one would have to start the service at around six o'clock. I would like to have arranged an additional minyan at Chasdei Avot Synagogue that morning, in addition to the regular minyanim of 6.40 and 8.00 but such a "vatikin minyan" would not have finished before the worshippers starting arriving for the 6.40 minyan. The Religious Council had published that there would be a "vatikin minyan" in the Cave of Machpelah and also in the various Synagogues in Kiryat Arba. I enquired whether this included the

Nir Yeshivah, but was informed that it probably would not have such a minyan. From my further enquiries I learned that there was a minyan starting at 6.00 at the "Alon Yosef" Synagogue, which is situated in an annex to the Nir Yeshivah.

That morning, I went to this minyan. The service seemed at a rather fast pace and they in fact reached the amidah at about five minutes before sunrise. When they reached aleinu towards the end of the service, the gabbai announced that we would then go outside and recite Birchat Hachamah. It was then about a quarter of an hour after sunrise. We went outside but could not yet see the sun. There were buildings and trees blocking our view. We walked around in almost a complete circle, continually looking for a sign of the sun but in vain. We finally arrived at the plaza of the Nir Yeshivah which had been erected several years earlier by the Nachliel family, in memory of Avraham Nachliel (Borganin), for the recitation of the monthly Kiddush Levanah.

We could still not see the sun, but we began by reciting the various accompanying prayers to Birchat Hachamah, but still no sun! Whilst waiting, we then finished the morning service.

It is not specifically written that one should say the berachah Shehecheyanu over this mitzvah, but instead one should say the berachah over a new fruit or garment and bear this mitzvah in mind at the same time. The Rabbi of this Synagogue had a new tallit, and recited shehecheyanu over it asking the congregation to have in mind that this berachah was also for Birchat Hachamah.

Finally, the sun could be seen emerging between trees which had until then been blocking us seeing the sun and everyone then recited the berachah "oseh ma'aseh beraishit." We all then started singing and dancing.

A little later, I arrived towards the end of the 8.00 service at Chasdei Avot (the minyan I usually attended), and after the service the worshippers went outside, recited the Birchat Hachamah service and then danced.

After that I went home, and in accordance with the opinion that women recite this berachah, went outside with my wife, and a granddaughter who had already arrived to stay with us for the first day of Pesach, and they recited the berachah.

One of my daughters had gone that morning to the Cave of Machpelah, where amongst a multitude of people, the service was conducted, but she informed me that they did not dance afterwards.

Fortunately, the weather forecasters had been wrong. There was glorious sunshine during the entire period when this berachah could be recited!

FORTY YEARS AGO
Reminiscences of the period of the Six Day War

Anyone who was in Israel at the time of the Six Day War in the summer of 1967, will never forget that period. For a few weeks, a potential holocaust seemed to be looming on the horizon, but, with the help of the Almighty, within the subsequent few days, the enemy was utterly defeated, and Jerusalem, Hebron, Shechem and indeed Eretz Yisrael west of the Jordan river was liberated.

The prayers, fasting, supplications and tears before the Almighty, by world Jewry, ranging from the greatest Rabbis to the Jews in the street, enabled the Israeli armed forces to completely overcome all the Arab armies within just a matter of days. Israel's success was so swift that even University Professors in War Studies could not explain it academically.

Forty years have now passed since those days, and many people are now relating their reminiscences of those historic and miraculous days.

Here is my story....

I first arrived in Israel on 30 August 1966, the day that the new building of the Knesset was officially opened. I was met at the airport by relatives who had lived in Petach Tiqva since the mid-1920s, and I was taken to their home. About a week later I registered in Bet Brodetsky, a hostel for new immigrants, which

262

was situated in Ramat Aviv. I already had a job as a lecturer in Chemistry at Bar-Ilan University and a few weeks later started work there.

As soon as I arrived in Israel, I wanted to visit Jerusalem but was advised that since the border with Jordan went through the city, I should make my first visit with a tour group. I found such a group and booked a tour. The first place we went to was Mount Zion and the guide warned us that the border was adjacent to it and he had strict instructions from his company that we should not cross the border. Soon after, he showed us a low wall and said that wall was the border and he deliberately went a few metres beyond it! Later I learned that the border was in fact about one hundred metres beyond this wall. He also showed us the Mandelbaum Gate which was then a famous tourist attraction, since it was Israel's only crossing point to a neighbouring country.

On Chol Hamoed Pesach of 1967, I went to Mount Zion, climbed up the tower there and looked over to see what I could of the Old City. Little did we then dream that by Shavuot it would be in our hands.

Since the restaurant at Bet Brodetsky was closed throughout Pesach, I made arrangements with some friends of mine who lived very nearby, and whose parents had come over from Britain for an extended holiday, to eat with them throughout Pesach. It was just a couple of weeks after Pesach that Egypt began to move her army into the Sinai Peninsula and the preparations by the neighbouring Arab States for what they hoped to be the destruction of Israel intensified. My friends immediately realizing the potential danger, sent their parents straight back to Britain.

I had at about that period been invited to stay for a Shabbat with the Director of Public Relations of Bar-Ilan University. That Shabbat another guest who was present suggested I go and visit Yeshivat Hagev in Netivot. I took up this suggestion of his.

About ten days before the start of the Six Day War I took a bus to Netivot. I recollect reading a sign during the course of this journey, which said that the border was just ahead. It was the border with the Gaza strip. In those days buses did not go into Netivot, but stopped at the entrance to the city. I got off and went to the house of the Rosh Yeshiva, Rabbi Yissachar Mayer, who spoke perfect English.

I remember the exact date – Friday 16 Iyar (26 May). The reason I can be sure of this was that although Ashkenazim can shave on that day since Lag B'Omer was on the following Sunday, I had not done so, and Rabbi Mayer asked me if I was a Sepharadi. When I arrived in Netivot that day, the Yeshiva students were busy digging trenches to run to in case of air-raid attacks. Although the Yeshiva had recently built a dormitory block, it did not have a shelter. These trenches were in the shape of a zigzag.

After Shabbat I returned to Bet Brodetsky and in a letter to my parents told them I had gone to Netivot and mentioned in passing that the bus going there had gone near the border. I didn't realise at the time that the Jews in the Diaspora were in a terrible panic on account of the situation in Israel and my mother write back that I should not go near any borders. I later learned that parents who had children in Israel, were during those weeks crying during the Shabbat services in the Shuls. My parents had a booking to come to visit Israel – it would be their first visit – on the day the war started (or possibly the day before). However, because of the war, the flights were cancelled and instead they came after the war.

In the weeks before the war, parents were desperately trying to send telegrams to their children to return to the Diaspora. However, since the telephone lines were clogged full, they generally did not succeed, and this included my parents. I had a cousin in Israel at the time. Her father worked for a big firm in London and it had a direct communications line to Israel. He utilized this to send her a telegram to come home. She was furious when she received it and told them: "I would have expected it from anybody but you."

Just before the war began – I don't remember exactly when – there was a meeting between some of the residents and the Manageress of Bet Brodetsky at which some residents offered their services for various civilian tasks in Bet Brodetsky should a war break out. However, when it actually came to the war, I myself didn't notice many of these "volunteers" doing anything. I did not attend simply because I did not know about this meeting in advance.

The Manageress told me that some of the residents had told her that they would leave Israel should a war break out but they would return to Bet Brodetsky after the war! She replied to them that she didn't know whether there would still be a Bet Brodetsky after the war (from this answer one can see how seriously those in Israel regarded the Arab threats of annihilation of Israel) and even if there was, whether Bet Brodetsky would be prepared to take them back. I told her that I had no intention of leaving Israel and she answered that she had been sure that that was the case.

At that period (I don't remember whether it was before, during, or soon after the war) some English speaking journalists from abroad came to Bet Brodetsky and had a meeting with some of the residents, which included myself. I spoke at this meeting and knowing how journalists are likely to write down something quite different from what one says to them, I asked one of them to read back what he had written. What he read out, not only was not what I said, it didn't even make any sense!

During this pre-war period, I put up notices in my room concerning the trust we must have in the Almighty. These were the days when the noose was tightening around Israel. The Egyptians had moved their forces into the Sinai Peninsula. Nasser had ordered the United Nations to remove their peace keeping forces from Sinai, resulting in the immediate compliance by the United Nations. The Straits of Tiran were closed to Israeli shipping thus cutting off Israel's trade to the Far East. King Hussein of Jordan signed a defence treaty with Egypt. Syria and Jordan amassed their armed forces around Israel's eastern border.

On the Thursday before the Six Day War, the Israeli Chief Rabbinate declared a fast and the Synagogues were filled with worshippers. I myself fasted and went to the Minchah service held at the Synagogue at Bar-Ilan University which was full with both men and women worshippers.

The war began on Monday 5 June. In fact, that morning I overslept and was awoken by the wail of a siren at about eight o'clock. Only when I got to the University did I learn that the war had started. The staff from the Chemistry department were busy moving expensive equipment and inflammable chemicals into a safer location. One of the staff was still busy with taking a final research reading on one of these machines!

During the course of that day, we were running in and out of the air-raid shelters at the bidding of the sirens. A story was being passed around that the Administrative Director of the University had heard that Israel had destroyed 400 Arab aircraft and that he was jumping for joy. However, at the time we dismissed this as wishful thinking. My immediate reaction was that someone had added a few noughts! As I recollect, the Staff were told to return home early.

I had heard that day that shortages could occur with food and so I immediately on returning to Bet Brodetsky went to the supermarket which was situated nearby and bought a large number of tinned goods. Due to the fact that in the end there were no food shortages, I didn't use any of these tins. After the war I offered to give them to my relatives in Petach Tiqva, but they told me they didn't use such tins. I don't recollect what finally happened to them.

Because of the danger of aerial bombardment, a blackout was imposed and during the course of that day instructions to its implementation were given over the radio. (There was not yet television in Israel.) Vehicle drivers were given instructions how to blackout their headlights and because of this, in order to avoid accidents, a strict speed restriction was imposed for night-time.

The lights in the corridors of Bet Brodetsky were the type that when one pressed a switch to turn them on, they remained on for a short period and then went off automatically. One could not turn them off manually. This was of course a problem when there is a blackout, since when these corridor lights are on, one can see the light outside through the windows. The residents would out of habit press these light switches during the war. The solution would have been to disconnect these lights at the main switch but as the Manageress pointed out this would also turn off the enormous refrigerator which had a compartment for every two residents and which was operated from the same main switch. I don't know if and how this problem was solved. I do recollect that on one occasion when a light was seen from outside, one of the civil defense people on duty outside, called out "Bet Brodetsky. Turn off the light."

That Monday night, as soon as it got dark, the sirens again sounded. I even remember the exact time 19.20 hours, since I was just about to daven Ma'ariv. All those in Bet Brodetsky ran to the shelter where we remained until the all-clear signal which was about an hour and a half later. The room used as a shelter had some small windows near to the ceiling and either on that Monday or the following day, the residents put sand bags by these windows. The public had been informed that they could take sand from where it was to be found but they should not leave a hole for passers-by to fall into.

In order to break the tension of just sitting in a shelter, some residents turned on their transistor radios to play some music, but someone called out hysterically: "Turn it off, people are at the moment being killed." Whilst in the shelter, I could hear bangs in the distance and I assumed that Tel Aviv was being bombed. When I finally came out, I could see a fire in the distance and assumed Tel Aviv was burning.

I went to bed full of apprehension, fully clothed, since I thought there might well be further air-raids that night. At about four o'clock in the morning, I was woken up to another siren, and wondered whether I had slept through any air-raids – but I hadn't. It was back to the shelter and I saw that almost no-one had changed into pyjamas that night.

Opposite Bet Brodetsky was the local Shul and about six o'clock or six thirty that Tuesday morning I went there to daven Shacharit. We had reached about the Shema, when the siren sounded. The Shliach Tzibur continued as if nothing was happening, although he did recite the shortened repetition of the Amidah. However, after the service he added some Tehillim. Someone, I think he may have been the gabbai, opened the big windows of the Shul when the siren sounded, presumably to minimize the effect of any possible blast. Meanwhile some civil defense people had arrived and immediately after these Tehillim, told the people to go straight to the shelter, and should there be an air raid in the future, they should continue davening in the shelter.

That day – Tuesday - I stayed in Bet Brodetsky. The previous night, when not in the shelters, some of the residents sat in the lounge. Having big windows, they of course had to sit in the dark. I felt that this should not have to be repeated and that black blankets should be nailed over these windows. The management supplied me with the materials and tools to do this job. The news that day was far better and the destruction of 400 enemy aircraft appeared in that day's newspapers, and I had my transistor radio by my side to hear updates of the news. It was not easy to nail up these heavy blankets single-handed but I struggled to do so. There was one other person at the time in the lounge. Instead of offering to help, he turned on my transistor and demanded I make less noise banging in the nails for these blankets since it disturbed him listening to the transistor. Afterwards I checked the efficiency of these blankets from the outside of the building, but apart from one very tiny spot of light shining through a flaw in the weave of the blanket when viewed from a certain angle, no light penetrated to the outside. I asked the civil defence person on duty whether this tiny spot mattered and he said it was of no significance.

As that day progressed, the news became more exciting, especially in the case of Jerusalem. I would go round to people, especially those I thought would be in the know, asking how the war around Jerusalem was progressing. One person even drew me a sketch showing which areas we had already captured and which areas were at the time giving more trouble in capturing.

The first thing the following morning – Wednesday 7 June - I listened to the BBC World News which said that the Old City of Jerusalem had been virtually captured by the Israelis. I went to Shul full of excitement and said to some worshippers that the Old City was in our hands. One of the worshippers asked how I knew this and told him in English what I had heard on the BBC. He told me he didn't understand English and I translated it into Hebrew. That day, the Likud daily newspaper "Hayom" had a cartoon of the Kotel with arms coming out of it embracing an Israeli soldier and saying: "I have waited for you for 19 years."

On that Wednesday I went to the University. I felt sure that there would be no more air-raids. On the way I decided to go into my bank which was in Ramat Gan. Whilst I was on the bus, the siren sounded. The bus immediately stopped and everyone ran off looking for the nearest shelter. After the all-clear sounded I went on to the bank and then the University. Throughout the day I tried to get further information on what was happening in Jerusalem and in Judea and Samaria. It wasn't until the mid-afternoon that I officially heard of the liberation of the Old City of Jerusalem.

I learned that day that Shechem and Nablus were the same place! Whenever I heard that a place in Judea and Samaria had been liberated, such as Bethlehem or Gush Etzion, I looked to see where it was on the map. I heard that Shechem had been liberated but wondered what had happened with Nablus!

That night whilst sitting in the lounge of Bet Brodetsky I would listen hour after hour to the news, which included the service at the Kotel immediately after it had been liberated. Even though I heard it numerous times, it was just as exciting each time. I afterwards heard from someone living abroad that not only could they hear the service, they could also see it on the television.

On the following day – Thursday 8 June – it was announced that there would be a ceasefire between Israel and Jordan and I was worried whether it would come into effect before the complete liberation of Judea and Samaria. Would Hebron be liberated? It took me a little time to discover that Israel had in fact managed to liberate all these areas.

That day, Bar-Ilan University made an impromptu celebration in their restaurant in which both academic and administrative staff participated. One of the Chemistry lecturers was full of excitement that he climbed on a table in the department and either drew or pointed to a map of the places Israel had liberated. Sadly, he received news in the subsequent days that two of his sons had been killed in this war. He heard this news regarding each son separately. When it was known that a second son had been killed, his friends were debating how to break the news to him.

By that Friday 9 June, the war with Egypt and Jordan was over and the battle continued for another two days with Syria on the Golan Heights. I decided to spend that Shabbat with my relatives in Petach Tiqva. The blackout restrictions were still in effect and I saw notices from Rabbi Lande of Bnei Brak that one should not have any lights in a place where it might be found necessary to extinguish them on Shabbat. In fact, just minutes before Shabbat it was announced that the blackout was cancelled.

Shavuot was on the following Wednesday and it was announced that the Kotel would be open to Jews from that day onwards. I was sure that it would be very crowded and that it would thus be near impossible to approach it and so I decided to wait a few days. On the Thursday I asked someone who had been there on Shavuot whether it was possible to get near the Kotel and he said it was possible. It was too late to go that day and I decided to go on the following Sunday.

The only road then open to the Kotel was via Mount Zion. I don't remember whether one entered the Old City via Zion Gate or the Dung Gate. The Jerusalem railway station was opposite Mount Zion and I therefore went by train from Tel Aviv – the train was crowded - to Jerusalem. I walked up Mount Zion, over the old border and excitedly approached and went through the gate in the Old City wall. I then walked along a path, with barriers at each side warning people that there might be mines across these barriers.

After a few minutes I reached the Kotel. The area in front of the Kotel which had been originally been full of dwellings had already been demolished by the Israelis, thus giving a much larger praying area. Whilst there that day, I recited the entire book of Tehillim. I afterwards wrote to my parents that this had been the best day of my life,

A few weeks later, the city of Jerusalem was unified and was brought under Israeli sovereignty. Jews could then go freely all over Jerusalem. A day or so later was Shabbat and I was in Jerusalem for that Shabbat, although I cannot remember where I stayed. It was probably in some Yeshiva. Incidentally, I had planned being in Jerusalem that Shabbat before I knew that the whole city would be open to Jews.

Already on the Friday. I walked to the Old City. I was not the only one with this idea, since its narrow streets were packed out. Again on the Shabbat I went for a walk in the Old City and again the streets were crowded.

A week or so later, Bar-Ilan University arranged a tour of Judea and Samaria. This took place on the Sunday of Rosh Chodesh Tammuz. I particularly remember the date since one of the participants said he was going to daven Mussaf at the Kotel during the course of this tour.

Since the tour was going to start early on the Sunday morning, I spent Shabbat at Bar-Ilan. One of the academic staff of Bar-Ilan acted as the tour guide giving explanations at every place that we visited. However, I can only recollect a few of the details of this tour. We first went, I think, to some archaeological site in Samaria. The Old City of Jerusalem was of course on the itinerary and at the Kotel we met up with the Chancellor of Bar-Ilan University who addressed us. We also went, amongst other places. to the Cave of Machpelah in Hebron. Although towards the end of the tour it was already getting towards night, some of the participants wanted to visit Jericho, and we quickly went there and back. During the course of the traveling, one of the men who had a pleasant voice sang a number of songs via the loudspeaker system of the coach. One of the songs was "Ata chonein leadam daat." During the final part of the return journey, when it was already dark and many of the participants were already sleeping, one of the boys on the coach suddenly starting singing through this loudspeaker system, not to the satisfaction of some of those on the coach!

Forty years have now past since those days, when with the help of the Almighty we succeeded in the course of a few days in getting Eretz Yisrael west of the Jordan River in our possession. Sadly, instead of massive settlement of Jews in all these liberated areas – and had we had the desire, there could be millions of Jews in Judea and Samaria today – groups of Jews have had to fight with the Israeli government to build almost every apartment. Let us now change our ways and instead of expelling Jews, build,

build and more build, and thus have a massive settlement of Jews in all the liberated areas of Eretz Yisrael.

⚜ ⚜ ⚜ ⚜ ⚜ ⚜ ⚜ ⚜ ⚜ ⚜ ⚜

60 HARROWES MEADE
Reminiscences of my first home 1942 - 1966

In the years following their marriage in 1933, my parents lived in a rented house in Northfield Road in the Stamford Hill area of North London, together with my maternal grandmother and her other three children. It was in 1939 that they all decided to move and someone suggested to them - Edgware. When I once asked my father why they decided to move from their house in Stamford Hill, my father answered that the house was rented and that they were paying someone else's mortgage. My father was a firm believer in, as he said, "bricks and mortar" – in other words buying one's own house and not renting one. He would say that 60 Harrowes Meade was his second-best acquisition – his best acquisition was my mother. I have likewise followed his dictum of house purchase, and as soon as it was possible bought a house first in Liverpool and then in Kiryat Arba and a few years later also bought out the neighbour's apartment in Kiryat Arba.

It was in 1939 that my parents bought 60 Harrowes Meade and at the same time my widowed grandmother bought a house about three-minute walk away in the next road, Francklyn Gardens. The price paid for 60 Harrowes Meade, as I was told, was £950. [In 2011, the price of such a house in Harrowes Meade is in the region of half a million pounds! – *information from the internet*]

The house my parents bought was the last one built in Harrowes Meade and only several years after the end of the Second World War were houses built up to the end of the road – I believe the last house was number 90.

It was about November 1939, which was a few months after the start of the Second World War, that my parents moved into their new house. The house was semi-semi-detached, namely, the front half of the house was detached, whilst the back half was joined to the neighouring house. The house had two floors. On the ground floor, one entered from the street door into a largish hall and on either side of the hall, there was a large room. A disadvantage of this type of structure was that one could not knock in a wall between the two large downstairs rooms to make a very large room. On this ground floor, there was also the kitchen. On the upper floor there were three bedrooms and a toilet and separate bathroom. At first, one of the bedrooms was used as my father's office, but during the 1950s, the garage was refurbished and became his office.

The house had both a front and back garden. A number of fruit trees were planted in the back garden – two apple trees, two pear trees and a couple of other fruit trees. We had a nice crop of fruit each autumn. When I was young, I remember the front garden being uprooted and being cemented over.

The kitchen appliances were quite different in design than those found today. The refrigerator worked by gas and to make it work, there was a place to light (as in a gas stove) underneath the refrigerator. The icebox was a tiny thing situated inside the refrigerator at the top right hand side corner. The refrigerator stood on longish legs which were visible.

To heat the kitchen, there was a boiler in that room which worked on coal. Every year, we would order a number of sacks of coal and when it was delivered it would be stored in a coalbunker in our back yard. Having such a coal fire was a boon on erev Pesach, since one could burn the chametz without having to specially make a bonfire. There was also an "ascot" in the kitchen to heat water and this hot water was stored in a tank in the bathroom.

The kitchen also had a lot of fitted cupboards. My mother had some more cupboards built near the ceiling to store the Pesach crockery. The Pesach pots and pans were stored in a big cupboard in the bathroom.

Until about the 1950s, we had no washing machine for clothes. All the washing had to be done by hand. We then bought a machine which one had to fill manually with water and the machine would then just swivel the washing around. The washing would then manually have to be put through a wringer powered by electricity. It was then transferred to a drier which one had to hold down to prevent it jumping all over the kitchen. The washing machine was stored just inside the kitchen by the side of the door, while the drier was kept in the cupboard under the stairs which was situated in the kitchen.

When my parents moved into 60 Harrowes Meade, there was no garage, and so they erected a shed. It was only after the Second World War that they decided to have a garage built. Strange as it may seem, it was not easy in those days to find a builder. We had no car and for a number of years we had a table-tennis table (slightly smaller than the regulation size) in the garage and we would often play table-tennis there.

A few years after building the garage, houses were built in the open fields adjoining our house. After they were built, we received a letter of complaint from the Local Council that the colour of the bricks of our garage did not match those of the adjacent new houses. My father who was an expert with his pen answered that it would require a large stretch of imagination to match the colour of bricks with houses which were not yet built!

There is a photograph extant taken in 1945 where one can see in the background the house shed which pre-dated the garage. One can also see that our house was then the last house in the street. (The purpose was not to photograph this part of the house but it was a photograph of me aged two and a half in my pram and the background is in fact incidental!)

Bombs were regularly falling on London in the Second World War, and since Edgware was not exempt from this, it was necessary to have some sort of shelter. My parents bought an indoor shelter which was placed in the dining room in place of a table and indeed served as a table during the war. I was born in the middle of the war and I heard that I was put in this shelter in my sleeping cot. However, I was only a baby at the time and so I do not remember this.

One bomb fell in the fields next to our house. Someone in the family thought it had fallen in our garden. Another fell on a house a few minutes' walk from our house and made a big crack in the outer wall and the house had to be rebuilt. Fortunately, no-one was in the house at the time.

There were also public shelters built in the streets. I remember one of them about two minutes from my house, since it was not demolished until well after the end of the war. I am told that there were places in Edgware where one would have to go a long way to find such a shelter.

My mother told me that one occasion, a relative who lived on the other side of Edgware came on a visit. The day seemed quiet from air raids and my mother took me in my pram to accompany her home. Soon after this relative left her, the sirens rang out warning everyone to go into the shelters, but we were then in a place far, far from any shelter. My mother started running with the pram as fast as she could until she came to the shops on Mowbray parade. She ran into the kosher butcher shop and the butcher's mother-in-law who was there at the time, advised her to get home as quickly as possible, which she did.

Naturally there was a strict blackout every night. One night my parents returned home to see at least one home-guard waiting by the house. What had happened was that a desk light in my father's office in the house which was near to a window had somehow come on – maybe it had a loose switch. The light could be seen about a mile away and the home-guards had traced it to our house. I seem to remember my mother telling me that she told them to take their shoes off before coming into the house. She also said that they carefully looked around the house – maybe they thought we were German agents signalling the enemy aircraft!

Although the Germans dropped a few bombs in Edgware, it was much safer than the centre of London. Therefore, numerous relatives who lived well inside London made extended visits to our house and also to the house of my grandmother in the next street. The wife of my mother's brother came for one weekend and stayed for six years! It is related that on one Shabbat they laid the table for 16 people.

The authorities had a right to billet people in someone's house and the authorities went around the houses to see in which houses they could do so. When they came to our house (or maybe my grandmother's house) and saw how many members of the family there were already there, they jokingly said that **we** needed a further house!

During the Second World War and in the following years, food was scarce and rationed. Every member of the family was given a ration book and I remember going with my mother to get our ration books. One of the items in the ration books was bacon. For people who did not eat bacon, this item was stamped "cancelled" and they got an allocation of margarine instead.

My mother told me that a family received a total of six eggs per month. Once my mother was carrying the month's ration of eggs home in a bag and she dropped the bag. She was near the kosher butcher shop and they gave her a cup to carry home what was left of the eggs.

In the fields next to our house there were allotments and many people used to grow their vegetables there, but my family did not. A neighbour across the road had a relative who had a farm and she would send her from time to time a cucumber. This neighbour would sometimes cut off a small piece and give it to my mother. Today this may sound funny, but in the war years it was a treat to even receive a bit of cucumber.

The price of food was also strictly controlled. My mother bought her groceries from a local Jewish grocer, a Mrs. Harris, and she was friendly with her. It seems that on one or more items, Mrs. Harris charged a halfpenny or even a farthing (which was half a halfpenny) more than the permitted price, but my mother did not object. Someone must have lodged a complaint, because one day as the delivery boy was bringing our order, a food inspector stopped him and obviously studied the bill. Mrs. Harris was summoned and my mother was called as a witness for the prosecution. My mother told me that at the Court, much to the consternation of the prosecution, she was happily chattering with Mrs. Harris. I assume Mrs. Harris was fined for overcharging.

Someone recommended to my mother that she gets her Pesach groceries from Selfridges. My grandmother was apprehensive – What! get her Pesach order from a non-Jewish shop! My mother therefore took my grandmother to Selfridges so that they could see for themselves. There they saw that all the Pesach food was in a separate section of the shop and there was a man – in a white coat, as my mother told me – watching over the food. My grandmother and mother were most impressed. Many decades later when I happened to be looking at the "Jewish Chronicle" for that period I saw that the Pesach section of Selfridges was under the supervision of the London Beth Din. The "man in the white coat" was obviously the shomer (Rabbinical supervisor). Selfridges was thus far better for Pesach than many small Jewish grocers where before Pesach the chametz and the Pesach foods are right next to each other.

My mother had a definite weekly routine for her housekeeping. On Wednesday she would go to the butcher to buy meat and chicken, which would then be delivered to the house. Unlike today, in those days the housewife had to do the salting ("koshering") process herself in order to remove all the internal blood. At first my great aunt did the salting process and a few years later it was taken over by my mother. The fowls in those days were quite mature and as I recollect, they weighed over 2 kilos each. Often partially formed eggs were found in them and they were a great delicacy in the chicken soup. After all the salting process had been completed, my mother would put the chickens in a bowl of boiling water ("breeing upp" as she would call it) and then clean the outside of the chickens

Thursday was "fish day" and on Thursday morning my mother would make the gefillte fish. The cleaned fish arrived from the kosher fishmonger. My mother did not have a mincer and all the chopping was done by hand using a chopper and a chopping board. If my great aunt saw my mother doing the chopping she would say "klap noch a bissel" (chop a bit more). After the chopping of the fish was completed, the other ingredients were added and the fish balls were put in a saucepan of hot water to which fish skeletons supplied by the fishmonger had been added.

I remember making up the name "geshaiach" for these fish skeletons – I don't know what made me make up this name! This liquid was then used a fish soup for our Thursday dinner which was always a fish dinner – (on the other days of the week we had a meat dinner). After about an hour, the gefillte fish were ready.

My mother could be classed as an authority on cookery. Over the course of the years, she gave about seventy recipes to the newspaper the "Jewish Review" on a strictly honorary basis. One of them was her gefillte fish recipe which was especially well welcomed by the readers. She had an enormous selection of cake and kichels recipes. For many years she would make them each week by hand without the use of a cake mixer. Eventually she bought a mixer but at first they did not turn out right. She then went to a demonstration class given by the manufacturers of this mixer and she learned that with this mixer one can overbeat a cake, something which never arose when using just one's hands to beat.

Over the years, my family made no major changes to the house. The minor changes involved closing in the porch, laying fitted carpets and of course periodic decorating and painting the inside and outside of the house.

My family lived in 60 Harrowes Meade from the autumn of 1939 until my mother came to Israel in the summer of 1978 – my father had died three years earlier. I lived there until the summer of 1966.

TWO YEARS IN BET HADASSAH
Reminiscences of a Pioneer 1981 - 1983

In the centre of Hebron are situated many Jewish owned buildings. After the Jewish community had been forced to leave Hebron in the period of the British Mandate, Arab squatters took over these buildings. These buildings include Bet Hadassah, Bet Romano, Bet Schneersohn, and the Avraham Avinu complex.

Sadly, with the liberation of Hebron, the Israeli Government did nothing to return these buildings to the Jews. Any action to reclaim them had to be done, over the opposition of the Israeli Government, by individuals "taking the law into their own hands."

It was soon after Pesach 1979 that a group of women in the dead of night "broke into" Bet Hadassah and set up residence. The Government put a siege on the place but the women stuck fast. Gradually the siege was lifted.

On the morning of the First Day of Rosh Hashanah 1979, a Minyan had been held in Bet Hadassah and in the afternoon, a message was sent to Kiryat Arba that people should come on the following day to strengthen the Minyan. I went along. At the time they had no Aron Hakodesh and the Sefer Torah was kept in a recess in the back wall.

For Yom Kippur, I, together with Meir Peretz converted a big wooden carton into an ark by lining it with a sheet. The guard at the gate of Bet Hadassah allowed us to take it in; in those days, one could not be sure what would happen! After my meal before Yom Kippur, I hurried down to Bet Hadassah. I arrived about five minutes before the start of the Fast and they asked me whether I wanted a drink but I declined. An hour or so later I was sorry; all the running down there from Kiryat Arba had taken its toll. All this added to the affliction which is the Mitzvah of Yom Kippur.

The following morning, I again went to Bet Hadassah, first going into the Cave of Machpelah to say some Tehillim. I spent the whole day in Bet Hadassah. During the break between Mussaf and Minchah, Rabbi Levinger brought some mattresses for people to rest on. After Yom Kippur, I asked someone to loan me some money, in the hope that I would find an Arab taxi to return me to Kiryat Arba. Fortunately, I soon found such a taxi.

I had wanted to join the pioneers in Bet Hadassah, but there was then a problem. The eating was communal and the Shemitta year was just starting and they were utilising the "Heter Mechira" which I did not use. However, in the summer of 1981, when the products were no longer Shemitta produce, I was able to realise this ambition. It was on Lag B'Omer, a Friday, that there was the consecration of the rebuilt Avraham Avinu Synagogue and on the same day the Levinger family moved from Bet Hadassah to a refurbished house next to this Synagogue. Two days later my family moved to Bet Hadassah.

That day, I asked Chai Sa'adia, who had a small van whether he could take our effects to Bet Hadassah. He told us that by coincidence his family were also moving there that day. He accordingly took the effects of both families there. Bet Hadassah became my family's dwelling place for nearly two years. I shall now briefly describe a few of the incidents during this period which come into my mind,

My family received a room which was situated on the top floor - the far room on the left-hand side. The room already had internal brick wall partitions and was internally divided into three rooms. When one entered the main door of the room one came to a narrow room - about 2 metres in width, which extended along the whole length of the room. Off this room were two squarish rooms which we utilised as bedrooms - one for Dina and myself and the other for the children, who then numbered six. A few months later the seventh was born. The latter room was filled with beds, a double bunk and cots. When we first received this area, the narrow room was filled with all sorts of furniture and junk and we spent some time clearing it and sorting it out.

Several families were living on the two floors of this building, each of them having received one room. The corridor of the lower floor was used as the communal dining room. One room on the upper floor served as the Bet Hamedrash. Every facility involving water was confined to the front area of the building.

In the city of Hebron, there were often water stoppages. In such cases, the army would bring along water in big tankards and from them fill our tanks. In 1982, Rosh Hashanah was on Thursday and Friday, meaning that there would be three days, when if there were stoppages of water, we would not be able to call on the army. We accordingly asked, Rabbi Lior, if on Yom-Tov we could get the Arab Hebron Municipality to fill our tanks from their tankards. I was told that he gave permission for Yom-Tov but added that such permission did not extend to Shabbat. In fact, all this was fortunately unnecessary, since the army instructed the Hebron Municipality to ensure that the water to Bet Hadassah would not be cut off during these three days.

During the period I was in Bet Hadassah, we managed to gain possession of other Jewish property in Hebron such as Bet Schneersohn and Bet Harokeach. As soon as we gained possession, we immediately "created facts" and transferred families there. The Sa'adia family went to Bet Rokeach and the Oriel family to Bet Schneerson. In the latter there was a problem. One of the rooms there prior to 1929 had been used as a Synagogue and the question arose whether one could now use it as a living room.

However, the major building which we regained possession of, was Bet Romano. This was a very large building owned by the Lubavitch. Up to that period, the Arabs were using it as a school. On the same day as we gained possession, Rabbi Levinger told us to go there and take out all the furniture. This was not a simple job. In any school there is a mass of school desks and other equipment. We moved most of it into the grounds at the back until it was chock-a-block with furniture. At a later date, the Hebron Arab Municipality took away the furniture. To make as much use as possible of the place, we immediately opened a Bet Hamedrash there in place of that at Bet Hadassah. Within a few weeks a Yeshivah, Shavei Hevron was opened there.

The Religious Council of Kiryat Arba extended the Eruv to incorporate all these buildings. I was asked to check each week that the wire near Bet Hadassah was still intact.

When my family first went to live there, we took only a limited amount of furniture but as time progressed, we took down more things. In the beginning we would eat in the communal dining room, but after several months, we decided we would install our own private kitchen in our room. We therefore employed a plumber to install a sink together with a draining board and cupboards underneath it. Since the source of water and the drainage was at the opposite side of the building, we had to install extensive piping. We also brought over our refrigerator and gas cooker from Kiryat Arba.

However, one cannot live without problems. One such problem was a fight with Ampa to service our refrigerator which had stopped working whilst we were at Bet Hadassah. This is discussed in detail in the next chapter.

On Sukkot, a big Sukkah was built in the grounds of Bet Hadassah. In addition, on the two Sukkot when I was there, I arranged for Chai Sa'adia to bring the sections of my Sukkah to Bet Hadassah. On one evening during Chol Hamoed, I went to a Simchat Bet Hashoeva out of town. I returned to Kiryat Arba in someone's car at about midnight. I then walked alone in the dead of night unarmed to Bet Hadassah. Then only sounds I could hear on the way were dogs barking.

The second Purim I was there, occurred on Motzoei Shabbat. The Ulpana at Kiryat Arba had asked me to read the Megillah for them that evening - my "unique style" of reading it was very popular - and it was arranged that they would collect me by car immediately after Shabbat. However, no-one knows what the weather will be like and that Shabbat it snowed; by the end of Shabbat the roads were blocked. I therefore ended up hearing the Megillah in Bet Romano.

On one occasion, the Israeli television came to film how we were living and at a later date I saw the programme. My daughter Hadassah was an expert in getting in front of the camera! She would conveniently appear several times wheeling a pram backwards and forwards and again "conveniently" appear to lay cutlery on the table.

The Bet Hadassah building was in a poor state of preservation. We lived on the top floor and we could see the metal girders in the roof which were very rusty and, as we learned towards the end of our stay there, very dangerous. It was on one Motzoei Shabbat that I was in my room, when I heard a loud bang. A sizeable chunk of the metal girder had fallen off hitting the fluorescent light during its descent. Fortunately, I was not in direct line of the projectile!

We then saw that we could not continue living in that particular room, and we moved to a room on the lower floor. Since this room was much smaller, we also partitioned off a part of the adjacent corridor. Soon after, the Government agreed to completely renovate Bet Hadassah and it was thus necessary for all the families to vacate it. We therefore returned to Kiryat Arba in time for Pesach 1983. We had been pioneering there for almost two years and thus had made our contribution to the resettlement of Jews in the heart of Hebron.

MY FIGHT WITH "AMPA"

A few months after my family went to Bet Hadassah, we transported our "Amcor" refrigerator there from Kiryat Arba. I wrote a letter to Ampa (who were the servicing agents for "Amcor" appliances) notifying them of my change of address.

After the initial one-year guarantee on such an appliance expires, one can take out a service contract with the company by virtue of which they have to come within a certain number of days and repair such an appliance when it breaks down. In Israel, this is in fact a statutory requirement. However, as I soon learned, when I was in Bet Hadassah, this statutory requirement at that period did not include Judea and Samaria, although Ampa did come to Kiryat Arba.

I must have heard from other people living in Bet Hadassah that Ampa refused to come to Bet Hadassah. Although my refrigerator was then in working order, towards the end of October 1981, I telephoned to Ampa and they informed me that people owning Ampa appliances who lived in Hebron did not qualify to receive the service set out in the service contract, even though they had paid the premium. To get service they had to bring the appliances to Kiryat Arba. I wrote them a letter asking them to let me know in writing whether this information was correct or, maybe I had misunderstood Ampa during my telephone conversation with them.

One should remember here that one is not dealing with a small portable appliance such as a toaster, but a very large heavy refrigerator, and what is more, transporting it from place to place to can cause further damage.

When I eventually received a reply from Ampa, after having sent them a reminder, they proudly stated that they were the first company to give service over the "green line." However, they quickly added that there was a limitation – they only gave it to Jewish settlements.

I passed this letter over to the lawyer Elyakim Haetzni, and he immediately wrote to Ampa. In his letter, Haetzni argued in three ways. The first was the public and moral angle. He asked why a large company should "punish" pioneers: "Is this how you encourage the return of the Jewish people to the city of Hebron?" he asked and furthermore asked whether Ampa wanted their conduct to be publicised in the media.

He then continued with the logical angle asking what disqualification is there in Hebron and whether it was the presence of Arabs. If so, argued Haetzni, then you should also disqualify Acre, Haifa, Ramla and Lod and he also asked whether they gave service to the wholly Arab cities of Nazareth, Shafaram, Taibe, etc.

Haetzni's final angle was the legal one. He expanded on Ampa's refusal to give service to the Jews of Hebron by asking whether there were Arabs in Hebron who had service contracts with Ampa and whether distinguishing between Jews and Arabs would stand up in court. He concluded his letter by asking them to reconsider the matter.

Ampa answered Haetzni that they were not prepared to enter into a political dialogue. They pointed out that they do not give service in "Arab settlements in these places" adding that the reason is not to endanger their technicians. They concluded that in my specific case, my permanent abode was Kiryat Arba and they will be happy to answer my requests for service there.

At the period of the above correspondence, I had no need for service from Ampa. However, there is a saying that one should not open one's mouth for the Satan.

It was during Chol Hamoed Pesach of that year that my refrigerator without warning suddenly stopped working.

Fortunately, there was a very big communal refrigerator in Bet Hadassah and my family transferred all our food there.

Despite the fact that Ampa had informed us that they did not give service to the Jews of Hebron, on 16 April 1982 I telephoned Ampa and ordered service for my refrigerator. The telephonist informed me that their technician does not come to Bet Hadassah and that I should bring my refrigerator to Kiryat Arba. I asked her what clause in the service contract enabled them not to come but she declined to argue. I told her that I would put the matter in other hands.

A few days later, I telephoned the Ministry of Commerce and explained to a clerk called Chezi what was happening. Chezi told me to write to his office enclosing copies of the service contract, and my notification of change in address. I explained the urgency of the matter since it was the summer season and I was without a refrigerator and he promised to contact Ampa straight away.

In my letter to Chezi, I gave the background to my problem and continued that Ampa had "informed me that the technician was under no circumstances prepared to travel to my house, something which was in clear breach of my contract with them and contempt towards a citizen who had paid for a service which was not being provided when needed." I added that this was not an isolated case. I concluded pointing out the urgency of the case and requesting their speedily action. I enclosed copies of both my refrigerator and washing machine service contracts and a copy of the letter notifying them of my change of address to Bet Hadassah.

Two days later my wife spoke to Chezi and he explained that there was not yet a law in force Ampa to give service over the "green line," but despite this he would try.

The office of the Ministry of Commerce investigated my complaint and informed me that Ampa had told them that they were not prepared to give service at Bet Hadassah but if I brought the refrigerator to Kiryat Arba they would service it there. The letter continued that the Israeli law did not yet apply over the "green line" and therefore they could not obligate Ampa to give me service in Bet Hadassah.

I then decided that the time had come to write the newspapers on this matter. Here is my letter written in June 1982 which I sent to many Israeli newspapers:

> Ampa performs repairs on Amcor appliances (refrigerators, washing machines, etc.) for customers who have taken out the annual service policy. According to the terms of this policy, repairs are carried out at the customer's home. Also, anyone who changes his address during the period of this policy need only notify Ampa of this change and the policy continues automatically at the new address.
>
> I took out this service policy for my Amcor appliances. After I moved to Bet Hadassah, which is situated in the re-established Jewish (Chabad) Quarter of Hebron, I notified Ampa in writing of my change of address. When my refrigerator ceased functioning, I requested service from Ampa but they informed me that they refused to come to my home and if I wanted service, I would have to bring my refrigerator to Kiryat Arba or Jerusalem!
>
> In my opinion, this is a fragrant breach of the terms of the service policy. It is also manifestly absurd – we are talking about a refrigerator, not a portable radio or cassette recorder! To move a refrigerator requires a large truck, together with porters, not to mention the fact that further damage may likely result during transit.
>
> Sadly, my experience with Ampa is not an isolated incident. All my neighbours in Bet Hadassah who have requested service from Ampa have received the same response.
>
> I would like to know how a major Israeli corporation is permitted to accept my premiums for a service policy and then refuse to grant me the required service.

I know that at least the newspaper "Hatzofe" published my letter and what is more, in its entirety. I also know that "Ma'ariv," "Yediot Aharonot" and "Davar" asked Ampa for their comments.

Ampa replied to these newspapers by enclosing a copy of the letter they had sent to Haetzni adding that their stand in this matter had not changed. Ampa argued that I had paid my premium on the basis of my Kiryat Arba address and that if I request, they will cancel my service contract with them and refund my money.

I immediately replied to these newspapers answering the arguments put forward by Ampa. I pointed out that Ampa was not doing a favour by giving service – it was a legal obligation, and that a change in address does not nullify the service contract. Ampa had argued that it was dangerous for their technicians to come to Hebron. In reply, I said that such a statement was very strange. They were prepared to send a technician all the way from Jerusalem to Kiryat Arba, a journey which goes via many Arab locations, and this was far more dangerous than the short journey from Kiryat Arba to Hebron. Several months earlier the Kiryat Arba Municipal Council stated that they were prepared to give a security escort for their technicians, but Ampa had not even given any response to this offer.

A day earlier "Yediot Aharonot" had written a longish article headed "Who is afraid to repair a refrigerator in Hebron" in which they summarized what had occurred up to date in this matter.

It was at the same period that the Ministry of Commerce wrote to me informing me that the regulations requiring the giving of service over the "green line" had not yet been promulgated and so they could therefore not obligate Ampa to give me service in Hebron.

I therefore then wrote a letter to the Yesha Council to put them in the picture. I pointed out that all that was preventing the solution to this problem was the signature of the Minister of Commerce and Industry on the regulations to give service over the "green line" and they should exert pressure on the Minister and on Knesset Members so that the Minister will sign these regulations.

At the beginning of August 1982, the renewal of my service contract with Ampa became due and I notified Ampa in writing that my address was Bet Hadassah. Thus their argument that when I paid my premium my address was Kiryat Arba was no longer valid. Furthermore, they took my money and made no

287

comment that my address was now Bet Hadassah. Yet Ampa still refused to give me service. I telephoned Chezi at the Ministry of Commerce but he replied which a very strange and unacceptable answer that he did not consider it sufficient just to write my change of address but I need to get a definite agreement of Ampa to such a change in address.

I did not accept this answer of Chezi's and I wrote to the Ministry of Commerce a further letter but received a negative reply. I replied reiterating that when I paid my current premium, I gave my address as Bet Hadassah. I have no record of any further correspondence with him.

When just before the following Pesach I returned to Kiryat Arba since we had to vacate Bet Hadassah since the Israeli Government had agreed to completely refurbish the place. I took my refrigerator to Kiryat Arba where Ampa immediately repaired it – the entire motor had to be replaced.

However, I had to pay a considerable sum to the porters and for the transport of my refrigerator and washing machine from Bet Hadassah to Kiryat Arba – a sum of one thousand (old) Shekalim. I wrote to Ampa pointing out that they had told me to bring it to Kiryat Arba for repairs and they should refund me the thousand shekels. Ampa replied that this transport was nothing to do with them. I replied to Ampa that I had informed them of my change in address and they had even recorded my address as Bet Hadassah on their computer. They replied admitting that I had notified them of my change of address adding that they had recorded this change without paying attention to it. They thus agreed that under these circumstances they had to pay the transport costs and they enclosed a cheque for one thousand shekels.

YESHIVAH STUDENTS ARE NOT STUDENTS!

When I went to inquire about my customs exemption for new Olim, on the grounds that my rights had not yet run out since I was a student, I was informed that "Yeshivah students are not students." I would not accept this absurd statement and fought a successful battle to have the regulations changed.

Although all this occurred whilst I was living in the Hebron Military Compound it was in no way directly connected with Hebron. This very same battle could have occurred were I to have been studying in a Yeshivah elsewhere in Israel. I feel that this is a chapter that should be recorded in the interest of the fights that go on to this very day in Israel to grant Yeshivah student the same rights as other students.

It was soon after Pesach 1970, that we decided that we needed a new refrigerator and washing machine. The customs dues on these items was high, and there was an exemption for new immigrants, with extensions in the period for students at an "Institute of higher learning." The official regulation added: "An 'Institute of higher learning' for this purpose, is an institute which grants, after completion of study, an academic degree...."

When I tried to utilise this regulation, I encountered problems, which did not come as a surprise to me. I had had the feeling that the wording was such that it would exclude Yeshivah students! I therefore went to speak to S. Dror, the official responsible for personal imports at the Customs. At the meeting I argued that "Semichah" was the "academic degree" awarded by a Yeshivah and that the Ministry of Education recognised it as a B.A. degree. Dror asked me to bring such a letter from the Ministry of Education.

I found that getting such a letter from an official of the Ministry of Education was not simple. Their clerks would give it to me verbally but when I asked for it in writing they shuddered: "It's an internal regulation," they said: "Let me have a photocopy," I requested. Again a refusal.

I went into Yeshivat Mercaz Harav and told them the problem and asked their advice. One said that I should ask the secretary of "Mossad Harav Kook" an organisation who utilised this Ministry of Education regulation, to give me a letter that such a recognition of Semichah exists. Understandably, the secretary there said she had no power to do so and that only the Ministry of Education could give such a letter.

Someone then recommended that I should ask Rabbi Dr. Yaacov Ross who was an inspector at the Ministry of Education. I had met Rabbi Ross when he had been Principal of Jews College in London, although I don't think that he remembered me. I thus went again to the Ministry of Education and explained to him the problem. Unlike all the other officials, he immediately agreed to give me such a letter and I should come back a few days later to collect it, which I did.

I then had another meeting with the Dror and showed him this letter. He agreed to consult with the legal adviser and that that I should write him a letter with my request for customs exemption enclosing Dr. Ross' letter. In reply to my letter, he wrote that it was only the "equivalent" of a degree and not the degree itself. On receiving his letter, I had a further meeting with him, at which he told me that he cannot go against his legal adviser in the definition of a "Institute of higher learning." I then tried to argue, but without success, that the regulation did not say a "University degree" but an "academic degree" and that is what Semichah was. (I should also mention that at a meeting I had with the "Va'ad Hayeshivot," they likewise held that Semichah was an academic degree.)

I saw that this approach was not getting me anywhere and so I decided on sending letters to the newspapers and the religious Members of the Knesset. I wrote:

New Olim are granted customs concessions for a specified period of time when purchasing goods, and such periods are extended for Olim who start to study at an institute of higher learning. However, the Management of the Customs and Excise Office have informed me that the definition of an 'Institute of higher learning' in the Customs Regulations does not include Yeshivot. Such discrimination against Yeshivot is very difficult to understand and is made far more serious by the fact that a large number of the student Olim study in Yeshivot.

Perhaps the Minister of Finance can prevent this discrimination in the future by undertaking to ensure that Yeshivah students receive the same customs concessions as students at other institutions.

A number of newspapers published my letter and some sent it to the Ministry of Finance for their comments. In their fairly long rambling reply, they spoke of the "impossibility of including Yeshivot" within the framework they themselves had set up. Surely the whole point of my letter was to state that their definition was discriminatory and therefore needed to be changed!

The Ministry of Absorption Yeshivah Department also obviously had a positive interest to resolve this problem and I met with their Director, Yonatan Ben-Ari to put him in the picture and he promised to look into the problem. A few weeks later he wrote to me saying that this matter was the business of the Customs.

Also during this period, I had several meetings at the Ministry of Religious Affairs with Rabbi Klein of their Yeshivah department and the Ministry's legal adviser. The latter admitted that an "academic degree" was a university degree and that I should ask the customs why their regulations were unclear and they should have specifically written that this exemption does not apply to Yeshivah students. I asked him whether there was a legal definition of a Yeshivah, or could any few people learning together call themselves a Yeshivah. He replied that there was a legal definition.

At my final meeting with this legal adviser, he said that he would write to Zerach Wahaftig, the Minister of Religious Affairs suggesting an addition to the Customs' definition of "Institute of Higher Learning" in order to incorporate Yeshivot. That very day, Wahaftig wrote to the Minister of Finance pointing out that there was no room for discrimination against Olim who were Yeshivah students, especially as they represented an important segment of the potential Aliyah from the West. To solve the problem, he proposed an amendment to the Customs regulation. This letter to the Finance Minister was either as a result of a letter I had written to Wahaftig about a month earlier, or by the legal adviser contacting him immediately, or a combination of both. Which of these three alternatives, I don't know?

Meanwhile other Knesset members were also acting on this question. Zevulun Hammer submitted a parliamentary question to the Minister of Finance. He asked whether the information on this non-exemption of customs dues for Yeshivah students was correct? Why was there this difference between them and other students? What does the Minister intend doing to eliminate this difference? I never received a copy of the answers given to these questions. I do know from a person who worked in the Finance Ministry, that the Minister's answer got lost in their office and there was a "panic" to find it.

In addition, about that time, there was a debate in the Knesset on the Ministry of Absorption and in the course of it the Agudat Yisrael Member of Knesset, Menachem Porush, read out my letter in its entirety. Following this he added: "It is difficult for me to understand the discrimination against Yeshivah students and the matter is even more severe, since a large number of student new Olim learn in Yeshivot. I hope that the Minister of Finance will cancel this discrimination and that Yeshivah students will receive the same exemption from customs duty as students in other organisations." Incidentally, I learned about his speech in the Knesset when I went soon after to visit Yeshivat Hanegev and one of the students there showed me an Agudah paper with the text of his speech.

Four months passed, yet there was no response by the Finance Ministry to Wahaftig's letter. A reminder was thus sent. This at last produced a response and on 21 December 1970, a senior official of the Customs officially informed the necessary parties of the amended regulations to include Yeshivah students. A few weeks later Zevulun Hammer sent me a handwritten letter, informing me of this change, summarising the new regulation and adding that he understands that this answers the problem.

Although this change came too late for me to utilise, it meant that other Yeshivah students would get the benefit of the new regulations, and for this alone, I felt that all my efforts had been worthwhile.

THE WRONG BODY

Every week the English edition of the magazine "Mishpacha" features a true story in the collection of A. M. Amitz. One of these stories which appeared on 10 December 2008 (Issue 237) was entitled "Rest in Peace."

This story related of a woman who after she became widowed went to live in an "assisted living" home. Daily she would be visited by a member of her family. One day the family received a telephone call from this home telling them that she had died and the home would make all the burial arrangements.

The family naturally went to the levaya and decided that they would all sit shiva together. On the fifth day of the shiva they received a telephone call from their mother asking why no-one had visited her for nearly a week. The members of the family were flabbergasted and some of the family members even fainted on hearing their mother's voice five days after attending her levaya! How could someone who had died nearly a week earlier telephone them?!

On enquiry it was found that it was a different woman in the home who had died and the home had made a serious mix up. However, this mix up turned out to be to the good, since the son of the woman who had been buried, had planned, against the wishes of his mother, to cremate her and as a result of this mix up, she had a proper Jewish burial.

This story by A. M. Amitz reminded me of an incident which happened in 1968, over forty years ago in London at the levaya of my father's twin brother, my late uncle. I was in Israel at the time and only heard about it much later. Since I only heard it at least second hand, I cannot vouch for complete accuracy of all the facts but in general this is what happened. However, in contrast to the Amitz story which turned out for the good, had the mistake in the case of my uncle not be spotted in time, it could possibly have resulted in my uncle being cremated instead of having a Jewish burial.

I therefore after reading this story in "Mishpacha" decided to write a letter for publication to this magazine and I sent it to them by e-mail. Here is an expanded version of the letter I sent them:

My uncle who was in his early 60s had developed stomach cancer. I heard that this made it difficult for him to digest food and he thus became thin. He was hospitalized and died in hospital aged 62.

After his death the hospital authorities handed over a body to the Chevra Kadisha who then did a taharah on it and put it in a coffin. However, the body the hospital handed over was not my uncle's body. How this mistake occurred I don't know for sure, but I heard maybe the regular staff were not in the hospital at that time. It goes without say that the Chevra Kadisha did not notice the mistake.

The levaya started from the area of my parent's house in Edgware. It then proceeded to the Jewish burial ground in Bushey. In the ohel of the cemetery the various prayers prior to the levayah were then recited.

Whilst the coffin was then being taken to the prepared grave for burial, one of the Chevra Kadisha happened to ask my father what they should do with my uncle's clothes. My father replied "but he was wearing pyjamas." "No" they replied, "he was fully clothed." My father immediately realised that something was wrong and demanded that they open the coffin. They did this and discovered that they had the wrong body, almost certainly that of a non-Jew.

The Minister who was conducting the burial service had been a Synagogue Minister for over thirty years and had said he had never known of such a case like this, (or possibly he said he had known only one case like before). Maybe there had been cases, but they went undetected and the wrong bodies lie to this very day in the graves!

Immediately, together with my father, the Chevra Kadisha drove back at top speed to the hospital with the body of this stranger, identified the body of my uncle, performed a taharah on it in the presence of my father, who insisted on being present this time to make sure there were no further mistakes. They then returned to the cemetery and my uncle was then given a proper Jewish burial.

The car journey from my parents' house to the cemetery is about 15 minutes duration and therefore the family should have returned home after about an hour. However, because of what had occurred it took much much longer. My mother, who had not gone to the cemetery, related that in the house they were getting worried that the family had not yet returned from the cemetery. (This was well before the days of mobile phones.)

In conclusion, one shudders to think what would have happened had the member of the Chevra Kadisha not made this chance remark to my father, or had the stranger been wearing pyjamas; it was surely Siyata Dishmaya and not just "chance." This non-Jew would have had a Jewish burial and in its place my uncle might have been buried in a churchyard cemetery, or even worse, been cremated.

After I had sent a shortened version of the above account to "Mishpacha," they replied to me: "Who knows? Maybe the stranger who received the taharah was really Jewish?" To that one can answer that in view of the fact that the percentage of the population of London who are Jewish is very small, it is statistically unlikely that it was in fact the body of another Jew.

A similar case of the wrong body being buried occurred in Jerusalem in February 2011. However, in this case, the error was only discovered after the actual burial had taken place.

CPSIA information can be obtained
at www.ICGtesting.com
Printed in the USA
LVHW112044270522
719946LV00006B/54